THE FIRST ENCYCLOPEDIA

Banner Press
New York, New York

Editorial

Editorial Consultants
Michael Dempsey
David Lambert

Editorial Assistants
Vanessa Clarke
Chin Cheen Horn

Editor
Jane Olliver

Managing Editor
Revised Edition
Kathryn Borys

Contributors
Jennifer Justice
Robin Kerrod
Brenda Ralph Lewis
Angela Sheehan
Brian Williams

Design
David Nash

First published in Great Britain 1977 by Ward Lock Limited,
116 Baker Street, London, W1M 2BB, a member of the Pentos Group.

About this Book

The World of Wonder Encyclopedia is planned, written and illustrated for children between the ages of 7 and 12. It has been designed to help you understand what other people are talking about and writing about or showing you on television. A great wealth of color pictures has been used because these are often the quickest and most reliable way of explaining something. Seeing is often the best way of understanding, and very often we are led on by seeing a picture to read the accompanying article. We hope this will happen to you as you browse through this book. For this is not only a reference book, a book in which to look things up. It is very much a book to browse through, to dip into.

Your encyclopedia is, of course, arranged alphabetically. But don't forget the index on pages 187–190. If there isn't an article on something you want to find out about, look in the index. The information you need may be contained in an article on something else.

AARDVARK The aardvark of Africa is a curious animal. It has no close relatives, although its way of life is like that of the anteater. Its name means 'earth-pig'.

Aardvarks have strong claws. They break open termites' nests and lap up the termites with their long, sticky tongues. They can also burrow at great speed.

ACID Acids are sour-tasting chemicals. The sour taste of a lemon is caused by citric acid. Sour milk contains lactic acid. Vinegar contains acetic acid. These acids are weak acids, which are not harmful. Some acids are very strong. They are poisonous and can burn the skin. Strong acids include sulphuric acid, nitric acid and hydrochloric acid. These acids not only burn flesh, but also attack metals.

ADVERTISING tells people what is for sale. In fact, a simple 'For Sale' sign on a house is an advertisement. To persuade people to buy their goods, manufacturers spend a lot of time and money on advertising.

The first advertisements were shop signs. Above a shoemaker's hung a shoe. Today, posters, store displays and television commercials are all common ways of advertising.

To sell goods, an advertisement must attract attention. Catchy tunes called jingles and easily remembered phrases called slogans are often written for advertisements.

AFRICA is the world's second largest continent. It has many different land forms and kinds of weather.

The Sahara Desert is the largest desert in the world. It is very hot and dry here, with only scattered water holes, or oases, and few plants. But in the lowlands, it is hot and almost always rainy. Rain forests with huge trees grow here. The savannas are high rolling plains where it is cooler. In the savannas there are rainy seasons and dry seasons.

Africa also has mountains. The most famous, Mt. Kilimanjaro, is 19,341 feet (5,895 meters) above sea level. The longest river in the world, the Nile, flows through Africa. Other rivers are the Zaire, the Niger and the Zambezi. In East Africa, there is a great crack in the earth called the Great Rift Valley. In this area are Africa's largest lakes: Victoria and Tanganyika.

Much of Africa is thinly populated. In the north are mainly Arabs and Berbers. They follow the Muslim religion. In the south though, there are many different tribes who speak many languages and have many different religions. Two tribes are the Pygmies and the Bushmen.

Most Africans are farmers. They grow maize, yams, sweet potatoes, beans and fruit for themselves. On large farms called plantations, they grow cocoa, coffee, oil palm, tea, tobacco, cotton and sugar to sell to countries all over the world.

Africa is rich in minerals. It produces gold, diamonds, oil, copper, cobalt, bauxite and uranium. So far, there are few factories, but they are slowly being built.

In the 1800's explorers began to discover Africa. Until then it was called "The Dark Continent" because so little was known about it, but explorers found some of the oldest rocks and fossils of human beings. They also discovered the ruins of the Ancient Egyptian civilization.

At first, European governments divided the land their explorers found. These were called colonies. Today, most colonies have become independent nations ruled by black leaders.

Many African countries are poor. Industries are being developed, but there are not enough schools and hospitals and there is not enough food for all the people. Too many Africans

Africa covers more than a fifth of the Earth's land surface. The Equator runs across the center of the continent. On the wide savanna plains of Africa live great herds of grazing animals, which are hunted by lions and other flesh-eaters.

Atlantic Ocean

AFRICA

Atlas Mts

S A H A R A

Nile

Niger

Zaire

Lake Victoria

Lake Tanganyika

Mt Kilimanjaro

Indian Ocean

Zambezi

Namib Desert

Kalahari Desert

The modern world is changing life in Africa. Many Africans now live and work in busy cities. Above is Nairobi, the capital of Kenya and an important business center.

This beautifully carved ivory mask was worn as an ornament by the king of the West African kingdom of Benin. Great empires grew up in Africa before the white men came.

for heat, electricity and manufacturing.

Pollution can kill plants and animals. In man it causes scratchy throats, irritated eyes and contributes to respiratory infection.

Strong winds help to blow the air pollutants away, and rain and snow "wash" the air. But in order to conquer this problem, man must develop new fuels and methods of engineering.

The American Glenn Curtiss flew his 'Golden Flyer' at the Rheims air festival (1909).

Santos-Dumont's '14-bis' made the first airplane flight in Europe (1906).

are leaving their villages to try and find jobs in the towns. African governments are trying to solve these problems.

See also COUNTRIES OF THE WORLD; NILE; SOUTH AFRICA.

AIR is the substance that fills the 'empty' space around us. Air is a mixture of gases. Its main gases are nitrogen and oxygen. Oxygen is the gas all animals must breathe to live. Air is invisible and has no taste. But we can feel air when it moves. Winds are air movements. A layer of air, called the atmosphere, surrounds the Earth. The air in the atmosphere presses down upon us. This is called atmospheric pressure.

AIR POLLUTION. When the air becomes full of dust or poisonous gases, we have air pollution.

Sometimes nature causes air pollution, as when strong winds fill the air with sand during a sandstorm. Most pollutants are man-made. They include automobile exhaust fumes and gases produced by burning fuel

AIRCRAFT Men have always wanted to fly like birds. But the first success in the air was not through wings, it was in a hot-air balloon. Two American brothers built and flew the first airplane in 1903. They were Wilbur and Orville Wright from Dayton, Ohio. They made their first flights at Kitty Hawk in North Carolina. Their first flimsy flying machine was made of wood, cloth and wire. It could fly only a few yards and could not travel much faster than a bicycle.

Balloons, gliders and airplanes are all forms of aircraft. So are helicopters. Balloons are craft which are lighter than air. Gliders, airplanes and helicopters are heavier than air.

Modern planes are very different from the Wright Brothers' flying machine. They are sleek and streamlined and made of aluminum. They have powerful jet engines which can thrust them to fantastic speeds. The airliner Concorde travels faster than a rifle bullet!

There are many different types of planes. There are commercial planes like airliners, which carry passengers, and cargo planes, which carry freight. And

In 1924 two Douglas biplanes flew round the world in 175 days.

The Spitfire was one of the fastest fighters of the Second World War.

In 1947 the Bell X-1 broke the 'sound barrier' in level flight.

there are military planes like fighters, bombers and interceptors. These planes are fitted with guns, rockets and guided missiles to attack other planes or ground targets. Most planes are designed to land on the ground, but a few sea-planes are built with floats instead of wheels so that they can land on water.

But whatever they are like, all planes have certain things in common. They all have wings that enable them to fly. The wings have a special shape, called an *airfoil*. Its front edge is rounded but it tapers to a point at the rear. When wings move through the air, this shape causes them to lift. The faster they move, the greater is their lifting force. A plane takes to the air when the lift of its wings is greater than its weight.

through the air when they spin. They may be spun by a piston engine or by a special kind of jet engine. A piston engine works much like an automobile engine and burns gasoline.

Planes are built with a shape which will move easily through the air. This streamlined shape lessens the air resistance, or *drag* on the plane. To reduce drag

The Anglo-French Concorde airliner flies at twice the speed of sound. Its delta wing shape is ideal for supersonic flight.

Slow planes have thick wings which stick straight out from the body, or fuselage, of the plane. Fast planes have thin wings which are swept back like a swallow's wings. Very fast planes like Concorde have a delta wing, shaped like a triangle.

All planes have a *tail*. The tail helps to keep the plane traveling on a straight course, just as the tail feathers of an arrow keep the arrow on a straight path.

To guide a plane through the air a pilot moves hinged panels, called control surfaces, at the rear of the wings and the tail. Moving these surfaces makes the plane's nose go up to the left or to the right. The pilot controls the movement of the surfaces by means of a hand control column and foot pedals.

Planes are thrust through the air either by a stream, or jet, of gases or by propellers. In a jet engine fuel is burned to make hot gases. As these gases shoot backwards, they cause the plane to shoot forwards. Propellers have a twisted, curved shape and 'screw' themselves

further, the plane's outer surface is made as smooth as possible. The plane's landing gear, or undercarriage, is folded into the body during flight for the same reason.

Engineers use wind tunnels to help them design planes. They blow air over scale models of their designs. This gives them a clue as to how the real plane will behave. They build their planes of aluminum alloys. These alloys are light but very strong, and do not corrode, or rust, when exposed to the weather.

AIRPORT Airports are places where planes take off and land. Big international airports like London's Heathrow Airport and New York's Kennedy Airport are very busy. Planes take off or land every few minutes. They may be going to or coming from places thousands of miles away.

Handling the passengers and their baggage in a large airport has become a great problem. This is because big modern airliners like the Boeing 747, or

In a turboprop engine the hot exhaust gases drive a propeller.

A turbojet sucks in air and shoots out hot gas. This drives it forwards.

A bypass turbofan sucks in more air, giving more power and less noise.

A simple ramjet. It has no moving parts and works best at high speeds.

'jumbo jet', can carry up to 400 passengers at a time. In a day an airport may handle up to 100,000 passengers – the population of quite a large town. And some airports have become almost like miniature towns, with parking lots, buses, shops, banks, restaurants, bars and movies.

The planes take off and land on concrete runways, often several miles long. Many airports have several runways laid out in different directions so that planes can land flying into the wind, which is safer. The planes have instruments that help pilots land safely. People in the airport's control tower, who watch the planes approach on radar screens, also guide the pilots by radio.

ALEXANDER THE GREAT (356–323 BC) was a mighty conqueror. At the age of 20 he became king of Macedonia, in Greece. A prophetess foretold that he would never be defeated in battle. In 12 years he conquered a huge empire, stretching from Greece to India. When he died, he was buried in Alexandria, a city in Egypt named after him. Alexander even named a city after his horse, Bucephalus. Many people believed Alexander was a god. But after his death, his empire soon broke up.

Airports handle huge aircraft like this Boeing 747 jumbo jet every day. They carry freight or over 350 passengers. Each 747 weighs over 300 tons.

Below left: Alexander united Greece and beat the mighty Persians. He conquered Egypt and led his army as far as India.

ALLOY When one metal is mixed with another, the result is an alloy. If copper and zinc are mixed, they form the alloy brass. Copper and tin make the alloy bronze. We use most metals in the form of alloys. Alloys are usually stronger and harder than pure metals. The most common alloy is steel. This is a mixture of iron and carbon, and often other substances.

Above: Coin portrait of Alexander the Great. He dreamed of making Asia part of the Greek empire.

ALPHABET An alphabet is a group of letters, or signs, which stand for sounds. It is used to write down a language.

Primitive people did not write words. They drew pictures. Later these 'picture-signs' became 'idea-signs'. The ancient Egyptians used a kind of sign-writing called *hieroglyphics*.

The English alphabet comes from the Roman alphabet. It has 26 letters. Many other languages use the same letters, but the pronunciation is different.

The letters of the Greek alphabet are used as signs by scientists. The first two Greek letters, *alpha* (A) and *beta* (B), give us our word 'alphabet'.

ALPS The Alps are rugged mountains in southern Europe which stretch from France east as far as Yugoslavia. The highest peak is Mont Blanc, which is 15,772 feet (4,807 meters) high. Road and rail tunnels run through the Alps. Many people vacation there and enjoy winter sports such as mountain climbing and skiing. There are also many beautiful lakes and glaciers to see.

ALUMINUM is our most important metal, after iron. It is light, does not rust, and can be made into strong alloys. Aluminum is therefore used in the building of airplanes and ships. Aluminum carries, or conducts, heat well, so it is often used to make pots and pans. It is also made into thin foil for "silver" paper, or "tinfoil." Aluminum comes from an ore called bauxite.

AMAZON The Amazon is the world's mightiest river. It flows right across South America from the Andes Mountains to the Atlantic Ocean.

Much of the Amazon is still unexplored. Thick forests line its banks. There are few roads and no railways. Primitive Indian tribes still live in the forests, although white men have begun to clear the jungle and settle there.

AMERICAN COLONIES. In 1583 Sir Walter Raleigh sent an expedition to North America to explore the coast and find the best place to start a colony. When they returned, the explorers described the riches of the "New World"

Shown above (top to bottom) are letters from our alphabet, the Russian, the Japanese phonetic, the Greek and the Arabic alphabets. Each letter stands for a sound. The 26 letters of our (Roman) alphabet were borrowed from the 24-letter Greek alphabet. Two ancient alphabets are shown on the right: a traditional Japanese ideogram (far right) and ancient Egyptian ideograms.

In the Alps, villages lie on the slopes beneath the mountains. The wooden houses are called chalets. In spring gay alpine flowers bloom in the pastures.

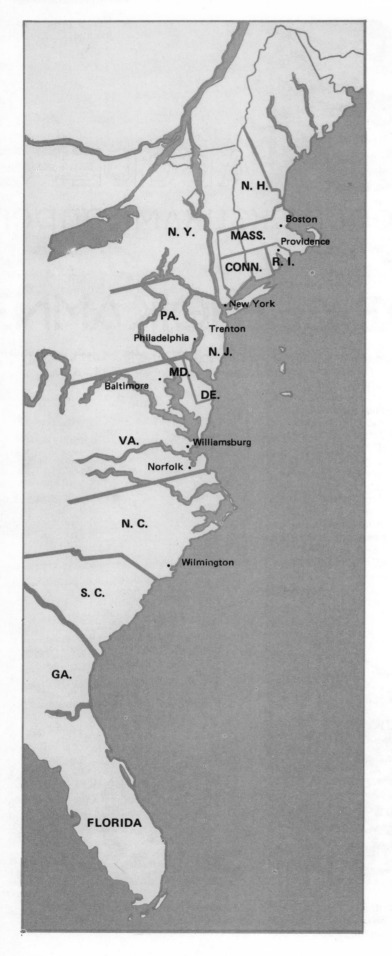

—herds of deer, fertile soil, friendly Indians. And excited by the wealth, Raleigh sent the first group of colonists in 1585, but the first colony did not survive, and the first successful colony, Virginia, was not established until 1624.

Why were people willing to leave the country they were born in to start life in an unknown wilderness? One reason was religious freedom. At that time each European country had an official religion. People had to support this religion with taxes even if they did not believe in it.

Also, in England most people were farmers. But only a few wealthy people owned the land. Others had to rent land as tenant farmers and live in poor huts.

As colonists they were offered passage to the New World, religious freedom and their own farms. Some were sent by business companies who saw the New World as a place to make more money. Others were sponsored by lords and nobles who wanted to increase their riches.

But the first group of settlers had a lot to learn. When they first arrived they should have prepared for winter by planting crops and building homes. Instead they wasted time searching for valuable minerals and gems to make them rich. And so without food or proper shelter, many of them died the first winter. But thanks to smart leaders like John Smith the colonies began to prosper.

John Smith saw the problems and made a rule: "No work, no food." He believed the wealth of the colonies was in its soil and forests. Tobacco, the first money crop, was sold to England. It

THE 13 ORIGINAL COLONIES

1. Virginia	7. New York
2. Massachusetts ·	8. New Jersey
3. Rhode Island	9. Pennsylvania
4. Connecticut	10. Maryland
5. Maine	11. North Carolina
6. New Hampshire	12. South Carolina
13. Georgia	

bove: Three of the
ost warlike Indian
ibes: the Iroquois (top)
e Apache (center) and
e Sioux (bottom).

turned struggling settlements into prosperous colonies.

In some colonies the Indians and the colonists fought. But in many cases, the Indians were friendly and helpful. Indians taught the colonists how to grow and store food, how to hunt and fish, and how to make clothes from the skins of animals.

See also AMERICAN INDIAN; CONSTITUTION OF THE UNITED STATES; DEMOCRACY; GOVERNMENT; UNITED STATES OF AMERICA, HISTORY OF.

AMERICAN INDIAN When the first European explorers reached America, they thought it was India. So they called the people living there 'Indians'.

In fact, the American Indians did come from Asia. Thousands of years ago they crossed the land which then connected Asia with Alaska, and moved southwards.

Few Indians lived like those we see in films. There were many tribes and each had its own customs and way of life. Some Indians lived by hunting and food-gathering. Others were farmers and fishermen.

The Indians of the forests lived in wigwams of bark or in great wooden

Below: An Indian family.

houses. Desert Indians built stone or mud houses, while plains Indians made tents from animal skins. Often several families shared a house.

On the rivers and lakes the Indians Traveled in canoes. On land they used sleds pulled by dogs to move their belongings from place to place. Then the Spaniards brought horses to America, and the Indians' way of life changed. Horses were used for hunting and for war. Some tribes gave up farming and moved out on to the wide plains of the west, where there were great herds of bison, or 'buffalo'.

When the first European settlers came to America, the Indians were friendly. But later there were quarrels and wars. The Indians were driven from their lands or killed.

In the 1800s, wagon trains of settlers and gold prospectors crossed the last Indian lands. Railways were built and the bison, on which the Indians depended for food, were hunted for meat. The United States Army fought the Indians until the few who were left were forced to go and live in special government reservations.

Many of their descendants still live in the same areas today. They try to keep the old Indian ways alive in the modern world.

AMPHIBIAN Amphibians are cold-blooded animals which spend part of their lives in water and part on dry land. Their name means 'double life'. The first prehistoric animals to adapt to life on dry land were amphibians.

Present day amphibians include frogs and toads, newts, salamanders and strange worm-like creatures called caecilians. Nearly all amphibians return to fresh water to lay their eggs. The young swim by wriggling their tails and breathe through gills. Later most develop lungs and can leave the water. Amphibians also breathe through their skins, which must be kept moist. So they like damp, shady places.

See also FROGS AND TOADS; NEWT.

ANDES The Andes Mountains stretch the length of western South America. The highest peak is Aconcagua.

Snail

Starfish

Crab

Earthworms, snails, starfish, crabs, bees and grasshoppers all belong to the group called invertebrates. They are animals without backbones.

Earthworm

Bee

Grasshopper

Shark

Herring

Animals with backbones include herrings and sharks (fishes), frogs (amphibians), cobras and crocodiles (reptiles), doves and storks (birds) and camels, antelopes and lions (mammals). Mammals are the most advanced creatures in the animal kingdom.

Doves

Stork

Frog

Antelopes

Camel

Cobra

Lion

Crocodile

The highest lake in the world, Titicaca, is also in the Andes.

The ancient Incas lived in the high Andes. Indians still live in the cool, green valleys. West of the central Andes are hot deserts. But from the eastern Andes rise many rivers, including the Amazon.

See also AMAZON; INCA.

ANIMAL All animal life developed, or evolved, from simple plant-like creatures. The lowest animals, like the amoeba, consist of one cell. To reproduce the amoeba divides in two. Higher animals are made up of many cells joined together. They breed by sexual reproduction. The females produce eggs which are fertilized by the males and become new animals.

The animal kingdom is divided into two groups. The larger is the *invertebrate* group. Invertebrates are animals without backbones. They include insects, worms, crabs, spiders, snails and starfish.

Animals with backbones are called *vertebrates*. The lowest vertebrates are fishes. Then come amphibians, reptiles, birds and the more advanced mammals. Most mammals give birth to live young. Almost all the others lay eggs.

Animals range in size from microscopic blobs of jelly to the huge blue whale. They live on and below the ground, in water and in the air. Many animals live alone, except during the breeding season. But others live in herds or smaller family groups.

Animals may travel long distances to find food or to breed. This is called migration. In winter, when food is scarce, some animals go to sleep. This sleep is called hibernation.

How long do animals live?
A rough rule is that large animals live longer than small ones.

Man lives longer than any other mammal and can live for more than 100 years. So can tortoises. Elephants can live to be 70, and the sturgeon, a fish, can reach 80. Eagles and cockatoos are the longest-lived birds at between 70 and 80. Lions live for about 30 years, sheep for about 15. The queen bee is one of the longest-lived insects, at 7 years. Many insects live for only a few days in adult form.

Animals which eat other animals are called predators. Some chase their prey; others hunt by making traps or lying in wait. Predators kill weak and old animals, and they help to stop the population from growing too large.

To escape their enemies, animals have many ways of defending themselves. One is camouflage, or trying to look like something else. Some animals are protected by armor or spines. Some are poisonous. Others run, climb, burrow or dive to escape.

Animals live in balanced communities, in which every kind, or species, plays a part. Human beings can upset this delicate balance by killing animals thoughtlessly or by destroying their homes. Because of this, many animals are becoming rare. Although zoos try to breed them in captivity, conservation is the best hope of preventing rare animals from dying out.

From the study of fossils, scientists know that many animals have become extinct. Millions of years ago strange prehistoric animals roamed the Earth. Now they have died out. Only animals which can adapt to change can survive. This process of change is called evolution.

See also BRAIN; CAMOUFLAGE; CELL; CONSERVATION; EVOLUTION; FOSSIL; HIBERNATION; MIGRATION; NERVOUS SYSTEM PARASITE; REPRODUCTION; SCAVENGER; SENSES.

ANIMATED CARTOONS are cartoons, or drawings that move. Snoopy and Donald Duck are animated cartoon characters. The artist makes them move by drawing hundreds of pictures which look almost, but not exactly alike. When the pictures are flashed very quickly in front of a movie camera they move, or become animated.

For example, if you wanted to make an animated cartoon of a girl singing, you would draw a picture of her with her mouth closed. In the next picture her mouth would open just a little, and in the picture after that a little bit more. Finally it would be entirely open. When these pictures were filmed by a movie camera, she would seem to be singing.

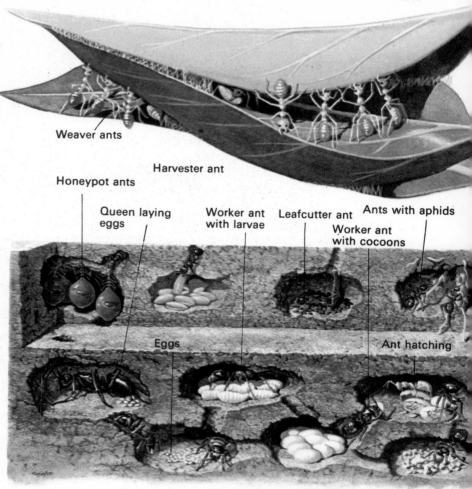

Weaver ants

Harvester ant

Honeypot ants

Queen laying eggs

Worker ant with larvae

Leafcutter ant

Ants with aphids

Worker ant with cocoons

Eggs

Ant hatching

ANT Ants mainly live in large groups. As many as a million ants may live in one colony. Ants build nests either on or in the ground or in trees. Inside are food stores and chambers for eggs, larvae and pupae.

Each ant colony has a queen. After mating with a winged male, the queen spends the rest of her life laying eggs. The small wingless female ants, called workers, cannot lay eggs. Their job is to look after the nest. They collect food and care for the young. Sometimes special workers called soldiers guard the colony against attack. Some ants will raid the nests of others and carry off their weaker victims as slaves.

Many ants eat other insects. Army ants march in vast columns, eating any animal in their path that cannot escape. Other ants 'milk' aphids for their honeydew. Harvester ants gather and store plant food. Some ants even grow fungus in special gardens inside their nests. Ants will mark a trail to guide other ants in their colony to food.

Many ants nest on the ground, but the weaver ants build their leaf nests in trees. Some ants store food, while others keep aphids as 'cattle'. Busy workers guard the queen and care for the eggs and young in the nurseries.

The large soldier ant can squirt stinging formic acid at enemies.

ANTARCTIC Unlike the Arctic, which is a frozen sea, the Antarctic is an ice-covered land mass or continent.

Its long coastline is a wall of capes and cliffs. There are mountains and volcanoes. Beyond lies a high, windswept plain, near the center of which is the South Pole. Over almost everything lies a sheet of ice, thousands of feet thick.

The Antarctic is colder than the Arctic. Even in summer, the temperature rarely rises above freezing point. In winter the sea freezes into an expanse of grinding pack ice. At its edge the ice breaks off in great icebergs.

Algae, mosses and lichens are the only plants. There are no land animals, apart from some tiny insects. But the sea is rich in plankton, fish, seals and whales, and there are penguins and other birds. The only people in the Antarctic are scientists. There is still much to learn about this vast frozen land.

See also EXPLORERS.

Few animals can live in the harsh Antarctic. But penguins live in huge colonies. The young birds huddle together for warmth.

ANTEATER The giant anteater lives in Central and South America. It breaks open the nests of ants and termites with its powerful claws. Then it thrusts its long snout inside and laps up the insects with its sticky tongue. Anteaters have no teeth.

Another kind of anteater, the pangolin, lives in Africa and Asia. It has scaly armor like an armadillo.

ANTELOPE The graceful antelopes are related to cattle. They run swiftly on two hoofed toes and, like cows, they chew the cud. Unlike deer, antelopes never shed their horns.

There are antelopes in Africa and Asia. Most live in herds on grassy plains. But some kinds prefer forests or marshes. The tiny duiker weighs no more than a rabbit, while the eland is as big as an ox. Some antelopes have corkscrew horns. Those of the powerful oryx are almost straight. The ungainly wildebeest looks like a horse with a cow's head.

Antelopes migrate in search of fresh grass during the dry season. They must always be on the lookout for danger.

The anteater's claws are a match for most enemies. Its long hair protects it from being stung as it raids ants' nests.

Nowadays husky dogs have been replaced by modern tractors which can pull much heavier loads.

Antarctic

Hartebeest

Greater
kudu

Sable
antelope

Four-horned antelope

*Male antelopes use their
horns to fight during the
breeding season. Some
female antelopes also
have horns.*
*The hartebeest (top) has
short, rather bent, screw
horns. More handsome
are the long corkscrew
horns of the greater
kudu. Longest of all are
the splendid curving
horns of the sable
antelope. Most
antelopes have only two
horns, unlike the curious
four-horned antelope
(bottom).*

Lions, cheetahs, leopards and wild dogs
all hunt antelopes. But antelopes have
keen eyesight and even the young can
run quickly. Impala and springbok bound
away from danger in great leaps.

APE Apes are the animals most like
human beings. Unlike monkeys, apes
have no tails. Sometimes they stand
erect. But usually they move about on
all fours, walking on the knuckles of
their hands. There are four kinds of
ape: the gorilla, chimpanzee, gibbon and
orangutan.

After human beings, apes are the most
intelligent of all animals. Even so, an ape's
brain is only half the size of a man's.
Young apes are playful and curious. They
are easily tamed. Apes use their hands
and feet skillfully and solve simple
problems. For example a chimpanzee
will use a stick to pull down food that is
out of reach. Few animals use tools in
this way.

The gorilla is as tall as a man, but
much heavier and stronger. Yet gorillas
are peaceful animals. They live in
African forests and spend most of their
time on the ground. At night each
gorilla builds a nest to sleep in.

Chimpanzees also come from Africa.
They are smaller than gorillas and more
agile. Chimpanzees live in family groups.
They eat plants, but also catch insects
and small animals.

The shy orangutan is a slow-moving
ape from Borneo and Sumatra. Its
name means 'man of the woods'.
Orangutans seldom come down from
the trees. Gibbons are slender apes
that also live in Asia. Their arms are so
long they almost touch the ground.
But in the treetops the gibbon is a
marvelous acrobat.

See also MONKEY.

AQUARIUM An aquarium is a tank for
keeping fishes and other water animals.
It usually has glass sides. A fresh-water
aquarium is quite simple to start.

Cover the bottom with gravel. Then
fill the tank gently with clean water.
Water plants make the aquarium look
attractive and also provide the fishes
with oxygen. Pond snails eat the algae
which grows on the glass. Stand the

*The gibbon (top) and orangutan (center) are
at home in the trees. The chimpanzee and
gorilla (bottom) live mostly on the forest floor.*

aquarium in a bright place, but not in sunlight.

Do not overcrowd the aquarium or the fish will not have enough oxygen and will die. Goldfish will eat dried fish food from pet shops, but they will enjoy live food such as water fleas occasionally, too. Do not overfeed them, as uneaten food goes bad. For tropical fish, the water must be kept warm with a heater.

ARCHAEOLOGY is the study of how people lived long ago through the clues they left behind – their tools, weapons, ornaments, coins, bones and buildings. Often these clues are buried underground.

Archaeologists excavate, or dig out, buried finds. The deeper they dig, the older the objects they find. Sometimes a ruin is hidden beneath a more recent building and is discovered by accident. To find out what shape the ruins are, the archaeologists first dig trenches. They remove the soil carefully and gradually uncover the remains below. From human bones, broken pots, kitchen rubbish and other remains they can learn how the people lived, what foods they ate and what skills they had developed. From ancient manuscripts and stone tablets, archaeologists have learned to read forgotten languages.

Graves are interesting, because ancient people often buried jewels, weapons, pottery and other possessions with the dead. Some pharaohs of ancient Egypt were buried inside huge pyramids, surrounded by treasure.

Sometimes even a whole town is preserved. This happened when the Roman towns of Herculaneum and Pompeii were buried beneath lava and ash when the volcano Vesuvius erupted in AD 79.

As a site is excavated, each find is **cleaned, labeled and handled with great** care for it may be very fragile. It is possible to tell how old an object is from

Archaeologists first mark off the site with a grid to make an accurate plan. They remove the soil to uncover ruined walls and the outlines of streets and houses. When they find a delicate mosaic pavement or a grave, they work very carefully, using trowels and brushes. Each 'find' is cleaned and marked. Everyone on a 'dig' dreams of finding treasure, such as the Greek mask of Agamemnon (below left). But even broken pots tell a fascinating story.

studying the soil and other remains found near it. A more accurate method, the carbon-14 method, measures how much natural radioactivity is left in certain objects.

Archaeologists do not always work on the ground. Photographs taken from the air can show the outline of ruins hidden beneath farmland. This is because crops grow shorter over the buried stones. Sunken ships can be studied by divers using underwater television cameras.

Most of what we know about ancient civilizations has been found out by archaeologists. But they are also in-interested in more recent times. Industrial archaeology is the study of old factories and machinery.

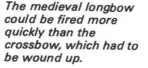

The medieval longbow could be fired more quickly than the crossbow, which had to be wound up.

ARCHERY The use of bows and arrows is called archery. Prehistoric men used bows for hunting and in battle. In the Middle Ages English archers were famous for their skill with the longbow, which had a longer range than the more complicated crossbow.

Bows and arrows became out of date when guns were invented. Today archery is practiced for sport.

ARCHITECTURE is the art and science of designing buildings. The architect draws the plans which the builders follow. Many different styles of architecture have been used through the ages. Architecture tells the story of how civilizations grow.

The first great architects were the ancient Egyptians. Their stone temples and tombs have lasted for thousands of years. The Egyptian architects were more interested in building tombs, such as the pyramids, than houses. Most people lived in simple homes made of mud and reeds.

In other parts of the Middle East people built huge mounds of mud bricks. These mounds, called ziggurats, had temples on top of them. The ancient

Architecture tells the story of Man's progress, from the first primitive shelters he built to the huge concrete and steel skyscrapers of the modern city. Many of the world's most famous and beautiful buildings were built as places of worship. They include cathedrals, temples, mosques and pagodas. Often they are richly decorated and took many years to build. Some of the many different styles and shapes chosen by architects over the centuries can be seen here.

Assyrians and Persians were skilled architects. They often decorated walls with magnificent carvings, showing hunting and battle scenes.

Some people think the architecture of ancient Greece was the most beautiful of all time. The Greeks tried to be perfect in everything they did. Their system of building was quite simple. Rows of tall marble columns supported heavy stone beams, on which the roof was placed. Greek temples were designed with great care, and decorated with carvings and sculptures.

The Greeks used different kinds of columns. The three main kinds were the Doric, Ionic and Corinthian styles, or 'orders'. These were later copied by the Romans. Many Roman buildings look like Greek buildings.

But the Romans were better engineers than the Greeks. They needed to build bridges, aqueducts and forts all over their Empire. They also needed big, roofed buildings. So the Roman architects developed the arch and the vault, a roof supported by arches. The arch was a good way of spanning a wide distance quickly. Small stones and cement could be used instead of heavy marble beams.

By using the arch, the Romans were able to build taller buildings. They built public baths, theaters and amphitheaters — arenas with seats arranged in rows. They built great arches and ceremonial columns as monuments to famous generals and emperors.

The great architecture of many civilizations is often best seen in its religious buildings. The Muslims built beautiful domed mosques, elaborately decorated both inside and out. Sometimes the shape of the building itself had a religious meaning. The Chinese thought of the tall pagoda as pointing the way to heaven.

In Europe during the Middle Ages stone was the natural building material for building strong castles and long-lasting cathedrals. At first architects followed Roman styles. This is called Romanesque architecture. But from around 1200 they began building tall, slender churches and cathedrals. The spires and pinnacles pointed to heaven, like the pagoda. Pointed arches were used instead of round ones. This is called the Gothic style.

Building a cathedral sometimes took hundreds of years. The stone for decoration was carved into delicate shapes. Often, stone figures of saints decorated the walls. Stained glass was set into the windows. For years this Decorated style, as it was called, was very popular.

During the Renaissance architects returned to the Greek and Roman styles. They liked the simple and regular 'classical' designs. But in time more decoration was added. By the 1600s the Baroque style was fashionable. It was very ornate. Even straight stone columns were twisted into spiral shapes.

During the 1700s architects designed many fine houses. Often they laid out parks and gardens as part of the design.

The Victorians of the 1800s liked the medieval Gothic style of architecture, and so many of their buildings look like much older ones. The Houses of Parliament in London are a good example.

A big change came with the use of steel and reinforced concrete. Architects could now build higher and more quickly. The first very tall buildings, dubbed 'skyscrapers' were built in the United States. Skyscrapers were soon being built in cities all over the world.

Modern architects prefer simple shapes. Steel, concrete, glass, plastics and brick are the chief materials used. The architect tries to design a new building so that it will fit in well with other buildings near it. The inside is as important as the outside, for it is here that people will live and work. Roads and gardens are often planned around the building, as part of the 'living space' designed by the architect.

See also BUILDING; CASTLE; CHURCH; EGYPT, ANCIENT; GREECE, ANCIENT; ROME, ANCIENT.

Above: A ruined portico at Knossos in Crete, the capital of the Minoan civilization of 4000 years ago. Below: French kings and queens lived in the chateau of Chenonceaux, built across the River Cher in 1515.

The History of Architecture	
BC	
3200	Ancient Egypt
400	Ancient Greece
200	Great Wall of China
100	Ancient Rome
AD	
800	Romanesque (architects imitate Roman styles)
1200	Gothic period begins
1300	Decorated style begins in England
1400	Renaissance style begins in Italy
1600	Baroque style begins in Italy
1715	Georgian style begins in England
1837	Victorian period begins
1868	First skyscraper in the United States
1920	Modern architecture

Doric   Ionic   Corinthian

The roofs of the beautiful Greek temples were held up by tall columns. At first these were in the simple Doric style. Later more decoration was added.

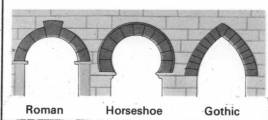

Roman   Horseshoe   Gothic

The Romans copied many Greek ideas and added one of their own – the arch. The arch made it possible to build larger buildings. Later, different arches, for doors and windows, were developed.

The map labels: Asia, North America, North Pole, Greenland, Europe

ARCTIC The Earth has two cold, frozen zones. At the South Pole lies the Antarctic. At the North Pole is the Arctic.

Most of the Arctic is frozen sea, surrounded by land. The line of latitude marking its boundary is the Arctic Circle, 66°N. Snow and ice cover everything in winter. But during the short Arctic summer, the snow melts and grass, flowers and moss grow on the tundra plains. The soil is thin and only a few inches down it is frozen all year round. There are no trees within much of the Arctic Circle.

Around the North Pole, the ice never melts. Further south the ice breaks away in huge floating chunks called icebergs. At the North Pole the sun never rises in winter. For six months there is darkness. In summer the sun does not set at the North Pole, even at midnight.

Arctic animals include seals, walruses, whales, polar bears, foxes, owls, weasels, musk oxen and reindeer. The only people native to the Arctic are the Eskimos. There are valuable minerals in the Arctic, including coal, oil and iron.

See also ESKIMO.

In the Arctic winter the ptarmigan's white feathers camouflage it in the snow. Eskimo hunters build snow houses or igloos for shelter. In summer, Arctic flowers bloom briefly and the Eskimos live in skin tents. Now the ptarmigan wears its brown summer plumage.

Armadillo means 'little armored one' in Spanish. The armadillo's armor is made of plates of bone. It can roll itself into a ball, but will also run away or dig a burrow to escape from its enemies.

ARMADILLO This South American mammal looks rather like a small pig. But it is armored like a tank. It is a timid animal and, when frightened, rolls itself into a ball. Armadillos eat worms, insects and roots. They dig burrows in the ground with their strong claws.

ARMOR Before gunpowder was invented, soldiers fought in hand-to-hand combat. To protect their bodies, they wore armor.

Leather made good, light armor and could be made stronger by adding plates of bronze or iron. The Greeks and Romans wore helmets, breastplates and leg armor. Their armor was tough but easy to move about in.

Later armorers learned to link together tiny iron rings to produce coats of mail. Mail gave good protection

against sword and spear. But steel plate was even stronger. Plate armor covered the whole of a man's body. There was even armor for his horse.

Only a rich knight could afford full armor. He wore a special emblem, or device, on his helmet so that other knights could recognize him. But even steel armor was no defense against the cannon. By the 1600's soldiers needed to move more quickly, so they began wearing less armor. Finally they stopped wearing it.

The modern soldier's helmet is a reminder of the armor worn in the past.

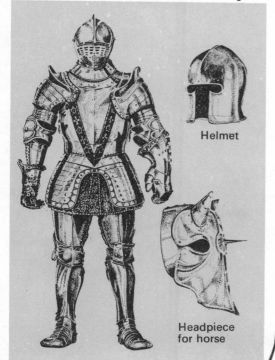

Helmet

Headpiece for horse

Above: Armor developed throughout the ages from simple metal shields to elaborate metal suits covering the entire body. This fine example was worn in the early 1500s.

ASIA is the largest continent, stretching from the Arctic to the Equator. It covers nearly a third of the Earth's land surface. With a population of over 2200 million Asia has more than half of the world's people.

There are many different types of land and climate in Asia. In the north are evergreen forests, flat grasslands called steppes, and cold tundra plains. Most of this area is called Siberia and is part of the Soviet Union. In central Asia are the world's highest mountains, including the mighty Himalaya Mountains. The high plains of Tibet are known as 'the roof of the world'. From these mountains many great rivers flow into the rest of Asia. Asia has some of the world's longest rivers. They include the Ob, Lena and Yenisei in the north; the Euphrates in the west; the Indus, Ganges, Brahmaputra, Salween, Irrawaddy and Mekong in the south; and the Hwang Ho and Yangtze in the east.

Some parts of Asia are very dry. There are wide deserts, such as the cold Gobi Desert of Mongolia and the hot deserts of India and Arabia. There the land is dry and barren. In other places there is heavy rainfall, but only once a year during the monsoon season. In these areas there are tropical rain forests.

Asia's wild animals include tigers, leopards, wolves, rhinoceroses, pigs, deer, monkeys and snakes. The elephant and the water buffalo have been tamed to work in the forests and fields.

This Buddhist temple in Bangkok, Thailand, has a golden spire. Buddhism is one of the chief religions of Asia.

In the Middle Ages when warlords ruled Japan, armored knights called samurai fought fierce battles.

Arctic Ocean

Ural Mountains

RUSSIA

Black Sea

Caspian Sea

Caucasus Mts

MIDDLE EAST

Tibetan Plateau

Red Sea

Arabian Desert

Himalayas

INDIA

Because of its great size, Asia has many differences of climate, geography, wildlife and ways of life. The main regions are the hot, wet monsoon lands of the southeast, where most of the people live; the high barrier lands, with their deserts and snow-capped mountains; and the great plains and forests which lie beyond the mountain ranges to the north.

Indian Ocean

ASIA

CHINA

Pacific Ocean

S.E. ASIA

MALAYSIA

INDONESIA

Few people live in the mountains, plains and deserts. Those who do are mostly nomads (wanderers), grazing flocks of sheep, goats, horses and camels. Almost all Asia's people live either in the fertile river valleys, or on the coastal plains. Most of them are peasant farmers, scraping a living out of a small patch of land. But more and more people are going to live in the cities.

In the warm, wet monsoon lands of southern Asia, rice is the chief crop. Rice and fish are the main foods of many Asians. Other crops are tea, sugar, cotton, coffee and spices. Many of the people are very poor. They use old-fashioned farming methods and cannot grow enough food. If the crops fail because of flood or drought, many people starve.

Asia has few large industries, but valuable raw materials. The forests provide timber and rubber. There are minerals such as coal, iron, copper and tin. In the Middle East some countries have become rich because there is oil beneath the desert. The most important industrial country in Asia is Japan, which manufactures many products to sell in other countries. China and India are gradually developing their industries, as well as improving their agriculture.

Asia has a long history. It has had rich and powerful civilizations. The great religions of Christianity, Islam, Hinduism and Buddhism all began in Asia. The Asian peoples reached high levels of progress in the arts and sciences long before the Europeans did so. But the deserts and mountains kept the peoples of Asia apart, for only camel caravans could cross the dangerous lands between them. So each part of Asia developed its own languages, customs and ways of life.

European explorers came to Asia in search of riches and spices. They set up trading stations, and later founded colonies. Some parts of Asia were ruled by Europeans until quite recently. But now all the countries of Asia are independent and run their own affairs.

See also CHINA; COUNTRIES OF THE WORLD; EXPLORERS; HIMALAYAS; INDIA; JAPAN; MIDDLE EAST.

ASTRONAUT

An astronaut is a person who travels in space. The word 'astronaut' really means 'star-traveler.' Astronauts have not journeyed to the stars yet, but they have reached the **Moon. On July 20, 1969, Neil Armstrong, an American, became the first man to walk on the Moon.** He and fellow astronaut Edwin Aldrin visited for 22 hours and brought back the first samples of moon rock.

Traveling in space is one of the most exciting and dangerous things Man has ever done. The astronauts have to be well trained before they can go. For example, they are trained to withstand the great force caused by the thrust of the rocket when they take off. They grow accustomed to such a force in machines that whirl them around at high speeds.

When the astronauts are traveling in space, they weigh nothing at all. They just float about. There is no gravity to keep their feet on the floor. They have to eat and drink out of tubes. If they tried to eat food with a knife and fork, the food would simply float away. And liquids will not pour in space.

In space there is no air to breathe. So astronauts must take air with them in their spacecraft. When they leave their spacecraft, they must put on a spacesuit. This supplies them with air and keeps their bodies at the right temperature.

ASTRONOMY

is the study of the heavenly bodies. It is one of the oldest sciences. People became astronomers when they began noting the changes that take place in the heavens. They observed the Moon regularly changing its shape and saw different stars come into view every month. They also observed that some 'stars' wander, but they did not know then that these 'stars' were really planets, like the Earth.

Astronomers today know a great deal more about the heavens and the universe, thanks to the discoveries of great astronomers of the past, particularly Copernicus, Galileo and Newton. They now work in well-equipped observatories with a variety of instruments. Their most useful instrument is the telescope, which gathers and strengthens the feeble

Outside the spacecraft, the astronaut must wear a pressurized spacesuit. A liquid-cooled inner suit controls his body temperature. His back pack contains his air supply, radio and air conditioning. A gold-plated visor shields his eyes from the sun.

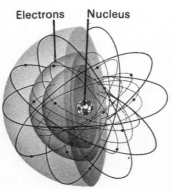

The structure of the atom looks rather like a model of the solar system. The heavy nucleus in the center is made up of neutrons and protons. Around it, like planets orbiting the Sun, are layers of electrons.

Electrons   Nucleus

light from the stars. In recent years astronomers have learned much from information collected by spacecraft.

ATHLETICS

Exercises like jogging and gymnastics; sports like track and field and wrestling; and games like football and baseball are called athletics. *Professional athletes* earn their wages by performing athletics. Some examples of professional athletes are football players, baseball players and golf and tennis pros.

One of the most popular demonstrations of athletics is the Olympic Games which are held every four years. The modern athlete must train hard to do well. Athletes spend many hours practicing their skills.

See also BASEBALL; BASKETBALL; FOOTBALL; OLYMPICS

ATLANTIC OCEAN

The world's second largest ocean is the Atlantic. It divides North and South America from Europe and Africa. Within the ocean, about one mile down, lies the world's largest continuous mountain range, The Mid-Atlantic range. In the western Atlantic is a strange calm area called the Sargasso Sea, where the ocean is thick with seaweed.

See also OCEAN, PACIFIC OCEAN.

ATOM

Every substance is made up of one or more chemical elements. Iron is an element. Wood is a substance made up chiefly of three elements – carbon, hydrogen and oxygen.

If you could cut a piece of iron into smaller and smaller pieces, eventually you would be left with tiny particles called atoms. They are the smallest particles of an element that can exist.

Every element has a different kind of atom. Atoms of different elements combine to form molecules of a new substance. Two atoms of hydrogen (H) combine with one atom of oxygen(O) to form one molecule of water. We can therefore represent water like this: H_2O.

It is difficult to imagine something as small as an atom. There are millions more atoms in a speck of dust than there are people in the world. Yet every atom is made up of even smaller particles. It is

AUSTRALIA

Timor Sea

Coral Sea

Great Barrier Reef

Great Dividing Range

Great
Sandy
Desert

Ayer's Rock

Gibson
Desert

Great Victoria
Desert

Nullarbor
Plain

Indian Ocean

not solid, but is made up mainly of space.

At the center of the atom is a solid *nucleus*. This contains two kinds of particles called *protons* and *neutrons*. The protons have an electric charge. At the outside of the atom are tiny particles called *electrons*, which circle the nucleus. They also have an electric charge, which keeps them attracted to the nucleus.

The atoms of different elements contain different numbers of particles. The simplest atom of all is the hydrogen atom. It has a single proton in its nucleus and a single electron circling around. An atom of the heavy metal uranium, on the other hand, has a nucleus containing 92 protons and 146 neutrons, and has 92 circling electrons. The uranium atom is very special because it can be made to split. When it does, an enormous amount of energy is released. This is the basis of nuclear power.

Australia is a huge island. Most of the center is hot and dry. All the fertile, well-watered lands are near the coasts. Australia's plants and animals are unlike any others in the world.

AUSTRALIA The smallest continent is a vast, dry island. A grassy plain lies in the center, but to the east lie the dry Nullarbor Plains and to the west a sandy desert. Most people live in the southeast where there is enough rain for crops.

Australia is a farming country. It produces wool, dairy foods, meat, fruit and wheat to sell to other countries. Minerals including gold, silver, lead, copper, tin, uranium, and oil are also mined.

Until it was discovered by the Dutch

Sydney, New South Wales, is a busy port. Near here the first settlers from England landed in 1788.

in the 1600's Australia was called *Terra Australis Incognita,* which means "unknown land of the south." Because it was so far away, Australia was one of the last continents to be explored.

The Aboriginies, Australia's native people, live in the dry bush. They still make stone tools and hunt with spears and boomerangs.

Australia is the home of many strange plants and animals—like the platypus—which are not found anywhere else in the world. The Kangaroo, koala, wombat and emu are some of Australia's native animals.

See also EMU; KANGAROO; KOALA; MARSUPIAL; PLATYPUS.

FACTS AND FIGURES:
Area: 2,967,000 square miles
        (7,687,000 square kilometers)
Population: 13,300,000
Capital: Canberra
Government: Federal republic
Money unit: Dollar
Longest River: Darling, 1,702 miles
        (2,739 kilometers)
Highest Mountain: Mt. Kosciusko, 7,300
        feet (2225 meters)

AUTOMOBILE. Many people from many countries contributed to the design of the automobile. However until Henry Ford invented the mass production, or assembly, line cars were very expensive. With the assembly line, cars could be made quickly and cheaply. But Ford's Model "T" was a far cry from the automobile as we know it today

A modern car is a collection of 10,000 or more separate parts. These parts make up several basic units: the body, the engine, and the transmission are the main units. The transmission carries power from the engine to the driving wheels. The other units are the steering, the braking and the suspension systems.

An ordinary car engine consists of a heavy block of cast iron. Inside are four or more closed tubes, or cylinders, in which pistons can travel up and down. A mixture of gasoline and air is burned in the top of the cylin-

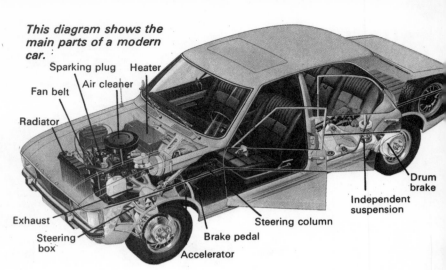

This diagram shows the main parts of a modern car.

Sparking plug   Heater
Air cleaner
Fan belt
Radiator
Drum brake
Independent suspension
Exhaust
Steering box
Steering column
Brake pedal
Accelerator

ders. The gases produced push the pistons down. The movement of the pistons turns a rod called a crankshaft. This turning motion is then carried by the transmission to the car's wheels.

Today there are nearly 200 million cars in the world. The exhaust from automobiles is a major contributor to air pollution. Scientists have been trying to invent devices which help to purify or eliminate these fumes. They are also trying to invent new cars which use less fuel to operate, and help to conserve energy. One recent invention is a car powered by electricity. It actually "runs" on a giant battery which gets "charged up" when it runs down.

A car's transmission system carries the turning motion of the engine from the crankshaft to the driving wheels, which are often at the rear of the car. The most common system consists of a clutch, a gearbox, and shafts connecting the gearbox to the driving wheels. The clutch connects the gearbox to the engine. By shifting the gears in the gearbox, the driver can make the car go faster or slower for the same engine speed.

The first car made by Gottlieb Daimler in 1886.

AZTEC The Aztecs were rich and powerful people of ancient Mexico. They had schools and hospitals but were also cruel. They sacrificed humans and practiced slavery.

By 1519 when the Spaniard, Cortes, entered Tenochtitlan, the capital, the civilization was at a peak. But after a two-year war the city and its gold fell to the Spaniards.

The Model T Ford.

A family of badgers at their set. Badgers come out at night to look for food, often making well-trodden paths to and fro. They are clean animals and gather bracken as fresh bedding.

BABOON Baboons are large monkeys which live on the rocky grasslands of Africa and Arabia. They roam about in large bands called troops. The males are strong and fierce, with powerful jaws. Young baboons ride on their mothers' backs. Baboons eat plants, eggs and insects; sometimes they raid farm crops. In ancient Egypt the baboon was sacred.

Baboons spend the day in the open and at night sleep among the rocks or in trees for safety.

BACH, Johann Sebastian (1685–1750) is the most famous of a great family of German composers and musicians. As a musician, Bach was master of the organ. He composed hundreds of pieces of music, including many choral works. Bach also wrote music for church services, for orchestras and for the harpsichord. Several of his many children also became composers.

BACTERIA are among the smallest living things. Each one is made up of just a single cell, and can be seen only under a microscope. There are millions of bacteria all around us. They are in the soil, in the water and in the air. And they are inside our bodies.

Most bacteria are helpful. Some feed on dead creatures and waste matter, and cause them to decay. Bacteria make the soil rich and help plants to grow. They also cause changes in food. Without bacteria, we could not make cheese or wine.

But bacteria also turn meat rotten and milk sour. So some foods must be protected against them. And some bacteria cause disease. These harmful kinds are often called germs. They can be controlled by vaccines and drugs.

Some bacteria look like tiny rods. Others are shaped like balls or screws. Bacteria multiply by dividing into two. If there is plenty of food for them, they can increase very quickly.

BADGER The badger is a relative of the weasel. It is a powerfully built animal with short legs and a black and white striped head.

Badgers dig deep burrows called sets, from which they emerge after dark to forage for food. They eat snails, eggs, insects, worms, berries and roots and will fight fiercely if attacked. But left alone, badgers are peaceful animals.

BALLET is a classic form of dance performed on the stage. It may tell a story or act out an idea or feeling. Classical ballet is based on a number of set positions and movements which a

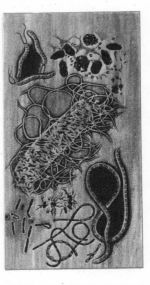

All bacteria are made of a single cell. Some have tiny hairs, which help them to move about.

In classical ballet there are five basic positions of the feet. Below are the fourth and fifth positions.

BANK A bank is a place where people keep money. Banks started when merchants needed a place to keep their gold where it could not be easily stolen.

Today banks play an important part in our lives. The money which people keep in banks is lent to other people, and a charge, called interest, is made for the loan. A person with a bank account can pay bills by writing a check, telling the bank how much money is to be paid and to whom.

choreographer arranges in various ways for each dance. Modern ballet allows the dancers more freedom of movement.

Ballet began over 450 years ago in Italy and France as court entertainment. Now, many countries have Ballet companies or troupes.

BALLOON Two Frenchmen, Joseph and Etienne Montgolfier, built the first hot-air balloon in 1783. Since then, man has used balloons for sport and in scientific investigation.

Balloons float because the air or gas they contain is lighter than the air surrounding them. Helium, hydrogen and hot air are used to fill balloons because they are lighter than the cooler air and other gases in the atmosphere.

The hot air balloon made it possible for scientists to study the air high above the earth. Recently, experiments conducted from balloons helped pave the way for space trips. Even today, balloons are circling the earth sending back information about weather conditions.

BAMBOO is a kind of giant grass that grows in the tropics. The bamboo stem is hollow and jointed. Bamboos can grow as tall as 90 feet (35 meters). It is used in Asia to make houses, boats, water pipes and flutes.

Two of the greatest stars of ballet today, Margot Fonteyn and Rudolf Nureyev, dance together in a scene from 'Swan Lake'.

The Montgolfier's hot-air balloon made the first manned balloon flight over Paris in 1783.

The pointer of an aneroid barometer shows whether the air pressure is rising (good weather) or falling (bad).

BAROMETER A barometer is an instrument that measures air pressure. The pressure of the air varies from day to day as weather conditions change. Weathermen take readings of air pressure to help them forecast changes in the weather.

The most common kind of barometer is the aneroid barometer. It consists of a drum from which most of the air has been removed. When the pressure of the air changes the size of the drum changes. This change in size is recorded by a pointer on a scale. Some barometers are fitted with a pen and, as the pointer moves, the pen records the pressure on a roll of paper. These barometers are called barographs.

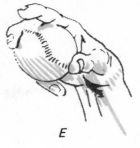

A   B   C   D   E

The pitches used in baseball: (a) the slow, change-of-pace ball; (b) the knuckle ball; (c) the fast ball; (d) the curve ball, held off-center by the pitcher and then (e) released from the middle finger by the pitcher.

BASEBALL. Abner Doubleday of Cooperstown, New York is considered the founder of baseball. However, stick and ball games like baseball were played as far back as Ancient Egypt. In fact, today's game actually comes from an English game called "rounders" where posts were used instead of bases.

Baseball is played by two teams each having nine players. The equipment consists of a ball, bat and gloves. The playing field is divided into an *infield* and an *outfield*. The four bases or the *diamond* make up the infield. The outfield stretches to the fence or the stands surrounding the ball park.

The visiting team has the first turn at bat. It remains at bat until the home team puts "out" three of the visiting players. While the team at bat tries to score runs, the opposing team in the field tries to stop them from scoring.

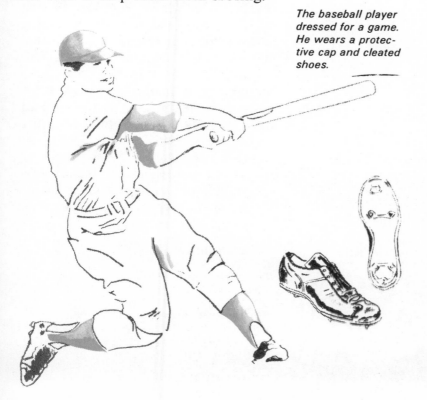

The baseball player dressed for a game. He wears a protective cap and cleated shoes.

Each team member has a specific responsibility.

The *pitcher* has one of the hardest jobs. He must throw a variety of balls to keep the batter from hitting them. He must also field batted balls that fall near him, and keep an eye on base runners so they don't advance.

The *catcher* stands behind home plate. He must catch all the pitcher's throws that are not hit by the batter, and guard home plate against base runners who are trying to score a run. He also studies the batters and signals the pitcher telling him what kind of ball is best to throw.

The *infielders* guard the bases and the area around it. The *first baseman* guards first base and the *third baseman* defends third. The *second baseman* guards the area between first and second; and the *shortstop* guards the area between second and third. Both of them defend second. Three *outfielders* guard the territory behind the infield or the outfield.

A player can be put "out" in several ways. He can be struck out by failing to hit three fair balls. Or a fielder can catch a "fly" ball before it hits the ground. If the batter hits a "ground" ball which is caught by a fielder and then thrown to the base before the runner arrives, he is also out.

BASKETBALL is an indoor game played between two teams of five players. The players bounce and pass a ball to each other and try to score goals. A *goal* is scored by throwing the ball into a basket which is defended by members of the opposing team.

Basketball begins with a *jump ball* into the air between two players who stand in the center circle on either side of the center line.

Each team has five players on court: one center, two forwards and two guards. Each team may also use up to five substitutes. Each game is divided into quarters. Each quarter is 10 minutes long.

Each time a basket is made points are scored. There are two ways of scoring points. A field goal is worth two points; a goal from a free throw is worth one point. A *field goal* is one scored during normal play from any part of the court.

Free throws are awarded when the opposing team commits certain offenses. The throws are taken from behind the free-throw line. During a free-throw, players of both teams line up alternately outside of the free-throw line. Other players may not try to stop a free-throw.

There are several ways for the team to get the ball to its basket. Players may pass the ball to each other using one or more hands. Or a player may *dribble* the ball by bouncing it on the floor. But a player with the ball may only take one step. If he takes more than one step he is called for running. However, he can *pivot*. That means he may step in any direction with one foot while keeping the other on the floor.

If a player is charged with a *personal foul* for pushing, charging, holding or blocking an opponent, the

DRIBBLING   PASSING   FAKING   PIVOTING

There are two ways to move the basketball: by dribbling (bouncing the ball along the floor) or by passing (throwing the ball from one player to another). Faking is used to confuse an opponent by making it look like the player is moving in one direction but is actually going in another. This is usually done with a fast pivot.

opposing team gets possession of the ball from the nearest sideline.

However, if a player is fouled in the act of shooting, or if the foul was either intentional or committed in the last three minutes of the game, the fouled player is awarded two free throws. *Technical fouls* such as deliberately delaying the game also give the opponent two free shots.

If a violation is called against a player, the other team is awarded *possession*. This means the ball is thrown in from the side of the court nearest the place the offence occured. *Violations* include running with the ball, or striking it with the hand or foot.

There are also time restrictions. A player must not take more than five seconds to put the ball into play. Nor may a player whose team has the ball stay in a restricted area for more than three seconds. A team gaining possession of the ball must take a shot within 30 seconds. And in the last three minutes of a match or in an extra period, the team must move the ball from its back court to its front court within ten seconds.

There are many different types of shots and passes which the experienced ball player masters. Some of them are the two handed chest pass,

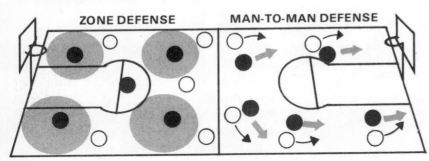

ZONE DEFENSE   MAN-TO-MAN DEFENSE

Each player is assigned to guard a specific area of the basketball court when playing a zone defense. In man-to-man defense, however, each player guards another player anywhere on the court.

the hook pass, the one handed set shot and the lay-up shot.

The referee's signals are the same for all basketball games: (a) start clock; (b) stop clock; (c) stop clock for jump ball; (d) holding; (e) traveling; (f) no score; (g) illegal use of hands; (h) technical foul

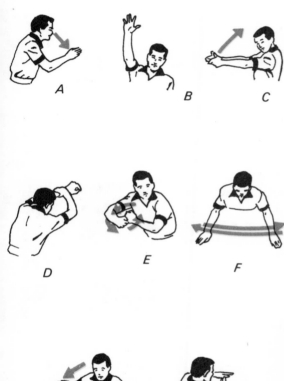

A B C

D E F

G H

BAT Bats are the only mammals which can fly. They sleep by day, hanging upside down in caves or other dark places. Fruit-eating bats are the largest. They have good eyesight. Insect-eating bats are smaller and cannot see well. Yet they can fly in the dark without bumping into obstacles. They send out very high-pitched squeaks and listen for the echo which bounces off the things around them. In this way bats also catch insects on the wing.

The vampire bat of South America feeds on the blood of other animals.

BEAR Although bears may look cuddly and playful, they are dangerous animals. They are very strong, and have sharp claws. Even though some bears can be tamed, they may still attack without warning.

Bears live mainly in forests and mountains. They are meat-eating mammals. But they will also eat almost any kind of plant food and insects. And all bears love honey.

Brown bears are found in Asia and North America. The largest kinds are the grizzly and the huge Kodiak bear of Alaska. The smaller black bear is an expert climber. The only bear in South America is the spectacled bear. The sun bear and the shaggy sloth bear live in Asia and often raid bees' nests. Another kind of black bear lives in the Himalaya mountains.

Polar bears have creamy white fur. These bears roam the Arctic, hunting seals. They sometimes swim far out to sea. Female polar bears hibernate during the winter and give birth to their cubs in snow caves. Other bears also sleep during the winter, living on fat stored in their bodies.

In the Middle Ages dancing bears were shown at fairs in Europe, and

31 BEAR

Most bears live in cool climates. The female polar bear spends the winter in a snow den, and has her cubs there. Brown bears also sleep in winter. They often fish in rivers and are quite at home in the water.

Bats use a form of 'radar'. Listening for echoes, they can catch insects in flight and avoid obstacles.

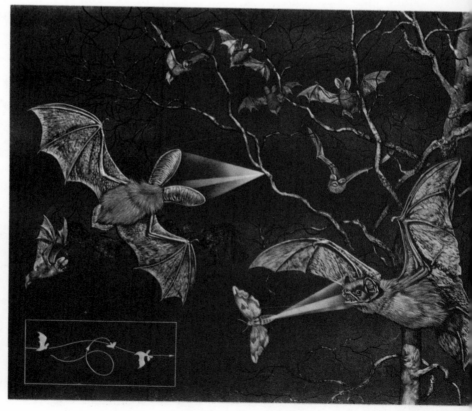

chained bears were 'baited' by dogs. Because man has hunted them, bears are now quite scarce in the wild.

BEAVER Beavers are always working, for these large rodents are the master builders of the northern forests.

Beavers live close to water. Their stout bodies and short legs make them clumsy on land. But they swim well with their webbed feet and paddle-like tails and can stay underwater for several minutes.

To make a home safe from enemies, beavers dam streams and small rivers with tree branches, stones and mud. They fell young trees by gnawing through the trunks with their sharp front teeth. In the pool formed behind the dam, the beavers build their lodge, a dome-shaped den of mud and sticks with an underwater entrance.

Beavers eat bark, twigs and roots. They store food underwater to eat during the winter. They live in family groups and warn of danger by slapping the water with their broad tails. In the past trappers killed many beavers for their valuable fur. Now the beaver is protected by law.

BEE Since ancient times Man has taken honey and wax from bees. But more important, these busy insects carry pollen from flower to flower. Unless they are pollinated, plants cannot make seeds.

Some bees are solitary. Others, such as the honeybee, we call social insects because they live in large colonies. A bee's nest is called a hive. In every hive there are many worker bees, a few male drones and a queen.

After mating with a drone, the queen bee settles down to the task of laying thousands of eggs. The workers are small female bees which do not lay eggs. They may live only six weeks. The workers build the wax cells of the honeycomb and gather nectar and pollen from flowers to make honey. A returning honeybee does a special dance to show other bees where food can be found. The workers also feed the queen and the larvae and guard the hive. Drones do no work and in the autumn they are driven from the hive to die.

Larvae which are fed on a special substance called royal jelly become new queens. But only one queen may rule a colony. When a new queen appears, the old queen may leave with some workers and a few drones to start a new colony.

Bees are expert builders. There are potter bees, mason bees, leaf-cutter bees, mining bees and carpenter bees.

Bumblebees nest in burrows. The drones and workers die at the end of the summer. Only the queen survives to continue the colony.

Worker

Queen

Drone

Every hive has three kinds of bees: workers, a queen and drones.

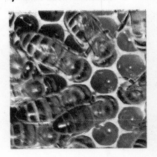

The bee's honeycomb has hundreds of cells for pollen and young. Each cell is made of wax and has six sides.

The beavers' lodge is an island home, safe from enemies. The beavers go in and out underwater, but sleep in a dry chamber.

BELL, Alexander Graham (1847-1922) is famous for inventing the telephone. Yet few people realize that his earlier experience as a teacher of the deaf contributed to his invention.

In teaching the deaf to speak, Bell learned how the vibrations of the vocal chords produced sound. He combined this understanding with his knowledge of electricity. The result was the invention of the telephone—a device which carries sound vibrations through electrical currents.

Bell was only 30 at the time of his invention. He spent the remaining 45 years of his life studying other scientific areas including heredity and flying.

BIBLE. The bible is the great book of the Christian religion. It is divided into two parts.

The Old Testament tells the stories of the Jewish people, their kings and

The first printed Bible was made by Johann Gutenberg in 1456. Each column had 42 lines of type, printed in black and color. The extra decoration was added to the book by hand.

BEETHOVEN, Ludwig van (1770–1827) was a German composer who wrote some of the world's greatest music. He began writing music while a boy and studied with the famous composer Joseph Haydn. Later he went deaf but still managed to finish nine wonderful symphonies and other music for instruments and singers.

BEETLE Beetles are one of the largest groups of insects. Beetles have two pairs of wings. But only the back pair are used for flying. The front pair have become hard wing covers.

Many beetles live on the ground and fly hardly at all. Some live in water, breathing air trapped under their wing covers.

Beetles and their larvae can be harmful. The Colorado beetle attacks potato crops. Grain weevils damage corn. Woodworms, larvae of the furniture beetle, bore tunnels in timber.

But beetles can be useful, too. The ladybird eats greenfly. And some beetles are scavengers, burying dead animals and laying their eggs on them so that the larvae will have plenty of food.

See also SCAVENGER.

Right: Dung beetles or tumblebugs are scavengers. They roll away and bury the balls of dung on which they feed.
Below: The ladybird and the diving beetle prey on other insects. But many beetles eat only plant food. Despite their fierce-looking horns, the large stag and rhinoceros beetles are quite harmless. The longhorn beetle gets its name from its long, slender antennae.

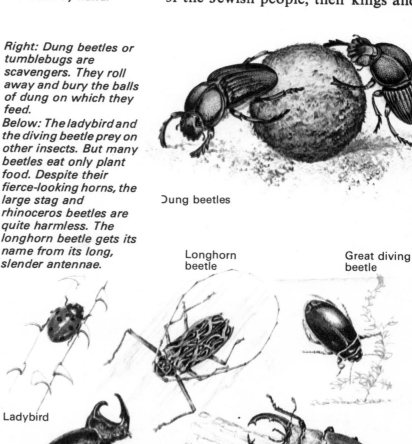

Dung beetles

Longhorn beetle

Great diving beetle

Ladybird

Rhinoceros beetle

Stag beetle

prophets, and their journey to the Promised Land. The first story tells how God created first the world, and then Adam and Eve, the first man and woman. Other stories are about Abraham and Moses. The Old Testament is held sacred by both Jews and Christians.

The second part of the Bible, the New Testament, is sacred only to Christians. Here in the gospels of Mark, Matthew, Luke and John we find stories of Jesus' life: his birth in Bethlehem, his teaching and his death on the cross. "Gospel" means "good news."

BICYCLE The bicycle is a form of transport that most people can use. It is easy to ride and is cheap to run because it needs no fuel. The rider uses the power in his leg muscles to move it forward.

The first bicycle, although very unlike the modern bicycle, was built in about 1790 by a Frenchman named De Sivrac. In 1816 a German, Baron Karl Von Drais, built an improved model called a *draisine*. He is usually given the title 'father of the bicycle'. The early bicycles were steered by the front wheel and propelled by the rider pushing his feet on the ground. Later bicycles had

pedals to propel them. The famous penny farthing bicycle had the pedals attached to its huge front wheel. More and more improvements were made to the bicycle. These included two wheels of equal size; rubber tires filled with air; ball bearings; spring saddles; and gears. By the end of the 1800s, bicycles resembling today's models appeared.

The modern bicycle is propelled by pedals attached to cranks. The cranks turn a toothed chain wheel which is attached to a cog on the rear wheel. When the rider pedals, the chain transmits 'power' to the rear wheel.

BIRD Birds are unlike any other animals. All birds have wings, although some cannot fly. All birds have feathers. All birds have beaks instead of jaws.

Birds are more advanced animals than insects because they have backbones. Like mammals, birds are warm blooded. But like reptiles, birds lay eggs.

The first birds were descended from reptiles. Probably birds learned to fly by gliding from trees. They had lost a scaly skin and gained feathers. But birds still have scaly legs.

Most birds are perfectly built for flying. Their bones are hollow and light but strong. Their wing muscles are

Owls are birds of prey. Their eyes are in the front of their heads, so that they can judge distance well. Their broad wings allow them to fly silently as they hunt.

Little owl

Great spotted woodpecker

Hobby

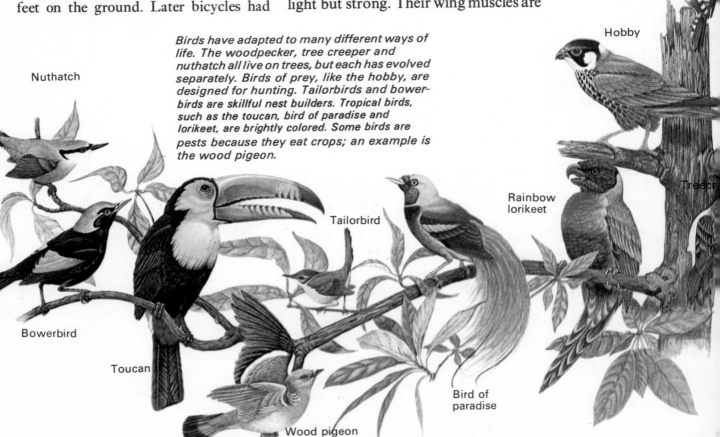

Birds have adapted to many different ways of life. The woodpecker, tree creeper and nuthatch all live on trees, but each has evolved separately. Birds of prey, like the hobby, are designed for hunting. Tailorbirds and bowerbirds are skillful nest builders. Tropical birds, such as the toucan, bird of paradise and lorikeet, are brightly colored. Some birds are pests because they eat crops; an example is the wood pigeon.

Nuthatch

Bowerbird

Toucan

Tailorbird

Rainbow lorikeet

Treecreeper

Wood pigeon

Bird of paradise

powerful. Their feathers help them fly, but also keep them warm and dry.

Flying is hard work and birds use up a lot of energy. So they spend a lot of time eating. They eat many different kinds of food. Birds rely mostly on eyesight to find food, but their taste and hearing are also good. Their sense of smell is poor. Birds are born with all the skills they will need. Much of their behavior is not learned but comes from instinct.

Birds reproduce by laying eggs. In the breeding season many of the male birds, or cocks, have bright colors and special songs to attract the females, or hens, and warn off rivals.

Many birds make nests in which to lay their eggs. The nest may be a skillfully woven basket of grass and leaves, or it may be a rough platform of twigs or even just a hollow in the ground.

In order to hatch, the eggs must be kept warm. To do this the parents sit on them. When the young hatch, they are helpless and must be fed by their parents. But they grow quickly and soon fly away.

Birds such as penguins cannot fly. But the penguin can swim well. The ostrich is another flightless bird. It uses its long legs to escape from enemies. The kiwi of New Zealand cannot fly, but it hides during the day and feeds at night when it is safer.

Man has domesticated some birds, keeping poultry and ducks for their eggs and meat. Some birds, including sparrows, live happily close to Man in towns. Others have become rare through contact with Man: some are killed by the chemicals farmers use to destroy insect pests.

See also CUCKOO; DODO; DUCKS AND GEESE; EAGLE; EMU; HUMMINGBIRD; KIWI; NESTS; OSTRICH; OWL; PARROT; PEACOCK; PENGUIN; STORK; SWAN.

BISON are wild cattle. They are large, powerful animals with humped shoulders, thick fur and short horns.

The North American bison is sometimes called the buffalo. Vast herds of bison provided food for the American Indians. But white men killed so many that the bison nearly died out. Now it is a protected animal. The European bison, or wisent, is also rare.

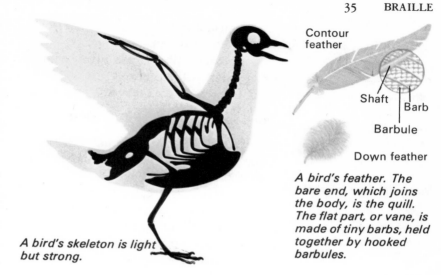

A bird's skeleton is light but strong.

Contour feather

Shaft

Barb

Barbule

Down feather

A bird's feather. The bare end, which joins the body, is the quill. The flat part, or vane, is made of tiny barbs, held together by hooked barbules.

The feet of birds are suited to the lives they lead. Shown here are (left to right): woodpecker (tree climbing), osprey (catching prey), coot and duck (swimming), and finch (perching or holding on to tree branches).

BLOOD Your heart pumps blood round your body. Blood carries food and oxygen to the body cells and removes waste such as carbon dioxide and water. Blood also fights disease and infection.

Blood is made up of red and white cells, or corpuscles, floating in a liquid called plasma. In warm-blooded animals blood is kept at a steady temperature. The blood of cold-blooded animals like fish and reptiles gets hotter or colder according to the temperature outside their bodies.

See also HEART.

BRAIN The brain is the body's control center. It receives messages from the senses and sends out orders to the muscles. Our brains control everything we do – our thoughts, memory, speech, sight, hearing and movement.

The brain is a soft mass of millions of nerve cells. Mammals have the best brains of all animals. But no animal has a brain as big, compared with the size of its body, as the human brain.

See also SENSES.

BRAILLE is a form of writing used by blind people. Instead of printed letters, a braille book has raised dots on its pages. The dots are arranged in patterns which represent letters or words. By touching the dots with their finger tips, blind people can read. They can also type in

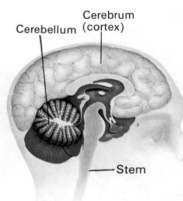

Cerebrum (cortex)

Cerebellum

Stem

The brain is protected by the skull. Its main parts are the cerebrum, cerebellum and stem.

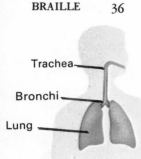

Human beings (above) breathe through lungs. Air passes into the lungs through the trachea and bronchi. Fishes (below) breathe through gills.

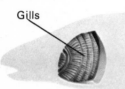

braille, using a machine which stamps out the dots through the paper.

The braille alphabet was invented by a Frenchman called Louis Braille. He lived from 1809 to 1852, and was blind from the age of three.

BREATHING All animals breathe. They need oxygen from the air to burn their food and make energy.

Human beings breathe through lungs. Lungs are spongy bags inside our bodies which fill with air when we breathe in. Oxygen from the air goes into the blood, and we breathe out carbon dioxide.

Fishes breathe through gills, which trap the oxygen dissolved in water. Insects and spiders breathe through tiny holes on the outside of their bodies.

Plants use carbon dioxide to make their food. In return they give off oxygen.

Beam bridges of reinforced concrete are still built today, but they can only span small gaps. To cross larger gaps, steel or concrete arch bridges are often used. For the longest spans, suspension bridges must be used. These are the most spectacular bridges of all. A suspension bridge is so called because the roadway is suspended from thick steel cables which run up and over steel towers. The Brooklyn Bridge in New York was the first modern suspension bridge. Another famous suspension bridge is the Golden Gate in San Francisco.

Some of the strangest bridges are moving bridges. Tower Bridge, a draw-bridge over the River Thames in London, has a roadway that opens upwards to let river traffic through. Swing bridges open by swinging sideways. Lift bridges are raised to allow ships to pass underneath.

The diagrams on the right show four kinds of bridge: suspension, arch, cantilever and beam. The arrows show the direction of the load, or weight, carried by each bridge.

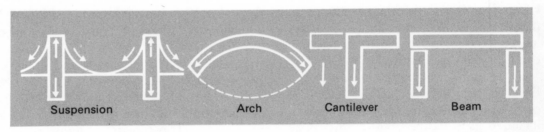

Suspension   Arch   Cantilever   Beam

Buddhist monks wear saffron-colored robes. On the face of Buddha is an expression of peace — the aim of all Buddhists.

BRIDGE From very early times Man has built bridges in order to cross rivers and ravines. The first bridges were probably simple tree trunks. Later bridges were stone slabs resting on stone supports, or piers. This type of bridge is called a beam bridge.

BUDDHA Buddhism is one of the world's great religions. Its founder was Gautama, the son of an Indian king. He was rich, yet he was sad for he knew the world was full of poverty and suffering. So he gave away his riches, and spent many years trying to find the answer to the world's unhappiness. Finally, as he sat beneath a banyan tree, the truth came to him. He taught people to be kind to others, and not greedy or selfish. He also taught that there are eight 'paths' to perfect peace. For this he was called Buddha, meaning 'Enlightened One', and today millions of Buddhists in Asia follow his teachings.

BUFFALO are wild cattle from Africa and Asia. There are several kinds. The Indian water buffalo likes muddy swamps. It is a useful working animal, and also gives meat and milk. The African or Cape buffalo cannot be tamed. It has massive horns and is most dangerous when wounded. The American bison is often called a buffalo.

BUILDING A few years ago American engineers finished the tallest building in the world. It is the Sears Tower in Chicago. It is 1,453 feet (443 meters) high and has 110 stories.

Like all skyscrapers, the Sears Tower is built with a steel frame set in concrete. This makes it very strong. Steel and concrete are used to build other things, too, such as bridges, dams and roads. They are our most important construction materials.

Ordinary houses and small buildings are usually built with other materials, especially wood, stone and bricks. Wood is often used in countries where there are lots of trees. In dry climates some houses are built of mud. But in most countries houses are built of bricks and mortar.

See also ARCHITECTURE.

BULB Plants make their own food and some are able to store this food to use later. Extra food is stored in special leaves called bulbs.

An onion is a bulb. When it is cut in half you can see the closely packed layers of fleshy leaves. Daffodils, tulips and hyacinths also have bulbs. In spring the plant uses food from its bulb to make new leaves and shoots.

BUTTER is one of the best energy-giving foods. We eat it as a spread on bread and as a cooking fat. Butter is made from cream, the richest part of cow's milk. The cream is shaken, or churned, until it becomes solid. Modern butter-making factories are called creameries.

The water buffalo is used to pull ploughs in the flooded rice fields of Asia. It is bigger than most domestic cattle.

BUTTERFLIES AND MOTHS

Butterflies are some of the most beautiful insects. They fly by day and their scaly wings are often brilliantly colored. Most moths are less colorful. Moths usually fly at dusk.

Butterflies and moths belong to the same family. Moths have hairier bodies, and they fold their wings flat when resting. Butterflies hold their wings upright instead. Butterflies have club-shaped feelers, or antennae, but moths have antennae without knobs.

Female butterflies and moths lay eggs. The eggs hatch into larvae called caterpillars. Caterpillars eat almost non-stop

The scaly skin of a bulb protects the fleshy leaves inside. The bud grows from the center. If a bud forms between the scales, it splits off to make a new bulb.

and grow by shedding their skins. Some caterpillars, like that of the cabbage butterfly, are harmful to crops. Others, like the silkworm are useful to Man.

When the caterpillar is fully grown, it stops eating. It fastens itself to a leaf or twig and becomes a chrysalis. The hard case of the chrysalis does not look alive. But inside, the caterpillar changes its shape. Soon the chrysalis splits and out crawls the adult insect. As soon as its wings are dry, it flies away.

Butterflies and moths feed on nectar. Like bees, they help pollinate flowers. To escape their many enemies, they

Brimstone moth

Hawk moth

A moth at rest holds its wings flat, while a butterfly holds its wings together over its body. All butterflies and moths have their own food plant, on which they lay their eggs. The caterpillars eat the leaves.

Red admiral

Magpie moth

often use disguise, or camouflage. When they stay still, it is very hard to see them.

Some kinds taste bad to eat and some are even poisonous. They are boldly marked so that hungry birds will recognize them and keep away. But other butterflies, quite good to eat, look just like them. So the birds avoid these butterflies as well. This is called mimicry, meaning imitation.

Butterflies can hear, taste and see, and they can smell through their feet! Moths cannot see so well, but they are attracted to light. In the spring butterflies and moths use special smells to attract mates.

The barrel cactus from North America gets its name from its round shape and 'ribs'.

Egg Caterpillar Chrysalis Adult

The butterfly's life cycle: from egg to caterpillar, then to chrysalis and finally to adult insect.

To protect itself, the caterpillar (left) of the puss moth tries to look fierce. It can also squirt acid at an enemy.

The beautiful peacock butterfly (below) belongs to the fritillary family.

CACTUS Cacti are flowering plants which live in the hot and dry desert. They have spreading roots for finding moisture and they store water in their fleshy stems.

To protect themselves, most cacti are covered with spines. Otherwise, because they contain water, they would be good food for desert animals. Cactus spines are really leaves.

CALENDAR A calendar is a way of dividing up the year into months, weeks and days. Practically everyone in the world uses the same kind of calendar. The ancient Romans worked out our present calendar nearly 2000 years ago. They based it on the movements of the Earth around the Sun and the Moon around the Earth. In 1582, Pope Gregory XIII made some minor changes to the Roman's calendar. It is this calendar, called the Gregorian calendar, that is used today.

See also TIME.

CAMEL The camel is often called the ship of the desert. For thousands of years this strange-looking animal has been used to carry men and their goods. There are very few wild camels left.

The camel is well adapted to desert life. It stores fat in its hump and can go for days without water. Its wide, padded feet do not sink into the sand.

The Bactrian camel from Asia has two humps. It can live in quite cold regions. The Arabian camel has only one hump. The dromedary is a swift Arabian camel used for racing. The meat, milk and wool of the camel are also used by man.

CAMERA A camera is a light-tight box with a window, or lens, on one side. When we take a picture a shutter moves aside and lets light from the object we are photographing pass through the lens. The light falls on to a strip of light-sensitive film, forming an image of the object. When the film is treated with certain chemicals, or *developed*, the image shows up. The developed film is called a *negative*. The negative is printed into a positive picture on special paper. The picture can be color or black and white depending on the film used.

Some cameras have extra dials and lenses which give special effects. Other cameras are designed for scientific, military and medical use.

A Polaroid camera uses film which develops the negative into the finished picture. Movie cameras take a rapid series of pictures. When they are flashed on the screen, the eye sees them as one movement.

CAMOUFLAGE Many animals are colored or shaped to match their background. We call this camouflage. Camouflage makes an animal difficult to see, and so protects it from enemies.

Spots or stripes help to hide an animal by breaking up the outline of its body. The zebra's stripes blend with the long grass on which it grazes. The leopard's spots conceal it among the sun-dappled leaves of a tree.

Most fish have dark backs and light undersides. This makes them harder to see from above and from below. Many

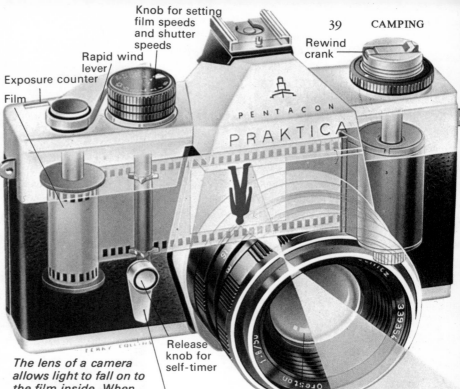

Knob for setting film speeds and shutter speeds
Rewind crank
Rapid wind lever
Exposure counter
Film
PENTACON PRAKTICA
Release knob for self-timer
Cocking device for self-timer
Lens

The lens of a camera allows light to fall on to the film inside. When this happens, an upside-down image of the scene in front of the lens is formed on the film.

insects and reptiles are so well camouflaged that it is hard to spot them until they move.

The chameleon can change its color to match its background. Flatfish can also do this. The fur of the brown snow hare and the stoat turns white in winter.

Some animals trick their enemies by looking like something else. This is called mimicry. Leaf insects look like leaves, stick insects look like dead twigs. Some flies look like stinging wasps. Some harmless insects look like others which are poisonous or bad to eat.

The camel can live in hot and dry deserts where most other animals would die. Arabian camels have been kept by Man since ancient times. But they have never become friendly. A bad-tempered camel will spit and bite if annoyed.

CAMPING. When people leave their homes to live outdoors for a time they go camping. The areas where they camp are called campsights.

A good campsight is away from gullies and cliffs. It is on high, firm ground that slopes away from the tent area. The campsight should have open spaces for pitching a tent, and some trees nearby for shelter from the sun. Camping directly under trees is dangerous.

A good camper knows how to survive in the wilderness. He knows how to collect wood and build a fire to keep warm and cook his food. He knows where to find shelter in a storm and how to figure out his direction if he gets lost. He also understands first aid in case he or a friend gets hurt.

It is always good to go camping in groups. Three people is perfect. If one person gets hurt there will be one person to stay behind and one to go for help.

Good campers clean up after themselves and take care not to harm the land, or waste its natural resources. This is called conservation.

See also CONSERVATION.

...

CANADA is the second largest country in the world. Only Russia is bigger. Yet Canada has only 22·7 million people. It covers the northern part of North America, stretching from the Atlantic Ocean to the Pacific and north to the Arctic Ocean. Canada is our northern neighbor.

Canada is a land of high mountains, such as the Rocky Mountains, thick forests and plains. The Great Lakes include the world's second largest, Lake Superior. The St Lawrence is an important river for trade. Canada has warm summers and cold winters. In the north, the ground is snow-covered for most of the year. Canada's animals include bears, wolves, beavers, foxes, caribou and moose.

The first Europeans in Canada were explorers and fur trappers. Now most Canadians live in towns. The farmers of the prairies grow wheat and the forests produce timber. There are rich minerals, such as coal, oil, natural gas, gold, uranium and asbestos. The rivers provide hydro-electric power.

About half of Canada's people are descended from British settlers. One third are French-Canadians, who speak French. The native people of Canada are Eskimos and American Indians.

Canada contains 10 provinces and two territories. The government of each province takes care of its own education, power, highways, land and forests. But the federal government in Ottawa makes laws for all of Canada.

Canada is part of the British Commonwealth of Nations. The Commonwealth is a group of nations which once belonged to the British Empire. The Queen of England is also the Queen of

Banff National Park, high in the Canadian Rockies, is a popular holiday resort.

Canada's population is very small for such an enormous country.

Canada. Though the governor general heads the Parliament as the Queen's representative, he has little real power.

CANAL Canals are man-made rivers. They are built to carry our cargo boats, barges and ships. Canals have many other uses. They provide water for irrigating the land. In some low-lying countries they drain the land. And in Venice canals form the 'roads' of the city.

Some canals have been in use for a very long time. Parts of the Grand Canal in China are over 2000 years old. It is the world's longest canal, over 932 miles (1500 kilometers) long. Many canals were built during the Industrial Revolution, when factory and mine owners needed better ways of moving coal and other goods.

Today, the most important canals are the ship canals of Suez, Panama and the

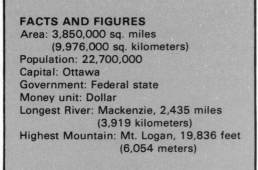

FACTS AND FIGURES
Area: 3,850,000 sq. miles
        (9,976,000 sq. kilometers)
Population: 22,700,000
Capital: Ottawa
Government: Federal state
Money unit: Dollar
Longest River: Mackenzie, 2,435 miles
        (3,919 kilometers)
Highest Mountain: Mt. Logan, 19,836 feet
        (6,054 meters)

St Lawrence. The Suez Canal cuts through sandy desert between the Red Sea and the Mediterranean Sea. It saves ships traveling between Europe and the Far East thousands of miles. The Panama Canal in central America is a short cut between the Pacific and Atlantic Oceans. The St Lawrence Seaway in Canada makes it possible for ships to travel from the Atlantic right into the heart of North America.

CARBON If you hold a plate above a candle flame, a black deposit forms on it. This is carbon. Burnt wood, or charcoal, and coke are also forms of carbon. And the 'lead' in pencils is a natural form of carbon called graphite. A diamond is another natural form. Yet graphite is very soft and a diamond is very hard. Carbon is one of the chemical elements. All living things contain carbon.

and thick. There were towers along the walls, with slits through which archers could fire arrows. Around the walls was a ditch, or moat, filled with water. In the center of the castle was a massive tower called a keep. Inside the keep, or in a separate building, was a great hall, in which lived the nobleman and his family, and a chapel. Elsewhere in the castle were kitchens, storerooms, barracks for soldiers, stables for animals and a well.

It was difficult to capture a castle once the defenders had pulled up the drawbridge over the moat. Inside they had enough food and water to last for weeks. From the shelter of the castle walls they could shoot at the attackers, or drop boulders and boiling oil on top of them.

When an army laid siege to a castle, they surrounded the castle walls. The soldiers tried to break down the walls by

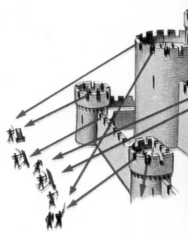

The battlements on top of the castle walls and towers protected the defenders, and gave them good positions from which to fire at the enemy.

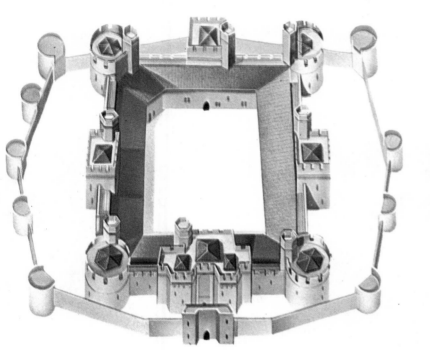

CASTLE Hundreds of years ago a castle was the safest place in time of war. Noblemen and kings built strong castles to defend their lands.

The earliest castles were wooden forts. They were built on hill tops and surrounded by banks of earth and ditches. Inside there was room for the local people and their animals.

During the Middle Ages castles were built of stone. The outer walls were high

The castle's strong outer walls were its main defense. Inside were the great hall, the chapel, kitchens, storerooms and barracks for soldiers.

digging tunnels beneath them or by hitting them with battering rams. Catapults hurled rocks at the castle while the soldiers used scaling ladders and wooden siege towers to try and climb over the walls. If all else failed, they starved out the inhabitants.

Although they must have been cold and damp places to live in, castles were good strongholds. When cannons were invented, castles were no longer safe. Stone walls were easily smashed by cannon balls.

CAT A fluffy, playful kitten does not look very fierce. But it is a close relative of the mighty tiger. All cats are flesh-eating mammals. They hunt by stealth, usually alone. They move silently because their claws retract into soft pads on their feet. They can see well, even at night, and they have a keen sense of smell.

Domestic cats are descended from the African wild cat. To the ancient Egyptians the cat was sacred. But in Europe cats did not become common mouse hunters until the 1700s.

Cats make good pets. There are many kinds. But they are independent animals, and go back to living in the wild quite easily. The European wild cat looks like a large tabby, but it is very fierce.

Cats breed twice a year. The female gives birth to five or six kittens. The young of the big cats, such as the lion and tiger are called cubs. All cats, even well-fed pets, are hunters, and the big cats are the fiercest hunters of all. But they only hunt when they are hungry.

See also CHEETAH; LEOPARD AND JAGUAR; LION; TIGER.

CATTLE For thousands of years farmers have kept herds of cattle. Like all mammals, the cow feeds her newborn calf on milk from her own body. Cattle provide us with milk, meat and leather made from their skins.

Cattle eat grass and leaves. Farmers also give them hay and special foods to make them fat. Cows 'chew the cud': that is, they eat quickly and then bring up the food again later to chew it properly. A cow's stomach has four parts. Food passes through each part as it is digested.

Domestic cattle are descended from wild cattle, such as the extinct aurochs. Zebu cattle from Asia have a hump on their shoulders. To the Hindus the cow is sacred.

There are many breeds of cattle. Dairy cows give the most milk. Beef cattle produce the most meat. In some countries oxen still pull carts and ploughs. Bison and buffalo are wild cattle.

See also BISON; BUFFALO.

CAVE Caves are found in the sides of hills and cliffs. They are hollowed out of the rock by the sea or by underground streams. Large caves are called caverns.

Caves are dark and damp. Inside may live bats, salamanders and a few insects. Fish and shrimps live in underground lakes. Some cave animals are blind.

Exploring caves, or pot-holing as it is sometimes called, can be dangerous. Strange rock formations called stalactites and stalagmites are found in some caves.

Cattle have worked as beasts of burden for thousands of years. In Turkey oxen are still used by farmers.

Cats are among the fiercest hunters of the animal world. Even the tame house cat is really a tiger in miniature. Shown here, from left to right, are: domestic cat, wild cat, caracal, lynx, tiger, black panther, snow leopard and lion.

CAVE MEN lived during the Stone Age. In earlier prehistoric times, people had lived by hunting and food-gathering. They lived out in the open, wandering in search of food and making rough shelters from tree branches. As the climate was mild, they did not need warm houses.

Then came the last of the great Ice Ages, and most of the northern parts of the world were covered by ice and snow. The Stone Age hunters had to find warm, dry places to live. So groups of people moved into caves, where they were safe from the storms and blizzards. Sometimes the people had to drive out animals like

After the Neanderthals came a more advanced people called Cro-Magnon people, named after a place in France. They were better tool-makers and on the walls of the caves they drew pictures of the animals they hunted – the mammoth, wild horse, reindeer, bison and woolly rhinoceros. These cave paintings were done in the flickering light of lamps made of moss soaked in fat. For paints, the cave men used earth and clay mixed with water. Sometimes their paintings had a magical meaning. They were made to bring the hunters good luck. Cave paintings can still be seen at Lascaux, France and Altamira, Spain.

the cave bear before they could live in the caves. Near the cave entrance they built a fire for warmth and to cook their food. Fire helped scare away hungry wolves and saber-toothed cats.

Cave men hunted animals for meat and used skins for clothing and bedding. They had wooden spears, hardened in the fire, and later bows and arrows. To make sharper arrow heads and spear points they used pieces of stone. They soon discovered a hard rock called flint. By hitting two flints together, they could chip off flakes and make simple tools, such as knives, axes and scrapers.

Cave men lived long before people had learned to write. But we know how they lived because they left piles of bones and flints inside their caves. They also buried their dead in caves. The first European cave men lived perhaps 100,000 years ago. They are called Neanderthal people after the place in Germany where their bones were first discovered.

Some caves were lived in for thousands of years. But when the Ice Age ended, people learned new ways of life. They began to grow crops and to keep domestic animals. They built houses near their fields. They discovered how to make metal tools. This was the beginning of civilization.

CELL All living things are made up of cells. Most cells are too small to be seen except under a microscope.

The animal called an amoeba has only a single cell. But the human body has millions of cells, each with a job to do. Cells reproduce by dividing. In this way worn out cells are replaced and new cells are added as we grow.

The center of a cell is the nucleus: around the nucleus is a blob of jelly called protoplasm. Cells join together to make tissues – the materials of which our bodies are built. Different cells build skin, bone, blood, nerves, muscles and glands.

The early cave men used rocks and sharpened sticks to kill animals for food. Later, men made weapons and tools by chipping flints. They used digging sticks as spades and learned how to make fire. Some Stone Age caves can still be seen today.

This painting of a spotted horse can be seen deep inside a cave in France.

Plants are also made up of cells. In many ways these are like animal cells, but they have a very thick cell wall made of cellulose, which gives plants their stiffness.

CENTIPEDE AND MILLEPEDE

Centipedes and millepedes are related to both insects and crabs. They have many legs.

Centipedes hide under logs and stones and come out at night to hunt. They run quickly and catch insects in their poisonous claws.

Millepedes have even more legs than centipedes. But they move more slowly. Millepedes burrow into loose soil and eat rotting plants.

CEREALS are important food crops. They belong to the grass family. The fruit or seed of the plant is called a grain. It can be eaten whole or ground into flour.

In tropical lands the most important cereals are rice, maize and millet. In cooler climates the chief cereals are wheat, oats, barley and rye.

See also RICE; WHEAT.

CHALK is a soft white mineral. It is a form of limestone, made up of the tiny shells of dead animals.

Chalk can be used as a writing material, as a fertilizer and, mixed with clay, as cement. Chalk is porous – it has tiny holes through which water can seep.

CHAMELEON

Chameleons are African lizards. They live in trees and move very slowly. But to catch insects, they shoot out their long tongues very quickly. The chameleon can change color to match its background. It does this partly as camouflage, to protect

The chief world cereals are from left to right: barley, maize, rice, rye, oats and wheat. Most of our bread is made from wheat flour. Maize, or sweet corn, can be eaten as corn on the cob. Rice is the chief food of most Asian peoples. Rye is an important crop in the cooler parts of Northern Europe, Asia and North America.

itself and partly as a way of showing it is angry or frightened.

CHEESE is made from the solid part, or curd, of sour milk. Bacteria are added to milk to make it sour. The curd is separated from the watery part, or whey. It is heated, pressed, cooled and stored until the cheese is ready. This is called curing.

During the curing process different kinds of bacteria are added to make the many varieties of cheese we know. In America, cheddar is the most popular variety. Others are Swiss, which is filled with holes and mozarella which tops pizza.

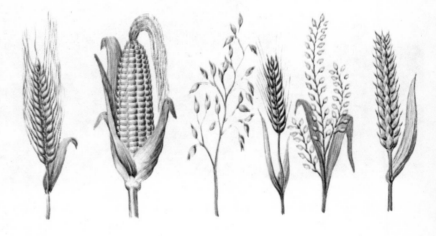

CHEETAH The cheetah of Africa is the fastest land animal. It hunts by stalking its prey and then chasing it at great speed. Not even the swift antelope can escape, for the cheetah can run at over 68 miles (110 kilometers) an hour, though only in short bursts. Cheetahs cannot retract their claws.

CHEMISTRY is one of the main branches of science. The people who practice chemistry are called chemists. They look into the properties and make-up of matter. They try to find out what substances are made of; how they are put together; and how they react with other substances. Over the years they have found, for example, that all substances are made up of certain basic units – the chemical elements.

Cheetahs are sprinters, not long-distance runners. These graceful hunters are becoming quite rare in the wild.

ISHOP KING

QUEEN

PAWN

ROOK KNIGHT

CHESS

CHESS is a challenging game of war strategy where two players pit their armies against each other as they try to capture their opponent's king. It is played on a board with 64 squares.

The "royal game" as it is often called was invented in India and Persia 13 centuries ago. In fact the word "chess" comes from the persian word *shah* meaning "king."

As the game starts, each side's king and queen are safely surrounded by their army of rooks, bishops, knights and pawns. But as the game progresses, each player must do more than just plot how he is going to advance and attack. He must also carefully guard his own king; for in one false move he can be *checkmated* and lose the game.

Each player has 16 playing pieces or *chessmen*. The more important pieces are the king, the queen, and the two rooks, knights and bishops. There are eight lesser pieces or pawns. One reason chess is so interesting is that each piece seems to have its own "personality" and can only move in certain directions.

Such wonders, and the splendor of the Chinese court, astonished Marco Polo, who was the first European to bring back stories of China. He completed the long journey over land to China in 1275 and stayed there for 17 years.

Finely carved stone work is a feature of the churches built in the Decorated style of the 1300s.

For centuries, China was ruled by emperors. But gradually it was weakened by civil wars and bad government. Finally, in 1911 a revolution broke out. The emperor soon surrendered and in 1912 China was declared a republic.

Later China was split by fighting between Communists and Nationalists. By 1949 the Communists won and China became a Communist state. Today many things in China are based on the thoughts of Mao Tse Tung.

CHURCH The early Christians had to worship in secret, sometimes in underground caves. Later they built churches in which to meet and worship.

Many churches, especially old ones, are built in the shape of a cross. At the eastern end is the altar and the chancel, where the priest takes the service. At the west is the nave where the congregation sits. In some modern churches the altar is in the center of the church.

Many churches have tall spires which point to heaven. Sometimes

Workmen toiled for hundreds of years to build the great cathedrals of the Middle Ages. A massive bell tower was often built where the transepts, nave and choir met. Some buttresses supported the outside walls.

windows made with colorful stained glass tell Bible stories. Churches built in different centuries follow different styles of architecture. During the Middle Ages, many great churches called cathedrals were built. A cathedral is the main church of a bishop's diocese.

CHURCHILL, Winston, Leonard Spencer (1874-1965) was Prime Minister of Great Britain during World War II.

He is one of modern history's greatest men. He is best remembered for the strong leadership and stirring speeches which gave people encouragement in the war against Hitler's Germany.

CIRCUS The circus is a popular entertainment, often held inside a large tent. The circus show features clowns, acrobats, jugglers, trick riders and performing animals. It may have daring high wire walkers and trapeze fliers. Elephants, lions, sea lions, dogs and chimpanzees are trained to do tricks. The biggest circus of all is Barnum and Bailey's Circus. It is called 'The Greatest Show on Earth'.

In ancient Rome the circus was a huge race track. Thousands of people came to watch chariot races. The charioteers had to be strong and skillful to drive the horses round the tight bends of the track.

CITY In prehistoric times people lived in groups for protection. They built a village with a wall or ditch around it.

Gradually, some villages grew into towns. People learned how to farm and began trading with each other. The most important towns or trading centers became the first cities.

Thousands of years ago the Egyptians built great cities. The ancient Greeks built Athens, with its beautiful temples. The city of Rome was the center of the Roman Empire.

In the Middle Ages European cities such as London, Antwerp and Venice became rich through trade. Art and learning flourished in the cities. But they were still small, compared with our cities today.

When the Industrial Revolution began in the 1700s, cities grew rapidly as people left the countryside to work in the new factories. Many of them had to live in terrible slums without proper houses or sanitation. It took a long time to improve conditions in many cities.

Cities are still growing as people arrive in search of jobs and better lives. In parts of Asia and South America people live in 'shanty towns' on the edge of modern cities. In the city centers building land is so scarce that very tall buildings called skyscrapers have had to be built.

Many people work in cities, but live outside and travel to their jobs every day by car, bus or train. The world's largest cities have more people than many countries. This causes problems such as traffic jams, shortage of houses, overcrowding and pollution.

Athens was one of the most beautiful cities of the ancient world. The ruins of the Parthenon still stand on the rocky hill known as the Acropolis.

In the busy modern city of New York are some of the world's tallest buildings. The city's skyscrapers dwarf the people in the streets far below. New York is the second largest city in the world; Tokyo, Japan is the largest.

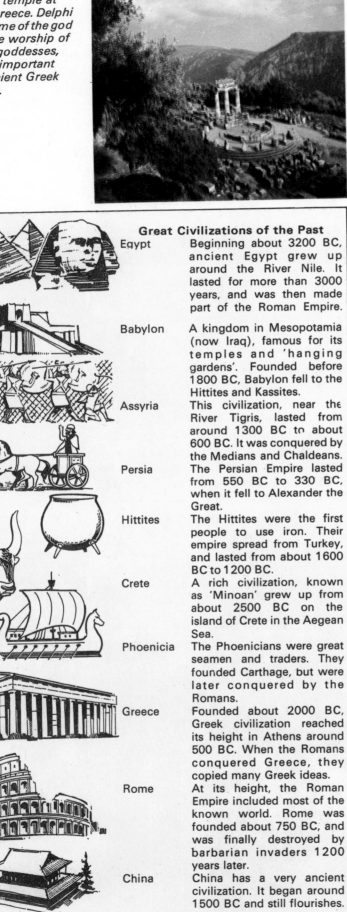

An ancient temple at Delphi in Greece. Delphi was the home of the god Apollo. The worship of gods and goddesses, played an important part in ancient Greek civilization.

CIVILIZATION means an advanced way of life. Civilized people are able to develop arts, skills, trade and learning. Civilization began when people no longer had to spend all their time searching for food. Thousands of years ago tribes began joining together to form communities. Farming and trade developed as people settled in one area, instead of wandering from place to place. As they grew more prosperous, they built cities, temples and roads. Strong and safe from enemies, people felt proud of their land and treated the uncivilized 'barbarians' of other countries with scorn.

Most civilizations in ancient times had strong armies to protect them against greedy rivals. Mighty empires spread their way of life by conquest. They grew so powerful that their rulers felt they would last for ever. But none did. Some civilizations grew weak and fell apart. Others were destroyed by enemies.

Only the ruins of these great civilizations of the past now remain. But they have left their mark on our lives. Modern civilization in Europe, for example, owes a great deal to the ideas of the Greeks and Romans. Civilization in America owes a great deal to the first settlers and our ancestors who came here from different countries in Europe. Today we share in the way of life known as the "industrial civilization." This refers to changes in living and working habits which resulted from the Industrial Revolution.

CLAY When rocks are worn down and crumbled by weather over a long period of time, they form clay.

Clay soil is heavy. When wet, it becomes mud; when dry, it hardens and cracks. Bricks, tiles and pottery are made by heating clay in a kiln. Many fossils are found in clay beds. Water cannot soak through clay, so underground reservoirs are sometimes formed where there are thick clay deposits.

CLIMATE The climate of an area is the combination of sunshine, moisture, wind and temperature over a time. Different parts of the world have different climates. The polar climate at the North and South Poles is cold and icy.

Great Civilizations of the Past

Egypt	Beginning about 3200 BC, ancient Egypt grew up around the River Nile. It lasted for more than 3000 years, and was then made part of the Roman Empire.
Babylon	A kingdom in Mesopotamia (now Iraq), famous for its temples and 'hanging gardens'. Founded before 1800 BC, Babylon fell to the Hittites and Kassites.
Assyria	This civilization, near the River Tigris, lasted from around 1300 BC to about 600 BC. It was conquered by the Medians and Chaldeans.
Persia	The Persian Empire lasted from 550 BC to 330 BC, when it fell to Alexander the Great.
Hittites	The Hittites were the first people to use iron. Their empire spread from Turkey, and lasted from about 1600 BC to 1200 BC.
Crete	A rich civilization, known as 'Minoan' grew up from about 2500 BC on the island of Crete in the Aegean Sea.
Phoenicia	The Phoenicians were great seamen and traders. They founded Carthage, but were later conquered by the Romans.
Greece	Founded about 2000 BC, Greek civilization reached its height in Athens around 500 BC. When the Romans conquered Greece, they copied many Greek ideas.
Rome	At its height, the Roman Empire included most of the known world. Rome was founded about 750 BC, and was finally destroyed by barbarian invaders 1200 years later.
China	China has a very ancient civilization. It began around 1500 BC and still flourishes.

But the tropical climate near the equator is warm and rainy. The climate of an area affects the way people live, the food they eat and how they dress.

See also WEATHER.

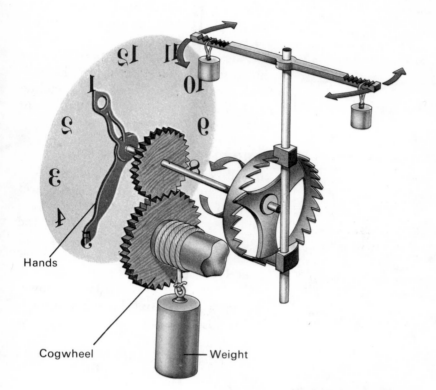

A simple clock is driven by a falling weight or pendulum. Cogwheels and smaller weights control the movement and regulate the mechanism.

Hands

Cogwheel

Weight

CLOCKS AND WATCHES These are timepieces – instruments that tell us the time. A clock divides the day into hours and minutes. A watch may also show seconds. Watches are small enough to wear on the wrist.

Most ordinary clocks are powered by a spring (mainspring). When you wind such a clock, the spring is tightened. As it unwinds it moves the clock's hands. A device called a rocking lever stops it from uncurling too quickly. This lever is rocked by another spring (hairspring) at a precise rate. This action regulates the clock by making the hands move round at the right speed.

Some big clocks, such as grandfather clocks, are powered by weights. They have a swinging pendulum to regulate them. Other clocks are powered by regular household electricity. Other kinds of watches are battery powered. They may have a vibrating tuning fork or a crystal to regulate them. Digital watches do not have hands; they show the time in figures.

CLOUD When it rains, the puddles soon dry. The water has turned into invisible water vapor.

The vapor rises into the air, and the higher it rises, the cooler it becomes. As it cools, the vapor turns back into water. Millions of tiny drops of water, so light they float in the air, make clouds.

The clouds rise, and more and more vapor turns to water. The drops get bigger and heavier. When they are too heavy to float any more, they fall as raindrops. When the air is very cold, these turn to ice, and fall as hail or snow.

By studying the different kinds of clouds, scientists can tell what kind of weather to expect.

See also FOG; RAIN; WATER; WEATHER.

COAL is one of our most important fuels. It can be burned to heat buildings. At power stations it is burned to make electricity. Coal is also made into coal gas and coke, which are both good fuels. A lot of coke is used in the steel industry. Many chemicals can be produced from coal to make dyes, plastics, medicines and explosives.

Coal is mined from the ground. It is formed from the remains of forests of huge ferns and strange trees which grew millions of years ago. When these died, they became covered by mud and sand. In time the mud and sand changed into rocks. The dead plants were squeezed until they changed into coal.

High cirrus clouds are made of ice. Fluffy cumulus clouds usually mean fine weather, but layers of low stratus clouds bring rain. The dark towering cumulonimbus are thunder clouds.

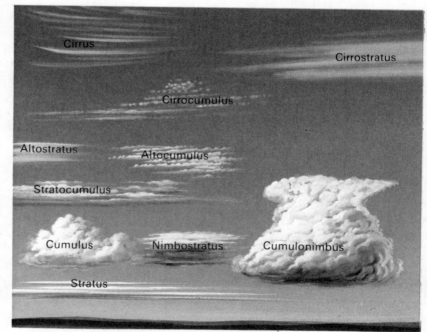

Cirrus

Cirrostratus

Cirrocumulus

Altostratus

Altocumulus

Stratocumulus

Cumulus

Nimbostratus

Cumulonimbus

Stratus

Sometimes the coal deposits, or seams, can be reached from the surface. But often they are buried deep underground. Underground mining is expensive and dangerous. Shafts are sunk deep into the ground, and tunnels are dug to the coal seams. Miners now use machines to cut out the coal. The coal is taken by conveyor belts or railway wagons to the shafts and lifted to the surface.

In a coal mine shafts are dug down to the seams or workings. The miners travel down in a 'cage', and fresh air is pumped down ventilation shafts.

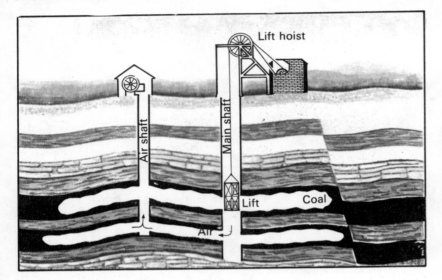

COCOA comes from the seeds of the cacao tree, which is grown in West Africa, the West Indies and South America. The beans are dried, roasted and ground until a thick brown liquid forms. When squeezed and dried, this makes cocoa powder. To make chocolate, sugar and other ingredients, such as milk, are added to cocoa.

Chocolate is an energy-giving food. Christopher Columbus brought cocoa beans to Europe from America in 1502.

CODES AND CIPHERS To send a secret message, either a code or a cipher can be used. In a coded message, the letters of each word are replaced by other letters. This is done according to a plan or key. For example, A might be replaced by B, B by C, C by D and so on. This way, the message 'COME NOW' would be written as DPNF OPX. Only people who know the key can read the message.

Such a simple code can be broken, or understood, quite easily. Ciphers are more complicated. The letters are often mixed up and replaced by numbers. The key to a cipher might be the first line of a book. For example, in the first line of

this article 'TO SEND A SECRET MESSAGE', T could be 1, O2, S3, and so on. Using this key, the cipher 14 4 12 1 7 13 19 7 1 20 reads 'MEET AT GATE'. Only someone knowing the key can decipher the message, especially since a letter can be represented by more than one number – E in the above example is 4,9,12, 15 and 20.

Codes and ciphers have been used for thousands of years, especially in wartime. Today, code books and coding machines are used to *encode* (write) and *decode* (read) secret messages.

COFFEE is made from the roasted and ground beans of the coffee plant.

Coffee bushes grow best in warm, wet highland areas. Inside each red berry are one or two beans. At harvest time, the beans are removed and dried in the sun. Then they are roasted and sold, either ground or whole.

The best coffee is made by slowly filtering or 'percolating' hot water through freshly ground beans. Instant coffee is

Cocoa beans (far left) look like nuts. They grow in pods on trees about 30 feet (9 meters) tall. Coffee beans (left) grow on bushes.

The semaphore code (below) is a system of flag signals. Each letter of the alphabet (starting with A top left, and reading from left to right) has a different signal.

made by drying liquid coffee until a fine powder is left. This powder quickly dissolves in hot water. Drinking coffee keeps some people awake. This is because coffee contains a mild stimulant called caffeine.

COLOR Everything around us has color—blue skies, orange sunsets, green trees and flowers of every color you can think of. In the animal world color is often used as a protection against other creatures. Some animals use their color to attract mates. With paint and dyes we color our houses, our clothes and our cars.

We see things in different colors be-

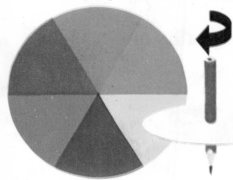

White light is made up of a mixture of colors. You can see this if you spin a colored top. The colors merge into white.

cause of the different ways they reflect light. Ordinary, or white, light is a mixture of all the colors of the rainbow. A rainbow in fact is caused by white light being split into its colors by raindrops. We see something as red, say, when its surface reflects only the red part of white light.

There are hundreds of different colors. But they are all made from only a few basic colors. We can make any colored paint by mixing red, yellow and blue paints together.

COLUMBUS, Christopher (1451-1506) was an Italian explorer who

discovered America. Europeans had long wished for a short route to Asia. And in 1492, believing that Asia was on the other side of the world, Columbus set out around the globe to find it. His ships, the Nina, the Pinta and the Santa Maria traveled nearly 3,000 miles before reaching land on October 12, 1492 . Columbus returned to Spain with gold and other riches but was disappointed he had not reached Asia. He died never knowing that he had discovered a New World.

The Sun's rays make the gas in a comet glow. In ancient times people thought that a comet in the sky warned of some great disaster to come on Earth. Today, we know when comets will appear next.

The three primary light colors are red, green and blue. Any other color can be made by mixing them. All the colors in a color television set are made from these three primary light colors.

Mixing paints is quite different from mixing lights. You can make any color of paint you want by mixing yellow, blue and red paints. But you cannot make white paint by mixing colored paints.

COMET Comets are heavenly bodies. They are glowing balls of gas and dust which travel in an orbit, or path, around the Sun. Some of them have a long tail. But they only start to glow when they get near the Sun. Some comets take only a few years to circle the Sun, others take thousands of years. The most famous comet is Halley's comet, which orbits the Sun every 77 years. We should be able to see it again in about 1986.

COMMUNISM is a way of thinking, or philosophy, which some governments use in ruling people. The main idea of Communism is that all of the wealth should be shared. And so the government owns and controls all the factories, mines, farms and shops. Communism is a harsh system of government. Religion is discouraged and there is little political choice. However, Communism has improved the living standards of people who were once poor.

COMPASS A compass is an instrument used to find directions. A simple compass has a needle which always points in the same directions – north and south. This kind of compass is a magnetic compass. About 2000 years ago the Chinese noticed that when they spun a spoon made from a special metal called lodestone, one end always pointed north when it stopped spinning.

Most ships and planes use a gyro-compass. This device contains a spinning drum and, once set, its axle always points in one direction, no matter which way the ship or plane turns.

See also GYROSCOPE.

A compass needle always points to the magnetic north pole. The Earth's magnetic poles are not in the same places as the North and South Poles.

COMPUTER Computers are a special kind of calculating machine that can work out complicated problems very quickly. They are sometimes called electronic brains. In seconds they can solve mathematical problems that would take a scientist a month to do. They can store and sort out all kinds of information about such things as wages, hotel reservations, airline bookings, paths of missiles and bank balances. Computers can run chemical plants, fly airplanes and steer ships. Some can translate languages; others can play chess.

Most computers handle information fed to them in the form of numbers, or digits. They are called digital computers. A set of instructions, called a program, tells the computer what to do. It stores the program and other information in a memory unit.

The smallest kind of computer is the pocket calculator. The numbered keys are linked to simple 'off and on' circuits, and the calculator can work out complicated sums in a few seconds.

CONSERVATION is the protection of nature, including natural resources such as water, soil, minerals, forests and wildlife. For centuries people have made use of these resources without any thought of preserving them for future generations. Forests have been cut down

to make room for farms and factories. The soil, air and water have been polluted, or poisoned, by waste. Many animals have been killed for their skins, captured for zoos or driven from their breeding grounds. Today, conservationists try to give rare animals safe places to live in. Even the seas are in danger. Unless people stop killing whales, for instance, there will be none of these huge sea mammals left.

Conservation means taking care of the Earth. We must have respect for all living things and use our resources more wisely. People are only beginning to see how much damage they have done by being greedy and thoughtless. Conservation concerns us all.

CONSTITUTION OF THE UNITED STATES The Constitution of the United States is perhaps the most important document in the history of America because it set the framework for government as we know it today. The Constitution was ratified on June 21, 1788.

After the Revolutionary War, the colonies had been united under a loose system of government based on The Articles of Confederation. But some of the delegates to Congress noticed problems in the government under the Articles of Confederation, and they agreed to meet in Philadelphia to see if they could work out a better system. There they drafted and ratified the Constitution.

The Constitution established the government we have today which consists of three branches: Executive (the President and his Cabinet); Judicial (the Supreme Court); and Legislative (Senate and the House of Representatives). In order to avoid the kind of tyranny they experienced under England, the Founding Fathers also developed a system of checks and balances whereby each of these branches could veto the decisions of the other.

The Constitution also outlined the various rights which were guaranteed to individuals. Though these were not included in the original document, they were proposed and ratified on

September 25, 1789. The rights are called the Bill of Rights and are the first 10 amendments to the Constitution. Other amendments have been added over the years in order to meet the people's needs in a changing world. Some additional amendments to the Constitution include: the 13th which abolished slavery; the 15th which granted equal voting rights regardless of race or color; the 16th which permitted the government to levy income tax and the most recent amendment the 26th passed in 1971 which gave 18 year olds the right to vote.

See also AMERICAN COLONIES; DECLARATION OF INDEPENDENCE; DEMOCRACY; GOVERNMENT; UNITED STATES OF AMERICA.

COPPER was one of the first metals to be used by Man. Today, a great deal of copper is used to make electrical wiring because copper carries electricity well. Pennies are made out of copper. And both quarters and dimes contain thin layers of copper. Brass is another metal containing copper. Brass fittings and copper piping are widely used by plumbers. Copper is also used to make jewelry, ornaments and cooking utensils.

CORAL looks like rock, but it is made from tiny algae or the skeletons of tiny sea animals called polyps.

Polyps are soft, like jellyfish. They build hard cases of limestone around themselves for protection. When the polyp dies, the hard shell remains. Over millions of years, the coral can grow into a great undersea wall called a reef.

COTTON is a very useful plant. Inside its round fruits, called bolls, are masses of white fibers. When the fruits ripen, they split and the fibers are blown away, spreading the seeds. But in the cotton fields, the bolls are picked before this can happen.

A machine called a cotton gin removes the fibers from the seeds and presses them into bales. At the cotton mill, the fibers are washed and spun into yarn. The yarn woven together makes thread, and the thread can be woven into cloth.

Cotton grows best in warm, wet lands. It is grown in the southern United States, Russia, India, China, Egypt and Brazil. Cotton seeds contain a valuable oil and also make good cattle food.

See also SPINNING AND WEAVING; TEXTILES.

COUNTRIES OF THE WORLD

There are over 160 independent countries of the world. They vary enormously in size, from the Vatican City (the world's smallest country) to the world's largest country – the USSR. The kinds of government are also very different from country to country. Some are ruled by a king or queen and others by a president.

The table (Page 56) shows all of the independent countries of the world with their capital city, population and kind of government.

Today cotton is picked by machine. The fluffy bolls are taken to the cotton gin for cleaning.

Coral polyps (below left) are animals, living in colonies. Each polyp feeds by using its waving tentacles as a 'net' to catch tiny sea creatures.

1. Coral grows in warm waters around a volcanic island.

2. Coral continues growing as the island sinks or the sea rises.

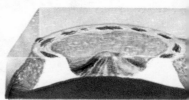
3. The coral reef remains after the island has disappeared forming an atoll.

Moscow (above) is the capital of Russia (the USSR). Russia is the largest country in the world. The picture below shows the Pope in St Peter's Cathedral in the Vatican City – the smallest country in the world.

The magnificent Niagara Falls (right) are situated between Lake Erie and Lake Ontario on the border between Canada and the USA.

Indians (below) from Ecuador in South America gather in the market to sell their goods.

1 Belize (Br.)
2 Guatemala
3 El Salvador
4 Honduras
5 Nicaragua
6 Costa Rica
7 Panama
8 Cuba
9 Jamaica
10 Haiti
11 Dominican Republic
12 Bahamas
13 Barbados
14 Trinidad & Tobago
15 Grenada

Canada

USA

Mexico

Colombia

Ecuador

Peru

Bolivia

Chile

Argentina

Paraguay

Uruguay

Brazil

Venezuela

Guyana

Surinam

French Guiana (Fr.)

16 Ireland (Republic of)
17 East Germany
18 West Germany
19 Netherlands
20 Belgium
21 Luxembourg
22 Liechtenstein
23 Switzerland
24 Austria
25 Czechoslovakia
26 Hungary
27 Yugoslavia
28 Albania
29 Malta
30 Vatican City
31 San Marino
32 Monaco
33 Andorra
34 Portugal

One of the hundreds of canals in Amsterdam, the capital city of the Netherlands.

Thousands of people live in floating homes in Asia because there is not enough space on the land.

59 Cyprus
60 Lebanon
61 Israel
62 Jordon
63 Syria
64 Kuwait
65 Bahrain
66 Qatar
67 United Arab Emirates
68 Bhutan
69 Bangladesh
70 Thailand
71 Khmer Republic
72 Singapore

The people of Africa are mostly Negroes. They make up 70 per cent of the total population of the continent.

The unusual sail-like domes of the opera house in Sydney, Australia.

35 Senegal
36 Gambia
37 Guinea-Bissau
38 Guinea
39 Sierra Leone
40 Liberia
41 Ivory Coast
42 Upper Volta
43 Ghana
44 Togo
45 Benin
46 Cameroon
47 Central African Republic
48 Equatorial Guinea
49 Sao Tomé & Principé
50 Congo
51 Lesotho
52 Swaziland
53 Rhodesia (Zimbabwe)
54 Malawi
55 Burundi
56 Rwanda
57 Uganda
58 Afars & Issas (Djibouti)

COUNTRIES OF THE WORLD

Country	Kind of government	Population	Capital
Afars and Issas (Djibouti)	Republic	125,000	Djibouti
Afghanistan	Republic	18,800,000	Kabul
Albania	Communist republic	2,400,000	Tiranë
Algeria	Republic	16,300,000	Algiers
Andorra	Principality	22,000	Andorra la Vella
Angola	Communist republic	5,800,000	Luanda
Argentina	Republic	25,100,000	Buenos Aires
Australia	Federal state	13,300,000	Canberra
Austria	Republic	7,500,000	Vienna
Bahamas	Parliamentary state	200,000	Nassau
Bahrain	Monarchy	240,000	Manama
Bangladesh	Republic	75,000,000	Dacca
Barbados	Parliamentary state	240,000	Bridgetown
Belgium	Monarchy	9,800,000	Brussels
Benin	Republic	3,000,000	Cotonou
Bhutan	Monarchy	1,150,000	Thimbu
Bolivia	Republic	5,630,000	La Paz
Botswana	Republic	670,000	Gaborone
Brazil	Republic	104,200,000	Brasilia
Bulgaria	Communist republic	8,700,000	Sofia
Burma	Republic	30,300,000	Rangoon
Burundi	Republic	3,700,000	Bujumbura
Cameroon	Republic	6,300,000	Yaoundé
Canada	Federal state	22,700,000	Ottawa
Cape Verde Islands	Republic	290,000	Praia
Central African Rep.	Republic	1,700,000	Bangui
Chad	Republic	4,000,000	Ndjamena
Chile	Republic	10,400,000	Santiago
China	Communist republic	825,000,000	Peking
Colombia	Republic	24,000,000	Bogotá
Comoro Islands	Republic	300,000	Moroni
Congo	Republic	1,300,000	Brazzaville
Costa Rica	Republic	1,900,000	San José
Cuba	Communist republic	9,100,000	Havana
Cyprus	Republic	640,000	Nicosia
Czechoslovakia	Communist republic	14,700,000	Prague
Denmark	Monarchy	5,000,000	Copenhagen
Dominican Rep.	Republic	4,600,000	Santo Domingo
Ecuador	Republic	7,000,000	Quito
Egypt	Republic	36,400,000	Cairo
El Salvador	Republic	4,000,000	San Salvador
Equatorial Guinea	Republic	300,000	Malabo
Ethiopia	Republic	27,200,000	Addis Ababa
Fiji	Parliamentary state	560,000	Suva
Finland	Republic	4,700,000	Helsinki
France	Republic	53,000,000	Paris
Gabon	Republic	520,000	Libreville
Gambia	Republic	520,000	Banjul
Germany, East	Communist republic	17,200,000	East Berlin
Germany, West	Federal republic	62,000,000	Bonn
Ghana	Republic	9,600,000	Accra
Greece	Republic	9,000,000	Athens
Grenada	Parliamentary state	100,000	Saint George's
Guatemala	Republic	5,500,000	Guatemala City
Guinea	Republic	4,300,000	Conakry
Guinea-Bissau	Republic	530,000	Bissau
Guyana	Republic	790,000	Georgetown
Haiti	Republic	4,600,000	Port-au-Prince
Honduras	Republic	3,000,000	Tegucigalpa
Hungary	Communist republic	10,500,000	Budapest
Iceland	Republic	220,000	Reykjavik
India	Republic	600,000,000	New Delhi
Indonesia	Republic	130,000,000	Jakarta
Iran	Monarchy	32,000,000	Tehran
Iraq	Republic	11,000,000	Baghdad
Ireland	Republic	3,100,000	Dublin
Israel	Republic	3,450,000	Jerusalem
Italy	Republic	55,600,000	Rome
Ivory Coast	Republic	4,800,000	Abidjan
Jamaica	Parliamentary state	2,030,000	Kingston
Japan	Monarchy	105,000,000	Tokyo
Jordan	Monarchy	2,700,000	Amman
Kenya	Republic	13,000,000	Nairobi
Khmer Republic	Communist republic	7,900,000	Phnom Penh
Korea, North	Communist republic	15,500,000	Pyongyang
Korea, South	Republic	33,500,000	Seoul
Kuwait	Monarchy	990,000	Kuwait
Laos	Communist republic	3,300,000	Vientiane
Lebanon	Republic	2,800,000	Beirut
Lesotho	Monarchy	118,000	Maseru
Liberia	Republic	1,700,000	Monrovia
Libya	Republic	2,400,000	Tripoli
Liechtenstein	Monarchy	24,000	Vaduz
Luxembourg	Monarchy	360,000	Luxembourg
Malagasy Republic	Republic	8,000,000	Tananarive
Malawi	Republic	4,930,000	Lilongwe
Malaysia	Monarchy	12,000,000	Kuala Lumpur
Maldives	Republic	129,000	Malé
Mali	Republic	5,700,000	Bamako
Malta	Republic	320,000	Valletta
Mauritania	Republic	1,300,000	Nouakchott
Mauritius	Republic	870,000	Port Louis
Mexico	Republic	60,000,000	Mexico City
Monaco	Principality	25,000	Monaco-Ville
Mongolia	Communist republic	1,470,000	Ulan Bator
Morocco	Republic	16,900,000	Rabat
Mozambique	Communist republic	9,250,000	Can Phumo
Nauru	Republic	7,000	—
Nepal	Monarchy	12,500,000	Katmandu
Netherlands	Monarchy	13,600,000	Amsterdam
New Zealand	Parliamentary state	3,100,000	Wellington
Nicaragua	Republic	2,100,000	Managua
Niger	Republic	4,500,000	Niamey
Nigeria	Republic	61,300,000	Lagos
Norway	Monarchy	4,000,000	Oslo
Oman	Monarchy	750,000	Muscat
Pakistan	Republic	70,000,000	Islamabad
Panama	Republic	1,700,000	Panama City
Papua—New Guinea	Parliamentary state	2,760,000	Port Moresby
Paraguay	Republic	2,600,000	Asunción
Peru	Republic	15,400,000	Lima
Philippines	Republic	42,000,000	Quezon City
Poland	Communist republic	34,000,000	Warsaw
Portugal	Republic	8,800,000	Lisbon
Qatar	Monarchy	190,000	Doha
Rhodesia	Republic	6,200,000	Salisbury
Romania	Communist republic	21,000,000	Bucharest
Rwanda	Republic	4,200,000	Kigali
San Marino	Republic	20,000	San Marino
Sao Tomé and Principé	Republic	80,000	Sao Tomé
Saudi Arabia	Monarchy	8,700,000	Riyadh
Senegal	Republic	4,300,000	Dakar
Seychelles	Republic	3,000,000	Victoria
Sierra Leone	Republic	3,000,000	Freetown
Singapore	Republic	2,250,000	Singapore
Solomon Islands	Monarchy	185,000	Honiara
Somalia	Republic	3,100,000	Mogadishu
South Africa	Republic	25,000,000	Pretoria
Spain	Monarchy	35,500,000	Madrid
Sri Lanka	Republic	13,900,000	Colombo
Sudan	Republic	17,300,000	Khartoum
Surinam	Republic	410,000	Paramaribo
Swaziland	Monarchy	510,000	Mbabane
Sweden	Monarchy	8,200,000	Stockholm
Switzerland	Republic	6,500,000	Berne
Syria	Republic	7,350,000	Damascus
Taiwan	Republic	15,000,000	Taipei
Tanzania	Republic	15,000,000	Dar es Salaam
Thailand	Monarchy	41,000,000	Bangkok
Togo	Republic	2,200,000	Lomé
Tonga	Monarchy	100,000	Nukualofa
Trinidad & Tobago	Parliamentary state	1,100,000	Port-of-Spain
Tunisia	Republic	5,600,000	Tunis
Turkey	Republic	38,300,000	Ankara
Uganda	Republic	11,500,000	Kampala
Union of Soviet Socialist Republics	Communist federation	253,000,000	Moscow
United Arab Emirates	Union	220,000	Abu Dhabi
United Kingdom	Monarchy	56,000,000	London
United States of America	Republic	211,900,000	Washington
Upper Volta	Republic	5,900,000	Ouagadougou
Uruguay	Republic	3,000,000	Montevideo
Vatican City	Ecclesiastical State	1,000	Vatican City
Venezuela	Republic	11,600,000	Caracas
Vietnam	Communist republic	43,200,000	Hanoi
Western Samoa	Monarchy	110,000	Apia
Yemen (South)	Republic	1,600,000	Aden
Yemen (North)	Republic	6,500,000	San'a
Yugoslavia	Communist republic	21,200,000	Belgrade
Zaire	Republic	24,000,000	Kinshasa
Zambia	Republic	4,800,000	Lusaka

CRAB Along with shrimps, prawns and lobsters, crabs belong to the group of animals called crustaceans.

Most crabs live in the sea. They have jointed legs, like insects, and walk sideways. They seize food in their strong pincers or claws.

Despite their armor, crabs have many enemies, including Man. Some crabs conceal themselves by sticking seaweed to their shells as camouflage. The hermit crab has no hard shell of its own so it takes over the empty shell of some other sea animal. Tiny pea crabs live inside the shells of mussels and oysters for protection.

The soldier crab lives on sandy beaches. As the tide comes in, it buries itself in the sand. In its little domed room, the crab is quite safe.

CRATER A crater is a bowl-shaped hole. The hole on top of a volcano is a crater. It is formed by the force of the explosion.

Another kind of crater is formed when big pieces of matter called meteorites fall to earth. The biggest crater in the world is in South Africa. It is 130 miles across. It was formed more than 250 million years ago. Moon craters are also formed by flying meteorites.

See also METEORS.

CROCODILE Crocodiles are large reptiles that live in rivers and swamps in hot countries. They eat fish and other animals which they catch with their powerful jaws and sharp teeth.

Crocodiles often bask on sand banks or lie in the water with just their eyes and nostrils above the surface. Like most reptiles, crocodiles lay eggs. Alligators and gavials are related to crocodiles.

CRUSADES The Crusades were a series of wars in which Christian armies fought to win back the Holy Land of Palestine from the Muslims. The First Crusade began in 1096 after Pope Urban II had called on the Christians of Europe to capture Jerusalem, which was a sacred city to the Muslims, too. Many knights answered the call, and the First Crusade was a great success. The crusaders captured Jerusalem in 1099.

But the Muslims were not beaten. In 1187, led by the great sultan Saladin, they recaptured Jerusalem. There were six Crusades in all. Thousands of crusaders went to the Holy Land. Some went because they loved war, others because they wanted to win riches and lands. 'Taking the Cross' (going on a Crusade) was the noblest thing a Christian knight could do. But it was also very dangerous. Before the Muslims finally defeated them in 1303, many crusaders had died of sickness or in battle. Many died at sea or were sold into slavery without ever seeing the Holy Land.

The Crusades brought Europeans into contact with the way of life of the East. They learned about Eastern medicine and science, and were encouraged to trade for the riches of the East.

CRYSTALS If you look closely at sugar, you will see that it is made up of thousands of tiny glassy pieces with flat sides. They are sugar crystals. Snow is made up of tiny crystals of frozen water. So are the beautiful patterns on a frosty window.

All crystals have a definite shape. They have smooth, flat sides that meet in sharp corners. There are many different

This rubbing of the brass plate on a crusader's tomb shows him in his coat of mail.

As a crocodile lies basking in the sun, small birds will often enter its open mouth to look for scraps of food and parasites.

varieties of crystal shapes and sizes. The differences are caused by the atoms in the crystals arranging themselves in different ways. Many crystals are so beautiful and hard that they are used as gems in jewelry. They are often called 'the flowers of the mineral kingdom'.

See also GEMS AND JEWELERY.

Snow crystals make many beautiful patterns, but always in the form of a six-pointed star.

CUCKOO The cuckoo of Europe does not build its own nest. Instead, it lays its egg in the nest of another bird.

When the young cuckoo hatches, it pushes out the other eggs and nestlings. The foster-parents do not seem to notice. They feed the cuckoo until it is bigger than they are. Finally the cuckoo flies away. Cuckoos winter in Africa and return to Europe in spring.

Below left: The baby cuckoo is soon larger than its foster parents, who are kept busy finding food to fill the cuckoo's gaping mouth.

Bottom: There are competitions in all the main ballroom dances. In formation dances, teams of couples take part.

An embankment dam is thickest at the bottom where pressure is greatest.

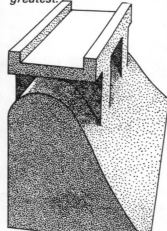

DAM When beavers want to make a river deeper, they build a barrier of tree trunks and branches across it. This barrier is called a dam. Human engineers also build dams to deepen rivers and lakes. Some dams are built to create a reservoir for storing water. Others are built to control flooding or to produce water power.

The biggest dams are great mounds of earth and rock. The Fort Peck Dam in Montana contains millions of cubic feet of earth and rock. Other dams are giant slabs of concrete. The Grand Coulee Dam in Washington state is the world's biggest concrete dam. It holds back the water by its sheer weight, and is known as a gravity dam. Other concrete dams, called arch dams, are much lighter and slimmer. They are strong because of their shape, which is arched towards the water.

At dams built to produce water power, pipes carry water through the base of the dam to a powerhouse. There the water is made to spin turbines. The turbines are connected to machines called generators, which produce electricity. This kind of power is called hydro-electric (water–electric) power.

An arch dam relies on its great strength to hold back the water.

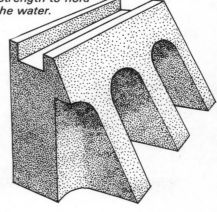

DANCING is as old as mankind. Thousands of years ago people often told stories by dancing. They danced to bring rain and to make crops grow. War dances made them feel brave before a battle.

In time dancing became an art. Today, dancers take part in religious ceremonies in many parts of the world. And many folk dances are still danced today, often

by dancers dressed in national costume.

Ballroom dancing and ballet are more formal types of dancing for they developed from court dancing in the 1600s. Dances such as the waltz and quickstep, danced by couples, have set patterns of steps. Some ballroom dances, such as the samba and tango, are really South American folk dances. In modern dancing dancers can happily dance on their own and make up their own steps.

See also BALLET.

DECLARATION OF INDEPENDENCE
On July 4, 1776, 56 men from the 13 colonies met in Philadelphia and signed the Declaration of Independence. And so a country called the United States of America was born.

Because they were part of Great Britain, the colonies at first followed the rules that King George and the Parliament made. They did not mind obeying these rules. Britain was a kind ruler, and protected the colonies from the French.

Finally, the British drove the French out of North America. Now the colonies were safe. But the war had cost a lot of money. And to pay for it, Britain began to tax the colonists. But the colonists had no representative in the British government. And they had no say about the taxes England was making them pay. So the colonists said there would be "no taxation without representation."

The Polish-Russian Vaslav Nijinsky (right) dancing in 'Le Spectre de la Rose'. Born in 1890, Nijinsky ranks as one of the greatest male dancers of all time.

This angered the British. They then imposed even more taxes and harsher rules. This lead to the beginning of the Revolutionary War. Finally, the colonists decided that they had to unite and stand together as a country. And so, they drew up and signed the Declaration of Independence as a statement of their unity.

The Declaration of Independence said that the 13 colonies stood united as one independent nation free from the rule of Britain. It said that all men were created equal. This meant that each man had the same freedom and opportunity. And it also said that all men in all countries had the right to be free from cruel and unjust governments.

Though the Declaration of Independence was a collection of everyone's thoughts, Thomas Jefferson was chosen to do the final writing.

Today, the Declaration of Independence is a statement of the rights of all of mankind. Each year we celebrate the birthday of our country, July 4th, Independence Day. The original Declaration of Independence can still be seen at the National Archives in Washington. It is one of the United States' most valuable possessions.

See also AMERICAN COLONIES; CONSTITUTION OF THE UNITED STATES; DEMOCRACY; GOVERNMENT; UNITED STATES OF AMERICA, HISTORY OF.

A red deer stag, with its antlers in velvet. The hinds do not have antlers. In the mating season the stags fight one another.

DEER are hoofed mammals, which run swiftly to escape their enemies. Like antelope and cattle, deer chew the cud.

Deer live in cooler climates than antelopes. Usually only the stags (males) have horns, or antlers. The antlers have branches or points. Unlike antelopes, deer shed their antlers every year and grow new ones, which are covered in soft skin called velvet until fully grown. Stags fight with their antlers during the breeding season.

Most deer live in woodland, feeding on grass and leaves. The reindeer, or caribou, lives on the cold northern tundra. The largest deer is the moose or elk of North America and Europe.

Some deer live in pairs or small groups, others in herds led by the strongest stag. Females are called hinds. Young fawns often have spots that help to camouflage them.

Deer are shy animals, always alert for danger. They have good eyesight and a keen sense of smell. For thousands of years men have hunted deer, both for food and for sport. Today, deer are often kept in parks, as well as in zoos.

DEMOCRACY The word democracy comes from the Greek word "demokratia." Demokratia is a combination of two other Greek words: "demos," which means people and "kratos," which means rule. Thus, the term democracy means rule by the people. Democracy is not a form of government, but a philosophy or a belief. In a democracy, people believe that all men have the same basic rights and that all men, not just a few, should make the rules.

In small communities, each individual votes on the issues or questions. This is called a direct democracy. However, this is only practical where the number of people is limited. Most democratic countries have a representative democracy in which the people elect public officials, and the officials act in accordance with the people's wishes.

In the United States, for instance, senators and congressmen are the elected representatives of the American people. These men and women were elected by the people because the people believed that these particular delegates would reach the same decisions about laws that they themselves would. So, as representatives of the people who elected them, senators and congressmen vote to pass or reject laws.

The following rights are guaranteed in a democracy: Freedom of Speech, Freedom of Assembly; Popular Sovereignty, Political Freedom, Religious Freedom and Educational and Economic Opportunity.

This map shows the world's deserts. About a fifth of the land surface of the world is desert. The biggest is the Sahara in Africa. There are also large deserts in North and South America, Asia and Australia.

Life in the desert. Most desert animals come out at night when it is cool.

DESERT Not all deserts are hot and

sandy. Some are cold. Many are rocky. But all get very little rain and snow. About a fifth of the Earth's land surface is desert.

Most deserts are in the middle of continents. There is little rain, because the moist winds from the sea are dry by the time they reach these deserts. Because there are no clouds, a desert may get very hot during the day. But at night, the dry soil quickly loses its heat and the desert becomes cold.

Strong winds blow away the soil, leaving bare rock, and sweep the sand into great waves called dunes. It is difficult for plants to live in such conditions. Some find moisture by sending long taproots underground. Others, like the cactus, spread their roots wide to catch as much rain as possible and store the moisture in their fleshy stems.

Many desert animals shelter from the sun by day and come out only at night. Some never drink, but get all the moisture they need from their food. Animals which can live in the desert include snakes, lizards, toads, tortoises, insects, and small mammals like the jerboa.

Most of the people who live in the deserts are nomads (wanderers). Often the only permanent settlements are near oases. An oasis is a place in the desert where there is water. Some deserts are rich in minerals, such as gold and oil.

The world's largest desert is the Sahara in Africa. There are other huge deserts in central Asia (the Gobi), in southern Africa, Australia, India, and in North and South America.

See also CACTUS; CAMEL; SAND.

DIAMOND Diamonds are our most precious gems. They are cut from crystals which are found in rocks. Diamonds are a form of carbon. If expertly cut, they sparkle with reflected light. Diamonds are expensive because they are rare and difficult to cut – they are the hardest of all the minerals. Because they are so hard, some diamonds are made into cutting tools for industry.

DINOSAUR Millions of years ago, long before people lived on Earth, the mighty dinosaurs ruled the animal kingdom.

The word *dinosaur* means 'terrible lizard'. The dinosaurs came from reptiles, and some of them were the largest land animals that have ever lived. The first dinosaurs appeared about 200 million years ago; the last dinosaurs died out about 60 million years ago. So no one has ever seen a living dinosaur. We know something of what they look like from their fossil remains in the rocks. Some were quite small, but others were huge. There were plant-eating dinosaurs and flesh-eating dinosaurs.

Among the plant-eaters were the biggest dinosaurs, such as *Brontosaurus* and *Diplodocus*. They walked on four thick legs, and had long necks and tails. Some giant dinosaurs were nearly 99 feet (30 meters) long. Others weighed 80 tons. They had to eat all day to get enough food for their enormous bodies.

Flesh-eating dinosaurs were smaller and most of them ran on their hind legs. The largest and fiercest was *Tyrannosaurus,* the 'tyrant lizard.' It stood 18 feet (5½ meters) high. It

There were many kinds of dinosaur. Some were flesh-eaters. Others were huge plant-eaters. For defense, some dinosaurs were armored, others ran swiftly.

A scene from over 100 million years ago. The fierce Tyrannosaurus attacks its prey, the plant-eating duck-billed Corythosaurus. The horned dinosaur Triceratops (right) gallops to safety. But the armored Ankylosaurus (center) continues to browse on leaves, while the long-legged Ornithomimus sneaks up to steal eggs from another dinosaur's nest.

had huge sharp claws on its legs and long sharp teeth in its cruel mouth.

As protection from such enemies, some dinosaurs had heavy armor. *Stegosaurus* had bony plates down its back and spikes on its tail. *Ankylosaurus* had a body like a tank and a tail that it swung like a club. *Triceratops* had three horns on its head and a bony frill to protect its neck.

Despite their great size and strength, dinosaurs had tiny brains. When they died out, mammals, which until then had been unimportant little animals, took their place. Scientists are not sure why dinosaurs became extinct. Perhaps the climate became cooler, and the vegetation changed. Unable to keep warm and without enough food for their huge bodies, the slow-witted dinosaurs were unable to survive.

See also FOSSIL; PREHISTORIC ANIMALS.

DISEASE When something goes wrong with part of our bodies, the cause is often disease. There are many different diseases, and they affect us in different ways.

Some diseases are *hereditary*. This means they can be passed on from parents to children. Many diseases are *infectious*. They are caused by attacks on the body by tiny living things. Bacteria cause diseases such as typhoid and tuberculosis. Viruses give us influenza, measles and the common cold. Fungi cause skin diseases. Protozoa live in the blood and cause diseases such as malaria and dysentery.

Diseases can also be caused by poor diet and lack of vitamins. Sometimes glands can go wrong and upset the body. Old age may bring various diseases. The serious disease called cancer alters the body's cells. Why this happens is not yet known.

Before the invention of the microscope, people had some very strange ideas about what caused disease. We now know how important cleanliness and proper sanitation are in preventing disease. Drugs can cure many diseases. And vaccination can protect us from others. Medicine has made great progress in the fight against disease.

See also BACTERIA; DRUGS; MEDICINE; VITAMIN.

DIVING For thousands of years pearl fishermen in Japan have dived to the sea bed to collect pearl oysters. And from early days divers have made repairs to ships beneath the waterline. At present divers are playing a big part in laying underwater pipelines for the North Sea oil industry. But people also dive into the deeps for pleasure as well as work.

Even skilled pearl divers cannot stay underwater for more than a few minutes. To remain underwater longer, divers must wear breathing apparatus. In fairly shallow waters divers use a device called an aqualung. It supplies them with compressed air through a mouthpiece.

Special suits, designed to resist crushing water pressure are worn by divers who go to depths of 325-650 feet (100-200 meters). Air is pumped into the suits through a pipe from a boat on the surface. To dive to even greater depths, people must descend in special diving vessels.

This small research submarine dives nearly 2,000 feet (600 meters) to explore the continental shelf.

A diver helps raise the anchor of a sunken ship from the sea bed.

DODO The dodo was a flightless bird which lived on the island of Mauritius in the Indian Ocean. The dodo was clumsy and helpless, but it had no natural enemies.

Then sailors came, introducing dogs, pigs and rats to the island. The dodos were killed and their eggs eaten. The last dodo died in 1681. Today we still use the expression 'as dead as a dodo'.

Right: The clumsy dodo could not fly. When men and their domestic animals came to its island home, the dodo had no means of escape and soon died out.

DOG The dog was the first animal to be tamed by human beings. Cave men probably reared wild dog pups and trained them to help with hunting. For thousands of years, the dog has been 'man's best friend'. Today, there are many different breeds, or kinds of dog.

Dogs are hunting animals. They have strong jaws and sharp teeth. Unlike cats, dogs cannot retract (draw in) their claws. The wild members of the dog family include wolves, foxes, coyotes, jackals and hunting dogs.

Dogs used for hunting are called *sporting dogs*. Terriers hunt small animals such as rats. Hounds chase larger prey. Greyhounds hunt by sight, while foxhounds and bloodhounds follow a scent. Gundogs, such as spaniels, setters, pointers and retrievers, are trained to find and fetch game birds shot by hunters.

Working dogs do many useful jobs. Huskies pull sleds in the icy polar regions. Sheepdogs are trained to herd farm animals. Alsatians make good police dogs and guard dogs. St. Bernards rescue people trapped in the mountain snows. Dogs can be trained to guide blind people.

In the Middle Ages mastiffs and bulldogs were bred for the cruel sports of bear-baiting and bull-baiting. But today most dogs are well cared for as family pets. The smallest is the chihuahua, which can sit on a person's hand. The largest is the Irish wolfhound. Pedigree dogs are those whose parents belonged to the same breed. But mongrels, or cross-bred dogs, often make better pets.

Even though the dog has lived close to people for so long, it still has the instincts of a wild animal. Before going to sleep, a dog will turn round and round – as if making a bed in dry leaves. Because wild dogs live in packs, or groups, the dog's instinct is to follow and obey the pack leader. This makes it

Below left: Some members of the dog family. Cynodictis (1) and Tomarctus (2) were extinct ancestors of today's domestic and wild dogs, including the bloodhound (3), coyote (4), collie (5), cocker spaniel (6), wolf (7), bulldog (8), sealyham terrier (9), fox (10), dingo (11) and chihuahua (12).

Below: The tiny Chihuahua (4 pounds or about 2 kilograms) is dwarfed by the Irish wolfhound (over 100 pounds or about 50 kilograms).

easy to train. Its master becomes the 'pack leader'. A male dog also marks out its own territory by 'lifting a leg'. When a pet dog buries a bone, it usually forgets all about it, because it is well fed. But in the wild, jackals and wolves will dig up buried food when they get hungry.

See also FOX; WOLF.

Dolphins are streamlined for life in the water.

DOLPHIN Dolphins are small whales. They live in the sea or in big rivers, and they eat fish. Dolphins are mammals, so they have to come to the surface to breathe.

They are marvelous swimmers and often play by leaping right out of the water and twisting this way and that. Dolphins are intelligent animals and can 'talk' to one another underwater. Porpoises are close relatives of dolphins.

The fast-flying dragonfly has huge eyes and powerful jaws. It catches other insects in flight with its front legs.

DRAGONFLY One of the fastest flying insects is the dragonfly. It hunts other insects, usually near water.

The dragonfly lays its eggs in ponds and rivers. The young dragonfly, or larva, lives underwater. When fully grown, the larva climbs up a plant stem, sheds its skin, and the adult dragonfly emerges. Millions of years ago there were dragonflies as big as pigeons.

DRUGS Herbs and chemicals that are used to cure diseases are called drugs. In ancient times sick people were often given strange mixtures made of the bones and fat of toads, bats, snakes and other creatures. These medicines usually did no good at all. But some mosses and herbs contain healing substances, and gradually people learned how to use them. By the 1600s nearly every town had an apothecary, or chemist who made up pills and mixtures in his shop. Drugs such as cocaine, obtained from plants, were used to ease pain. These were the first *anaesthetics*. In the 1800s the first man-made drugs, produced from chemicals, were used. A great step forward was the discovery of penicillin in 1928. This was the first *antibiotic* drug, which could kill harmful bacteria.

Today there are many kinds of drugs. They can be dangerous if they are not used properly. People can become addicted to certain drugs; this means they cannot live without them.

See also MEDICINE.

DUCKS AND GEESE Ducks are swimming birds, with short legs and webbed feet. They live on lakes and rivers or on marshes or the sea.

Some ducks 'dabble' for their food. They turn upside down in the water and use their broad beaks to sift worms and other small animals from the mud bottom. Other ducks dive underwater to find food.

Male ducks are called drakes. They are usually more colorful than the females. There are many different kinds of duck. Farmyard ducks were bred from the wild mallard. The eider duck lives at sea. Its soft feathers are used to make eiderdowns.

Geese look rather like large ducks with long necks. They spend much time on

Man has hunted ducks and geese for food for thousands of years. Only a few kinds have been tamed. The wild mallard is the ancestor of the farmyard duck, while the colorful mandarin duck from Asia is often seen on park lakes. The Canada goose is also seen in parks. It nests on islands in lakes and in swamps. The red-breasted goose nests on the tundra and cliffs in the Arctic. When migrating, geese often fly in a V formation.

Canada goose

Mallard

Red-breasted goose

Mandarin duck

land, nibbling grass or other plant food. The male goose is called a gander. Geese make good sentries, for they will honk loudly if a stranger comes too near. Wild ducks and geese often migrate for long distances.

DYES are substances used to color fabrics and other materials. Some dyes come from plants and animals. A red dye called madder comes from the roots of the madder plant. Cochineal is a scarlet dye obtained from the cochineal insect. But most of the dyes used these days are made from chemicals. Many of these man-made dyes have brilliant colors which do not easily fade.

EAGLE People have always admired eagles. These fierce birds of prey are the kings of the bird world.

Eagles can fly to great heights. The largest eagles can carry off lambs and even young deer in their strong claws. An eagle's nest is called an eyrie. It is usually built in a tall tree or on a rocky mountain ledge.

Because people have shot and poisoned many eagles, they are becoming rare. Today, eagles are protected by law.

EAR Our ears pick up vibrations, or 'shakings', in the air. The *outer ear* acts like an aerial; it catches the vibrations and passes them down a passage to the ear drum. When the vibrations hit it, the drum also vibrates, just like the skin of a musical drum. Three tiny bones in the *middle ear* pick up and pass on the vibrations. Inside the *inner ear* is a shell-like tube full of fluid. The vibrating air makes the fluid vibrate too. Nerves send messages about the vibrations to the brain. And when the brain has worked out what the messages mean, we 'hear' the sounds.

The inner ear also helps us keep our balance by means of *semi-circular canals*. These are tubes filled with fluid. If our bodies move, the fluid moves too. Nerves tell the brain. So we always know when we are standing upright, even if our eyes are closed.

See also SOUND.

The golden eagle (bottom) lives in the mountains, while the bald eagle (below) prefers sea coasts and rivers. The white feathers on its head give this eagle its name.

A cutaway drawing of the ear. Sound waves travel through the outer and middle ear passages to the delicate inner ear.

Inner ear   Eardrum   Eustachian tube   Canal   Outer ear

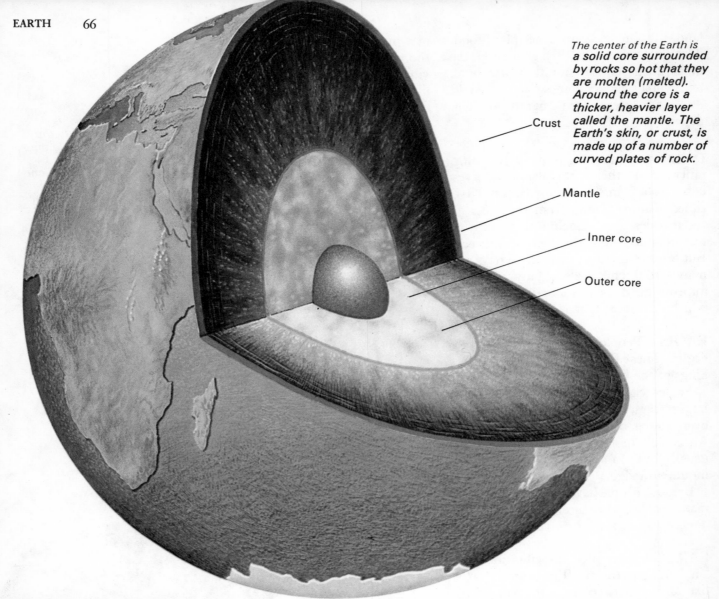

The center of the Earth is a solid core surrounded by rocks so hot that they are molten (melted). Around the core is a thicker, heavier layer called the mantle. The Earth's skin, or crust, is made up of a number of curved plates of rock.

Crust

Mantle

Inner core

Outer core

EARTH The Earth we live on is one of nine planets which orbit the Sun. Our Sun is only one of many millions of stars. The Earth is not even the biggest of its family of planets. But, so far as we know, the Earth is the only planet which has animals and plants living on it.

For a long time most people thought the Earth must be flat. But as long ago as the 500s BC, the Greek mathematician Pythagoras worked out that it was round. In fact, the Earth is a ball which bulges slightly at the Equator. The Equator is an imaginary line running round the middle of the Earth.

The Earth spins on its *axis*, an imaginary line running through the Earth's center from the North Pole to the South Pole. It spins round, or revolves, once in 24 hours, or one day. It takes the Earth about 365 days – one year – to travel once round the Sun.

Scientists think the Earth was probably formed from a spinning cloud of gas and dust. From the age of the oldest rocks we know that the Earth is more than 4,000,000,000 years old.

The Earth is like a huge spacecraft spinning through empty space. It has an invisible outer covering called the atmosphere. The atmosphere is in several layers. The outer edge is about 995 miles (1600 kilometers) from the Earth. The lowermost layer, called the troposphere is where life exits. It contains the gases, such as nitrogen and oxygen, on which life depends. The atmosphere protects us from harmful rays in space and also controls the temperature on the Earth's surface.

The Earth is the only planet with large amounts of surface water. Oceans and seas cover 70% of the Earth's surface. The water was formed by chemical

The Grand Canyon in the United States is a great gorge through which the 995 mile (1600 kilometer) long Colorado River runs. The canyon has been gouged out over millions of years by the river.

reactions after the Earth had become a solid ball of rock. It was in the oceans that life began.

The Earth is rocky, and very rugged in places. It is made up of igneous, or crystallized, rocks, and sedimentary, or deposited rocks. The surface is called the crust. Some parts are about 25 miles (40 kilometers) thick, others are much thinner. The crust is made up of huge plates of rock which carry the continents. The continents were once joined together. Over millions of years they have slowly drifted apart. Where the plates meet, they bend and fold. This is how mountains are formed.

Below the crust is the mantle. This is a thick layer of heavier rocks, up to 1,803 miles (2,900 kilometers) deep. Below this the rocks are molten (melted) because it is so hot. At the center of the Earth is a core of solid rock, made of nickel and iron. It is made solid by the enormous pressure acting upon it. The core acts as a giant magnet whose lines of force come together at the magnetic poles. That is why a compass needle always points north and south.

The Earth is still changing. In some parts of the world mountains are still being formed. Violent movements inside the Earth cause earthquakes and volcanoes. The surface also changes constantly. The rocks are eroded, or worn away, by the wind, by rain, rivers and seas and also by glaciers.

The study of the Earth is called geology. Geologists study the rocks and the fossil remains of plants and animals which the rocks contain.

See also CALENDAR; FOSSIL; MOUNTAIN; OCEAN; PLANETS; RIVER; ROCKS; VOLCANO.

EARTHQUAKE The ground beneath our feet feels solid. But in fact the Earth's skin, or crust, is made up of plates of rock, which can move and break. When they do, the ground shakes. This is an earthquake.

Earthquakes are caused by violent movements beneath the crust at the point where two plates meet. The rock bends and cracks. Buildings collapse. Thousands of people may be killed. Great waves called *tsunamis* are formed in the sea.

Instruments called *seismometers* can measure an earthquake's force.

Scientists know the regions where earthquakes are most likely, but they cannot yet tell when one will occur.

See also VOLCANO.

ECHO Sometimes when we shout, we hear our voice again a few seconds later. This is an echo. It happens when the sound of our voice is reflected back to our ears by an object some distance away. Bats use sound echoes to find the insects they eat. Ships and submarines use sound echoes (sonar) to detect objects under water. Airports use echoes of radio waves (radar) to 'see' aircraft in the sky.

See also RADAR.

ECLIPSE When one heavenly body passes in front of another and blots out its light, we say an eclipse is taking place. The Moon can cause an eclipse of the Sun. This happens when the Moon passes in front of the Sun and blots out the Sun's light. The Moon's shadow falls on the Earth, and the sky goes dark. Birds start to roost, and the stars come

The San Andreas rock fault in California caused the San Francisco earthquake of 1906. Over 700 people were killed.

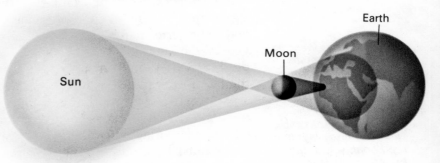

out. As the Moon's shadow passes, daylight returns and the eclipse is over.

The Earth also casts a shadow in space. Sometimes the Moon passes through the Earth's shadow. Then an eclipse of the Moon takes place.

EDISON, Thomas Alva (1847-1931) was an American inventor. Though his most famous inventions are the phonograph and the light bulb, at his death he held 1,093 United States patents and between 2,000 and 3,000 more in European countries.

In 1887 Edison set up the first fully equipped research laboratory, which

When the Moon is directly in line between the Earth and the Sun, people in its shadow see a total eclipse of the Sun. People farther away see only a partial eclipse.

Atlantic Ocean

Eels lay their eggs in the Sargasso Sea, in the Atlantic Ocean. The young eels swim back to the rivers of northern Europe and North America. They spend their adult lives in the rivers, returning to the Sargasso Sea to lay their eggs and die.

Egyptian kings were buried in great state. Professional mourners wept over the body as the funeral procession made its way to the tomb on the banks of the Nile. The body lay in a ⌐ ⌐ed boat, which the Egyptians believed would sail away and carry the dead king into the next world.

served as the foundation for today's research laboratories. Though Edison was born in Ohio, he invented so many new things during the time he lived in Menlo Park, New Jersey, he is called, "The Wizard of Menlo Park."

EELS Common eels live in rivers in Europe and North America. They travel downstream and sometimes overland into the Atlantic Ocean to lay their eggs. Then they die, and the young eels swim back to the rivers.

Some eels, such as the conger eel and the fierce moray eel, spend all their lives in the sea.

EGYPT, ANCIENT The civilization of ancient Egypt was centered on the River Nile. The Nile valley was hot and dry, but each year the river flooded and spread a rich silt (mud) over the land, making the soil fertile. The Egyptians took water from the Nile to irrigate their crops. They used the papyrus reed that grew along its banks to make boats and ropes, as well as a kind of paper. There were few trees, so homes were built of stone, mud and reeds.

The Nile was so important that the Egyptians worshipped the river as a god. They had many gods, such as Ra, god of the sun, and Osiris, god of the dead, and they built great temples and tombs. They studied mathematics and astronomy, and invented a kind of picture writing known as hieroglyphics, or 'sacred writing'. Because Egypt was surrounded by desert, it was safe from enemies for most of the time for 3000 years until it was finally conquered by the Romans.

The pharaohs (kings) of Egypt were very powerful. The people thought the pharaoh was a god. He owned everything and everyone had to obey his commands. The great pharaohs built huge tombs, often in the form of pyramids. Inside, the dead pharaoh was buried, surrounded by treasure and by all the things he would need in the next world, such as food, clothes, furniture and weapons. The dead body was preserved, or *mummified*, before being buried. From these tombs, archaeologists have learned much about ancient Egypt. Beautiful tomb paintings show men and women dressed in light, loose robes, their faces made up with cosmetics. Egyptian soldiers used bows and arrows and curved swords, and in later times drove small, two-wheeled chariots.

The workers who built the tombs and temples lived hard lives. But the rich Egyptians enjoyed lives of luxury in their fine homes. They had servants, slaves, dancers and musicians. They took perfumed baths, and slept on beds with thickly padded mattresses. Guests at a banquet sat with cones of perfumed oil on their heads. As the evening wore on, the cones melted and covered them with cooling oils.

Women had great power in Egypt. The pharaohs had to marry the queen or a princess if they wanted to rule. This was one of the reasons why the Roman leaders Julius Caesar and Mark Antony wanted to marry Queen Cleopatra of Egypt. After Cleopatra died in 30 BC, Caesar's nephew Octavian took over Egypt and made it a province of the Roman Empire. In this way the great empire of the pharaohs came to an end.

EINSTEIN, Albert (1879–1955) was one of the most brilliant thinkers of modern times. He completely changed our ideas about space, time and motion; about matter and energy. Einstein said that nothing can travel faster than light. He also said that mass and energy were different forms of the same thing. His ideas were set out in his famous laws of relativity. Einstein was born in Ulm, Germany. He spent the last 22 years of his life teaching at Princeton University.

ELECTRICITY In a thunderstorm brilliant flashes of lightning zig-zag between the clouds and the ground. Lightning is a form of electricity. It is very powerful and can destroy property and kill people.

The electricity we use in the house is man-made, and can also be a killer. But

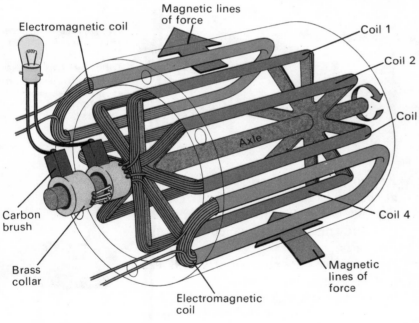

A generator works on the principle that when a loop of wire is rotated between the poles of a magnet, an electric current flows. In a practical generator coils of wire (called an armature) rotate on an axle between two electromagnets, which produce a magnetic field (shown by the arrows). The current produced by the rotating coils is collected by carbon 'brushes' which press against brass collars on the axle.

Magnetic lines of force

Electromagnetic coil

Coil 1

Coil 2

Coil 3

Axle

Coil 4

Carbon brush

Brass collar

Electromagnetic coil

Magnetic lines of force

battery. We use a battery in our flash-lights, radios and cars for example.

In a flashlight the battery is connected by wires to a bulb, through a switch. This forms an electrical circuit. Nothing happens when the switch is off. But when the switch is on, electric current flows through the circuit between one part of the battery and the other. As the current passes through the bulb, it heats up the fine wire coil (filament). This glows white and gives out light.

The flow of electric current is actually a flow of electrons. These are tiny particles present in all atoms. They are produced by chemical changes inside the battery. They flow easily in metals, which are called good conductors of electricity. Some materials, like glass and china, do not allow electrons to flow through them. They are called insulators. The strength of flowing electricity is measured by electrical pressure, or voltage. Flashlight batteries produce only a few volts. Household electricity is about 120 volts.

Electricity is produced by making coils of copper wires spin around in a magnetic field. Doing this sets up, or generates, electric current in the wire. In most power plants steam turbines spin the generator. In some they are spun by water turbines. These plants are called hydro-electric (water-electric) power plants.

Spacecraft produce electricity in different ways. Many have solar cells, which produce electricity when sunlight falls on them. Other spacecraft carry radio-active generators, which produce electricity from heat.

See also ATOM; MAGNET.

if it is used with care it is the most convenient source of energy we have. It powers our lights and electric fires; runs washing machines, vacuum cleaners, drills and television sets. In industry it powers all manner of machines and equipment, from small lathes to giant steel furnaces.

The electricity supplied to our homes is produced at electric generating stations, or power plants. For some purposes we need a portable supply of electricity. Then we use a

Thomas Edison made the first electric lamp in 1879 by passing a current through a wire filament inside a glass bulb.

ELECTRONICS is a science that explains how radio, television, radar, pocket calculators and computers work. Electronic equipment contains devices such as transistors and vacuum tubes – tubes from which the air has been removed. Transistors are special crystals which can control the flow of electrons through them. Electrons are tiny particles found in all atoms. In television the picture is produced by controlling a beam of electrons in a vacuum tube.

See also ATOM.

ELEMENTS are the building blocks from which all substances are formed. When a chemist splits up salt, he finds that it is made up of two substances called sodium and chlorine. No matter how hard he tries, he cannot split sodium and chlorine any further. They are chemical elements. In nature there are 94 elements. And scientists have made another 12. Most elements are found combined with other elements as chemical compounds.

Elephants are normally peaceful, but males will charge if they are annoyed or wounded.

ELEPHANT The elephant is the largest living land animal. A big male, or bull, may weigh 7 tons.

Elephants live in herds. If one elephant is injured, the rest will help it. Elephants eat huge amounts of grass and tree leaves every day. They also love to bathe.

The elephant uses its long trunk to breathe and to gather food. Although strong enough to lift a heavy tree, the trunk is so sensitive it can pick up a peanut. Elephants have long tusks, which are overgrown teeth. Hunters have killed many elephants for their ivory tusks.

There are two kinds of elephant. The Indian elephant can be trained to work. But the larger African elephant is not easily tamed.

See also MAMMOTH.

ELEVATOR An elevator is a box-like vehicle used to carry people and things up and down tall buildings. The first crude elevators used ropes and winches and date back to the Ancient Greeks. In the 1600's a "flying chair" was invented. Through a series of ropes and pulleys, people seated in special chairs were lifted up along the outside of buildings.

Until Elisha Otis demonstrated his safety invention in 1853, elevators were used only for freight because people were afraid to fall to their death in them.

EMBROIDERY Sewing designs on fabric is called embroidery. The patterns are made from hundreds of stitches sewn with a needle and thread.

Embroidered clothes were made in ancient Egypt and Persia, while in China and Japan beautiful pictures were stitched on to silk. In the Middle Ages church robes were decorated with elaborate embroidery, and huge wall hangings, or tapestries, were covered with large embroidered pictures.

The picture on the left shows a small part of the famous Bayeux Tapestry. The tapestry was embroidered on a strip of linen over 229 feet (70 meters).

EMU The emu is an Australian bird, almost as large as an ostrich. It cannot fly, but can run swiftly. The emu has long brownish feathers which look more like hairs.

Emus live in open country and eat mainly roots and plants. Once great flocks roamed the Australian plains, but hunters shot so many that emus are now rare in the wild.

ENERGY When a piece of wood is set on fire, it burns and gives out light you can see and heat you can feel. Heat and light are two common forms of energy. Wood is one kind of fuel, which releases energy when it is burned. Coal, gasoline and natural gas are others. When gasoline is burned in a car engine, the energy produced makes the pistons move. This turns the car wheels. The chemical energy in the fuel has been changed into mechanical energy to turn

The emu has long legs but hardly any wings at all. Like the ostrich and the cassowary it cannot fly. Male emus sit on the eggs to hatch them, while the females look after the chicks born in the previous year.

the car wheels. When the car is moving it has *kinetic energy*, the energy of motion. A rock balancing on top of a cliff has *potential energy* – the energy of position. When it topples over the edge, the potential energy is changed into kinetic energy.

See also HEAT; LIGHT.

ENGINE We use many kinds of engines in the modern world to work the machines in our homes and factories, in the air and on the roads. Most engines burn a fuel to produce energy to move the machine parts. A car engine burns gas while trucks and buses have diesel engines, which burn oil. Airplanes have jet engines which burn kerosene. There are all kinds of internal combustion engines, in which fuel is burned in an enclosed space. Steam engines and turbines are different because their fuel is burned outside the engine.

See also STEAM ENGINE.

ESKIMO The Eskimos live in the cold Arctic regions. They are a short, sturdy people, with plenty of fat on their bodies to keep out the cold. The Eskimos originally came from somewhere in east Asia. Now there are small numbers in Greenland, Siberia, Alaska and northern Canada.

Eskimos are skillful hunters. They travel in skin canoes called kayaks and on sleds pulled by husky dogs. If an Eskimo kills a seal, he eats the meat (sometimes raw), burns the fat as fuel,

makes clothes from the skin, uses the sinews as thread, and carves the bone into needles and ornaments.

The Eskimos' old way of life is changing. Many no longer live in tents during the summer or in snow houses (igloos) in winter. Instead, they live in modern settlements.

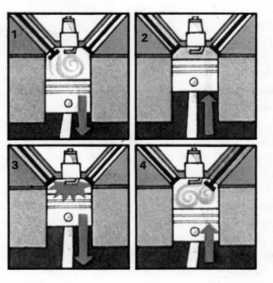

How a four-stroke internal combustion engine works. 1. On the induction stroke, fuel and air are sucked into the cylinder. 2. On the compression stroke, the piston compresses (squashes) the fuel and air mixture. 3. On the ignition stroke, an electric spark jumps across the points of the sparking plug and ignites, or lights, the mixture. Hot gases push back the piston. 4. On the exhaust stroke, a valve opens to let out the burned gases and the piston returns. Then the cycle begins again.

EUROPE The continent of Europe is smaller than any of the other continents except Australia. Yet one in five of the world's people lives in Europe, and no other continent has played so important a part in shaping the history of the world.

Europe has a mild climate, warm in the south near the Mediterranean Sea and colder in the north near the Arctic. It has many different kinds of scenery. There are fertile plains, especially in the east, and thick forests, although much of the forest has been cleared to make way

An Eskimo waits to harpoon a seal when it comes up through a hole in the ice to breathe. He is wearing a fur-lined parka and seal skin boots.

for farms and factories. Europe has high mountains, such as the Alps and the Pyrenees, and the Urals and Caucasus, which divide Europe from Asia. It has many rivers, of which the largest are the Rhine, Danube and Volga. The west coast of Europe is washed by the Atlantic Ocean.

Because Europe is such a crowded continent, with many towns and cities, there is not much room for the large wild animals, such as bison, bears and wolves, that were once common. But, there are many smaller mammals and birds, and plenty of fish in the lakes, rivers and seas.

Most of Europe has fertile soil and good rainfall. Europe's farmers produce meat, grain, fruit and vegetables. Most farms use modern machinery. Even so, few European countries are able to grow all the food they need. But Europe is rich in coal, iron ore and other raw materials. The Industrial Revolution began in Europe. Now there are many factories, making all kinds of goods which are sold all over the world. Most of Europe's people live and work in towns and cities.

Europe lives by trade. It has good roads, railways, airports and canals. Ships carry goods across the Baltic Sea, the North Sea and the Mediterranean Sea, and to all parts of the world. In the 1400s and 1500s the search for new trade routes sent European merchants to explore Africa, Asia and America. Later, European countries started colonies in these areas, and in the 1800s many people left Europe's crowded cities to begin new lives in new countries. European ideas, languages and discoveries spread throughout the world.

Since the time of the ancient Greeks and Romans, Europe has been a center of art and learning. It is often called the birthplace of western civilization. Its castles, churches and museums are full of fascinating history. Many tourists come to visit them.

The people of Europe are made up of many different nationalities. Each has its own language and customs. In the past European countries have quarreled with each other. European wars affected the rest of the world, because European

Important Cities of Europe

Paris	France
London	United Kingdom
Moscow	USSR
Leningrad	USSR
Madrid	Spain
Lisbon	Portugal
Rome	Italy
Athens	Greece
Berlin	Germany
Vienna	Austria
Brussels	Belgium
Amsterdam	The Netherlands
Prague	Czechoslovakia
Budapest	Hungary
Warsaw	Poland
Stockholm	Sweden
Oslo	Norway
Dublin	Ireland
Helsinki	Finland
Copenhagen	Denmark
Athens	Greece
Belgrade	Yugoslavia
Sofia	Bulgaria
Bucharest	Romania

Europe is a continent of contrasts – from cold frozen tundra and pine forests in the north, to the sun-parched plains of the south. There are lush green valleys and snow-capped mountains, open farmlands and crowded cities. Europe is a center of art and learning. Its many famous buildings show some of the continent's fascinating history. They are visited by thousands of tourists every year.

EUROPE

BRITISH ISLES

Atlantic Ocean

Pyrenees

SPAIN

Arctic Ocean

SCANDINAVIA

RUSSIA

Baltic Sea

GERMANY

The Alps

ITALY

Black Sea

GREECE

Mediterranean Sea

countries were so powerful. Two world wars in this century have begun in Europe.

Today, the European countries are among the richest in the world. They try to live peacefully together. But there are still divisions. Most of the countries of eastern Europe have communist governments. The western countries are democracies.

See also ALPS; COUNTRIES OF THE WORLD; FRANCE; GERMANY; ITALY; MEDITERRANEAN; SCANDINAVIA; SPAIN; UNITED KINGDOM.

EVOLUTION is the gradual process by which all living things have changed since life began millions of years ago. Fossils show us how creatures have changed. Early horses had several toes on each foot. The modern horse has only one. Other creatures have died out altogether.

The first creatures were microscopic forms of life. They evolved into more complicated plants and animals. Fishes evolved from smaller sea creatures. Some fish began breathing air and crawled on to dry land. These were the first amphibians. The amphibians evolved into reptiles. All birds and mammals, including man, evolved from reptiles.

The idea of evolution was first put forward by the scientists Charles Darwin and Alfred Russel Wallace. Darwin believed that animals compete for food and space. Only those which can change to meet changing conditions are able to survive. How such changes take place is explained by genetics.

See also CAMOUFLAGE; GENETICS; PREHISTORIC ANIMALS.

EXPLORERS Men have always had the urge to explore the unknown. Some explorers have gone in search of lands to settle. Others were greedy for riches, while some journeyed only in search of knowledge. All were very brave, for in venturing into the unknown, they faced many dangers.

To the ancient peoples of Europe, 'the world' meant the lands around the Mediterranean Sea. Only the Phoenicians dared sail out into the cold, grey Atlantic Ocean beyond. The Macedonian general

The Alcazar in Segovia, Spain is just one of hundreds of magnificent castles that can still be seen throughout Europe.

There are two kinds of peppered moth, one pale, the other dark. Until the 1800s the pale kind was most common, because its pattern matched the bark on trees and hid it from enemies. But when smoke from factory chimneys blackened the trees, the pale moths were easily seen and eaten. Now the dark moths escaped, and today the dark kind is most common. This is how evolution works.

Alexander the Great marched his armies east as far as India, and gradually maps were drawn, showing the 'known world' and the strange wild lands which were unexplored.

In the 900s the Vikings sailed in their small, fragile ships as far as North America. But until the invention of the magnetic compass in the 1300s, long sea voyages were very dangerous. Many people believed the world was flat, so sailors feared that if they sailed far enough, they would fall over the edge.

To reach the East, with its gold, spices and silks, European merchants had to travel overland. In 1275 Marco Polo reached China. He brought back many wonderful tales of what he had seen. The Portuguese discovered they could reach India by sailing round the coast of Africa. In 1492 Columbus tried to reach Asia by sailing west, across the Atlantic. Instead he reached America, the 'New World'. By 1522 Magellan's sailors had proved that the world was round by sailing round it.

After this explorers went out from Europe eager to find lands to settle as colonies. The Spaniards and Portuguese built empires in South America. The French and British explored North America. The Dutch sailed to the East Indies and found Australia and New Zealand. In the 1700s James Cook mapped the South Seas and neared the frozen continent of Antarctica.

The last continent to be explored was Africa. During the 1800s several explorers, of whom the greatest was David Livingstone, crossed the unknown 'Dark Continent'.

Yet, even after the last continent was explored, ever-curious man kept questioning the nature of the universe around him. Robert Peary reached the North Pole in 1909. This feat was followed by Roald Amundsen who explored the South Pole in 1911. In 1948, Thor Heyerdahl conducted a different type of exploration when he sailed from Peru to Polynesia on his famous balsa raft, the Kon Tiki. His purpose was to prove that the Peruvian Indians could very well have made a similar trip centuries ago. It took him 101 days to make the journey.

FAMOUS EXPLORERS

ASIA
Vasco da Gama (1460?–1524) Portuguese: Sailed round the Cape of Good Hope to India, and also founded a Portuguese colony in East Africa.
Marco Polo (1254?–1324?) Venetian: Traveled overland from Europe to China, where he stayed for 17 years.

NORTH AMERICA
John Cabot (1440–1498) Italian: Sailed from Bristol, England to North America. His voyage led England to claim North America.
Jacques Cartier (1491–1557) French: Discovered the St Lawrence river and explored the coast of Canada.
Christopher Columbus (1451–1506) Italian: His voyages to the West Indies marked the discovery of the New World (North America) by Europeans.
Sir John Franklin (1786–1847) British: Surveyed the Arctic and northern Canada.
Robert de La Salle (1643–1687) French: The first European to sail down the River Mississippi to the sea.
Meriwether Lewis (1774–1809) and **William Clark** (1770–1838) American: Lewis and Clark traveled the West, exploring the Missouri River and the Rocky Mountains.

SOUTH AMERICA
Vasco Núñez de Balboa (1475?–1519) Spanish: First European to cross the Isthmus of Panama and see the eastern coast of the Pacific Ocean.
Pedro Álvares Cabral (1467?–1519?) Portuguese: Claimed Brazil for Portugal and discovered the island of Madagascar in the Indian Ocean.

Hernando Cortes (1485–1547) Spanish: Conquered Mexico and discovered Lower California.
Sir Francis Drake (1540?–1596) English: Sailed round the world (east to west), 1577–1580.
Ferdinand Magellan (1480?–1521) Portuguese: Sailed round the southern tip of South America (the Strait of Magellan) and across the Pacific (which he named). His surviving crew completed the first voyage round the world, 1519–1522.
Francisco de Orellana (1500?–1549?) Spanish: Navigated and named the River Amazon in South America.
Francisco Pizarro (1471?–1541) Spanish: Conquered Peru and the Incas.

AFRICA
Sir Richard Burton (1821–1890) English: In search of the source of the Nile, found Lake Tanganyika. Also explored West Africa, Arabia and the South American Andes mountains.
Bartholomew Dias (1450?–1500) Portuguese: Sailed down the west coast of Africa and discovered the Cape of Good Hope.
David Livingstone (1813–1873) Scottish: Discovered the Victoria Falls and explored unknown Central Africa.
Mungo Park (1771–1806) Scottish: Navigated much of the River Niger in West Africa.
John Hanning Speke (1827–1864) English: Discovered Lake Victoria, rightly judging it a source of the Nile.
Sir Henry Morton Stanley (1841–1904) Welsh-born American: He went to look for Livingstone, explored Central Africa and followed the River Congo to the sea.

AUSTRALIA AND THE PACIFIC
Robert O'Hara Burke (1820–1861) Irish: The first man to cross Australia from south to north.
James Cook (1728–1779) English: Explored and mapped coasts of Australia and New Zealand and various South Pacific islands.
William Dampier (1652–1715) English: Sailed round Australia.
Matthew Flinders (1774–1814) English: Explored the coast of Australia, which he named.
Abel Janszoon Tasman (1603–1659) Dutch: First man to sail round Australia. Also discovered New Zealand and Tasmania.

POLAR
Roald Amundsen (1872–1928) Norwegian: First man to reach the South Pole. He also flew over the North Pole in an airplane.
Vitus Bering (1680–1741) Danish: Discovered the Bering Strait and Alaska.
Richard Byrd (1888–1957) American: Flew over the North and South Poles.
Henry Hudson (died 1611) English: Searched in vain for the NW Passage. Hudson Bay is named after him.
Fridtjof Nansen (1861–1930) Norwegian: Led the first crossing of Greenland, and explored the Arctic.
Robert Falcon Scott (1868–1912) Explored Antarctica and reached the South Pole, only to find that Amundsen had beaten him to it.

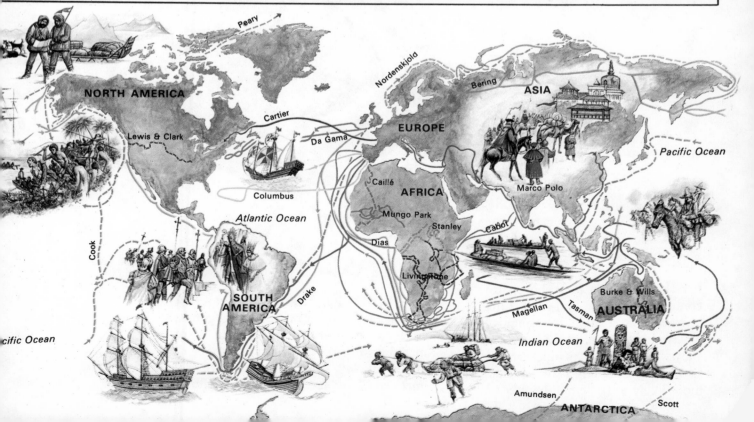

Today, there are still a few parts of the Earth which are unexplored. But aircraft and space satellites can map them from the air. The sea remains largely unexplored. And beyond the Earth is space. The Apollo astronauts began the exploration of the Moon from 1969 to 1972. Unmanned spacecraft are reaching out to explore the planets and beyond.

EYE Our eyes are very delicate. Each eye is a hollow ball full of liquid. In the center of the front is a black hole called the *pupil*. This lets in light. Behind the pupil is a *lens*. The lens focuses an image of whatever we are looking at on to a screen called the *retina*. Then messages are sent along a nerve to the brain. The brain arranges the messages into a picture again, and we 'see'.

The colored part of the eye is called the *iris*. It is a ring of muscle which makes the pupil larger or smaller. In bright light, the pupil gets smaller. But in dim light, it gets larger to let in as much light as possible.

Some of the most famous fables were told by Aesop in ancient Greece. They are still told today. An example is the story of the fox and the grapes.

'One hot day, a fox was walking past a vine, laden with grapes. The fox was thirsty. As he stared up at the grapes, thinking how juicy they looked, his mouth began to water.

The fox jumped as high as he could. But he could not reach the grapes. Again and again he tried, and each time he failed. It was no use. The grapes were too high.

Hot and cross, the fox gave up. "Oh well," he said to himself. "Those grapes were probably sour anyway." And he went on his way.'

Moral: When we can't get what we want, we pretend we never wanted it at all.

Other well-known fables are those told by the French poet Jean de la Fontaine.

Most birds have eyes at the side of their heads. They cannot judge distance well, or focus as well as birds with eyes in the front of their heads (such as owls). But they can see almost all around without turning their head. In this way they can keep a constant lookout for their enemies. To judge distance, they move their head from side to side, looking at an object with each eye in turn.

This cutaway diagram shows the main parts of the eye. Light rays from an object form an image, made up of nerve 'impulses', on the retina. The brain arranges these messages into a picture.

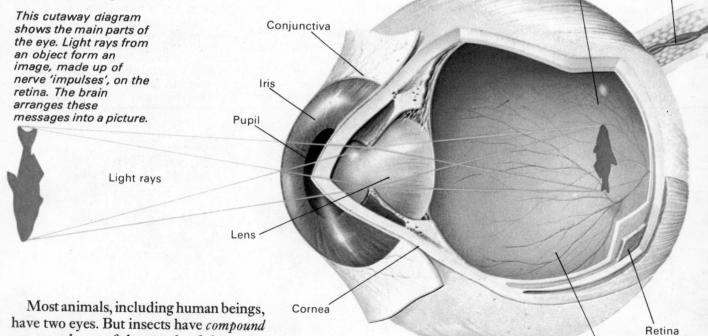

Conjunctiva

Iris

Pupil

Light rays

Lens

Cornea

Blind spot

Optic nerve

Retina

Vitreous humour

Most animals, including human beings, have two eyes. But insects have *compound* eyes, made up of thousands of tiny eyes. Some animals have no eyes at all.

FABLE A fable is a short story that contains a lesson, or moral. Often the characters in a fable are animals which behave like people. In this way, the fable shows how foolish people can be. And by making us laugh, it makes the lesson more likely to be remembered.

FACTORY Factories are buildings that are used to make, or manufacture, goods. In factories workers use all kinds of machines to produce a large number of goods quickly. This is called *mass production*. Many factories make products on an assembly line. Automobile factories produce cars in this way. The workers stand alongside a moving conveyor, which carries the shell of the car. Each worker adds a certain piece to the shell as it passes by, until at the end of the line there is a complete car.

FAIR A fair is a place where people gather to trade or to have fun. Fairs began in the Middle Ages. During local festivals, merchants and farmers would come to market. As fairs grew, they became specialized. There were horse fairs, goose fairs, timber fairs and so on. And to keep people amused, there were sideshows, games and performing animals. This is how the modern funfair or carnival began.

Today trade fairs are often called exhibitions. They are held to attract overseas buyers and to increase trade by displaying new goods.

A World's Fair is another kind of exhibition. In a World's Fair, many different countries gather in one place and build exhibits that show what life is like in each country. These exhibits are often buildings in themselves. A World's Fair gives you the chance to see and understand the many different ways people live and the various cultures and customs which make our world so interesting.

FAIRY TALE Fairies, tiny beings who look like people but have magic powers,

appear in folk tales from many parts of the world. These 'little people' are sometimes good, sometimes bad.

As well as tales about fairies, people have also told stories about spirits, gods, mythical creatures, giants, witches and imaginary kingdoms. Because the stories were originally told aloud, and not written down, new parts were added to them and they gradually changed or became mixed up. They were also taken from country to country; in this way the stories told in *The Arabian Nights* came to Europe from India by way of Persia.

A Frenchman, Charles Perrault, began to write down fairy tales in the 1600s, tales that included *Cinderella*. In the 1800s, the German brothers Grimm collected hundreds of fairy tales including *Hansel and Gretel*, *Snow White* and *Red Riding Hood*. Another famous writer of fairy stories was Hans Christian Andersen. He made up most of his stories, which include *The Ugly Duckling* and *Thumbelina*.

See also MYTHS AND LEGENDS.

On a mixed farm, cereals and root crops are grown. Cattle are kept for both milk and beef. The mixed farm may also have an orchard of fruit trees.

FARMING is the world's most important industry. By raising animals and growing crops, farmers provide us with food. Civilization became possible only when people started farming.

The cave men lived by hunting wild animals and gathering plants and fruits. Gradually, people learned how to plant seeds and grow crops, and how to keep and breed animals such as chickens,

cattle and sheep.

Primitive farmers grew just enough food for themselves. They had no tractors, and used wooden plows pulled by oxen or horses. They harvested by hand, using sickles. In winter in northern Europe they had to kill most of their animals, because there was no food for them. In hot, dry lands crops could be grown only near rivers, where irrigation helped water the fields.

Eventually the farmers divided the land into narrow strips. Later, these strips were joined together to make bigger farms. More people went to live in towns, and had to buy food instead of growing it. To feed them, the farmers began to 'specialize'. Arable farmers grew only crops, dairy farmers kept only cattle, and so on.

In the 1800s and 1900s machines were invented to do the work of men and animals. There were better plows, seed drills, threshers and reapers, and tractors replaced the horse and ox. Turnips and clover were grown as food for the animals in winter, and bigger, heavier animals were bred. Improved *crop rotation* – growing different crops on the same land from year to year – was good for the soil. Fertilizers, which helped to enrich the soil, and chemicals to kill insect pests allowed farmers to grow larger crops.

Today, different parts of the world are well known for different kinds of farming. On the vast North American prairies cereal crops are harvested by machines which not only cut the ripe wheat, but thresh it and put the grain into a tank or sacks. Today, many farms have cows milked by machine, and poultry and pigs reared inside special buildings. In South America beef cattle roam the pampas. Flocks of sheep graze in Australia and New Zealand. In much of Asia rice is grown in flooded paddy fields.

The most important crops are cereals (such as rice, wheat and corn), sugar, fruits, vegetables, coffee, cocoa and tea. Not all crops are used as food. Cotton, for example, is grown for its fiber and oil. Fish, bees and fur-bearing animals, such as mink, are also farmed.

In many parts of the world farming is still primitive, and people do not have enough to eat. So farming experts are teaching the people how best to use their land, and developing better seeds and animals which will resist disease.

FEDERAL BUREAU OF INVESTIGATION

The Federal Bureau of Investigation was founded in 1908. It is a branch of the United States Department of Justice.

The role of the FBI is to investigate and collect evidence in crimes in which certain federal (national) laws have been broken. Some of these crimes include kidnaping, bank robbery and assaulting or killing a federal officer. In fact, the men and women who make up the Secret Service and guard the President and his family are all FBI agents.

The FBI sometimes helps local and state police officers with special cases. Additionally, it runs the National Crime Information Center. This center has a computerized list of criminal information which is used by law enforcement agencies across the country. At the Identification Division in Washington, D.C., more than 160,000,000 fingerprint cards are on file. In a single year, more than 38,000 fugitives were identified by the use of these cards. It is the largest file of its kind known in the world.

In order to be considered for a job as an FBI agent, you must be a United States citizen, and at least 23, but not more than 35 years of age. An applicant must also have graduated from law school, or have an accounting degree; or he must have another special talent that would be of use to the FBI, like a special knowledge of science or a foreign language.

FIRST AID

First Aid is emergency care given to the victim of an accident, injury or illness before a doctor can arrive. The ability to recognize symptoms of a person who requires first aid can often save the victim.

Some instances where first aid is required include: 1) severe bleeding (hemmorage); 2) when breathing has stopped; 3) when poison has been swallowed; 4) when irritating chemicals come into contact with the eyes.

The prickly shield fern grows in the northern hemisphere. It grows in woods and on mountains.

Each fern leaf has a number of branches. New leaves uncurl from the bottom of the plant.

FERN Ferns are primitive plants. There have been ferns on Earth for over 300 million years. Some prehistoric ferns were as tall as trees.

Ferns have no flowers or seeds. Instead they have tiny cells called spores under their leaves. The wind scatters the spores onto the ground and they grow into tiny plants. Later these plants grow into new ferns.

Ferns like damp, shady places. Common ferns are bracken, male fern, hart's tongue and spleenworts.

FIORD Some coasts are pierced by long, twisting, narrow inlets of sea. These are fiords.

Steep cliffs rise on either side, and sometimes waterfalls plunge into the fiord far below. The largest fiords, such as Sognefiord in Norway, are more than 100 miles (160 kilometers) long and very deep. Fiords were formed by glaciers scraping out and deepening valleys, so that the sea ran in. There are also fiords in Alaska, Greenland, Canada, Chile and New Zealand.

See also GLACIER.

FIREFIGHTING Fire is man's enemy as well as his friend. It can kill and injure people, and destroy buildings. When a building catches fire, the firemen's first job is to rescue any people trapped inside. Then they must put out the fire as quickly as possible, before the flames spread. Most fires can be put out with water. But oil and electric fires can only be put out with chemical foam.

Until the fire pump was invented, people formed bucket brigades to put out fires. Standing in a line from the burning building to a well or river, they would form a human chain and pass buckets of water down the line to the firefighters who would then douse the house.

Forest fires are fought by dropping water 'bombs' from airplanes and by cutting down trees to make bare strips of land too wide for the flames to cross. To control fires, large buildings and ships have automatic sprinkler systems. As soon as the air becomes dangerously hot, water sprays come into action and alarms are sounded.

Sometimes firefighters wear special suits made of asbestos to resist the heat and protect them from the smoke and flames. They also wear breathing apparatus.

FISH Fishes are animals which spend their lives in water. They have fins for swimming instead of legs for walking. Fishes breathe by means of gills rather than lungs. All fishes are cold-blooded.

There are more fishes in the world than there are amphibians, reptiles, birds and mammals put together. Fishes live in salt water and in fresh water. Some spend part of their lives in the sea, and part in the rivers.

Most fishes have bony skeletons. But a small group including sharks have skeletons made of gristle, or cartilage. Like all animals, fishes have to breathe oxygen. Their gills take oxygen out of the water. Some fishes breathe through their skins as well, and a few have lungs.

Fishes eat water animals, including other fishes, and plants. In turn, many fishes are food for larger animals. Some people catch fishes for sport. But fishing is also an important industry in many countries, for fish is a nourishing food.

Fishes swim by bending their bodies from side to side, and by moving their tails. They use their fins to keep them upright and for steering and braking.

Most fishes are covered with scales. Some fishes have a line of special scales along each side of the body. This is called the lateral line. It helps the fish detect underwater vibrations. Most fishes have an air bladder inside their bodies to keep them at any level they choose. But the more primitive cartilage fishes do not

The seahorse carries its young in a pouch. The guppy is one of the few fishes which gives birth to live young.

Fishes often swim together in large numbers for safety. Many use camouflage to hide from their enemies. Some fishes have unusual and interesting habits. The archer fish shoots flies out of the air by squirting a jet of water at them. The puffer fish blows itself up into a spiny ball when frightened. The flying fish can glide over the waves using its fins as

Anchovies, herrings and cod are valuable food fishes. Anchovies and herrings swim in large shoals, close to shore. Cod live in deep water as far north as the Arctic. Most fish lay their eggs and leave the young to fend for themselves. But the Egyptian mouthbreeder (below) guards its young, which swim into its mouth if there is danger.

Anchovy   Herring   Cod

have this 'swim bladder'. If they stop swimming they sink.

During the breeding season some fishes migrate for long distances to their spawning grounds. Most fishes lay their eggs and leave them floating in the water. Out of millions of eggs, only a few survive. The rest are eaten by other fishes. If all the eggs survived the seas and rivers would soon be overcrowded. Other fishes lay fewer eggs, but take more care of them. The stickleback builds a nest, and the male fish guards the young.

wings. Some fishes, such as the electric eel, can give a powerful electric shock.

Deep sea fishes live at depths of nearly 29,500 feet (9,000 meters). No plants grow in the darkness, so the fishes eat each other or feed on dead fishes and plants which sink.

Some deep sea fishes are blind and have feelers to guide them. But many give off light to help them find food and mates.

The biggest fish is the whale shark. It is quite harmless. The oldest fish is

Egyptian mouthbreeder

Gill nets and purse-seines catch fish near the surface. Trawls catch deep-water fish. Long-lines and traps are also used.

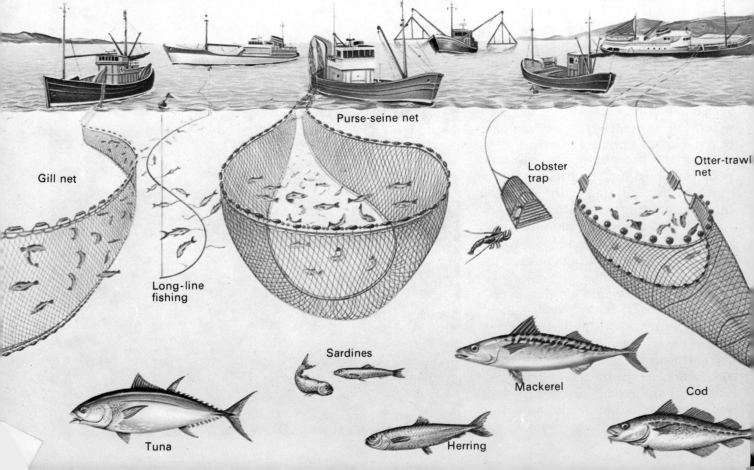

Purse-seine net

Gill net

Long-line fishing

Lobster trap

Otter-trawl net

Sardines

Tuna

Mackerel

Herring

Cod

the coelacanth. This fish was believed to have died out 60 million years ago. But in the 1930s one was caught in the Indian Ocean. There is still much to be learned about fishes.

See also EEL; SALMON; SEAHORSE; SHARK.

FISHING Fish is a tasty and valuable food. Most fish are caught in the sea; but in some countries river and lake fisheries are important. The best fishing grounds are in the Atlantic and Pacific oceans.

The most important food fish are cod, mackerel, haddock, herring, flatfish (such as flounder and sole) sardine, tuna and salmon. Shellfish such as lobsters, crabs and oysters also make valuable catches.

Most sea fish are caught in nets. *Trawls* are long, bag-shaped nets towed along under water. A *purse-seine* net is drawn round a shoal of fish, then pulled up. *Gill nets* look rather like curtains: the fish swim into them and are caught in the mesh. Fish can also be caught on baited lines. This is known as *lining* or trolling.

Deep sea fishing boats freeze their catch to keep it fresh. Once ashore the fish is either sold fresh, or preserved by freezing, canning or curing. Curing is done by drying, salting or smoking the fish. Smoked herring is one kind of cured fish.

Many people enjoy fishing as a sport and hobby. This is known as *angling*, and is done with a rod and a line, at the end of which is a baited hook.

FLAG A flag is much more than just a piece of colored material. It is a symbol. It represents a country, an organization or a person. Every country has its own national flag. Organizations such as the United Nations and the Red Cross have flags, and kings and queens have their own personal flags. Often flags are flown on special occasions and public holidays.

The first flags were ornamental streamers. In battle, flags, or standards, raised high on poles, were a rallying point for the soldiers. The emblems of the Roman legions were eagle standards. If the standard bearer fell, another soldier quickly took his place.

Flags were very popular in Europe during the Middle Ages. In fact, many royal families and nobles had their own flags with special symbols.

The first flag of the United States consisted of 13 stars in a circle on a blue background; and 13 stripes—7 red and 6 white. No one is sure about who thought of this design. But it is generally thought that George Washington asked Betsy Ross to sew the first flag.

Over the years, the American flag has changed many times. In the present design, the stripes represent the 13 original colonies. And each of the 50

1. Afghanistan 2. Albania
3. Algeria 4. Argentina
5. Australia 6. Austria
7. Belgium 8. Bolivia
9. Brazil 10. Bulgaria
11. Burma 12. Canada
13. Sri Lanka 14. Chile
15. China 16. Colombia
17. Cuba 18. Cyprus
19. Czechoslovakia
20. Denmark 21. Ecuador
22. Ethiopia 23. Finland
24. France 25. E. Germany
26. W. Germany 27. Ghana
28. Greece 29. Hungary
30. Iceland 31. India
32. Indonesia 33. Iran
34. Iraq 35. Ireland
36. Israel 37. Italy
38. Jamaica 39. Japan
40. Jordan 41. N. Korea
42. S. Korea 43. Lebanon
44. Liberia 45. Malaysia
46. Malta 47. Mexico
48. Morocco 49. Netherlands
50. New Zealand 51. Nigeria

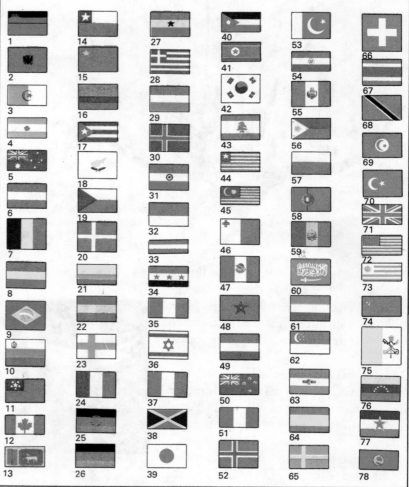

stars stands for one of the states. Each state has its own flag.

Each country of the world also has its own flag which symbolizes something about that country. A tricolor flag has three wide vertical stripes.

Flags are also used at sea to identify ships and to send messages. Normally flags are flown at the top of a flag pole.

52. Norway 53. Pakistan
54. Paraguay 55. Peru
56. Philippines 57. Poland
58. Portugal 59. Romania
60. Saudi Arabia
61. Sierra Leone 62. Singapore
63. South Africa 64. Spain
65. Sweden 66. Switzerland
67. Thailand 68. Trinidad & Tobago
69. Tunisia 70. Turkey
71. United Kingdom 72. USA
73. Uruguay 74. USSR
75. Vatican City 76. Venezuela
77. Yugoslavia 78. Zaire

Flown halfway down, at 'half-mast', they are a sign of mourning. To show a white flag means 'I surrender'.

FLOWER The flowers in our gardens and those that grow wild in the countryside are familiar to us. But in fact a great many more plants have flowers. Flowering plants grow in deserts, marshes and forests, and even in rivers and ponds. Some are tiny weeds; others are huge trees.

The diagram shows the parts of a typical flower. Some flowers have only one ovule. Others have hundreds. After they are fertilized, ovules develop into seeds.

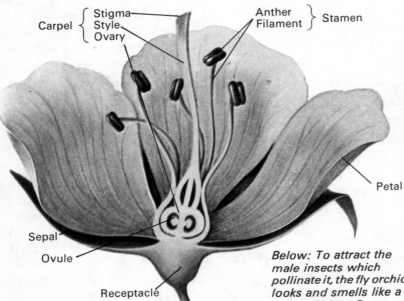

Carpel { Stigma Style Ovary }

Anther Filament } Stamen

Petal

Sepal

Ovule

Receptacle

Most plants have flowers. The flower is the part of the plant where the seeds develop. Without the flower, the plant could not reproduce itself. Inside each seed is all the 'information' needed to make a new plant grow.

Most flowers appear when the plant is fully grown. This is usually in summer time. Flowers come in all shapes and sizes, but all flowers have the same basic parts.

The most important parts are called *stamens* and *carpels*. The stamens are male parts, which produce a powder called *pollen*. The carpels are female parts. Each carpel has a sticky top, called a *stigma*. It is sticky so that pollen will cling to it. When this happens, the *ovule* in the lower part of the carpel can develop into a seed.

Some plants have separate male and female flowers. And some trees such as the willow have all male flowers on one

Below: To attract the male insects which pollinate it, the fly orchid looks and smells like a female insect. Bottom: The pansy's bright colors and 'guide lines' lead insects to the nectar.

tree and all female flowers on another tree.

In order to make seeds, the carpels of most flowers must be brushed with pollen from the stamens of another flower. Some plants rely on the wind to blow the pollen. Others are helped by insects. Insects play an important part in 'pollinating' flowers. Many flowers have **brightly colored petals, and a sweet** smell. Insects are attracted to them in search of the nectar which collects at the bottom of the petals. When an insect lands on the flower, it pushes its way inside to feed on the nectar. Pollen from the stamens rubs off on to its body, and when the insect flies to the next flower, it brushes some of this pollen on to the carpels.

Usually pollination only takes place between two flowers of the same species, or kind. If 'cross-breeding' between different species takes place, the result is a *hybrid* plant. After pollination the seeds begin to grow. Part of the carpel or of the flower stem turns into a fruit, which covers and protects the seeds until they are ripe. A pea pod is a fruit; so are nuts, apples, raspberries, cherries and grains of wheat. Some are soft and fleshy, others are hard and dry.

The brightly colored and sweet-scented garden flowers which are grown today have been developed from wild flowers. Often they look quite different from the original wild species.

Plants which have flowers are called *angiosperms*. Some plants have no flowers at all. Lichens, mosses, fungi and ferns are examples.

See also FRUIT; PLANT.

FLY There are thousands of different kinds of fly in the insect world. Some are harmless. But many flies carry germs and spread dangerous diseases.

Mosquitoes feed on blood and some spread the disease malaria. The tsetse fly spreads sleeping sickness. These flies live in hot countries. Some flies lay their eggs on living animals.

Houseflies and blowflies are common pests. They lay their eggs in animal dung or on rotting food. They pick up germs and carry them to our food. The housefly cannot eat solid food. It pours a special juice on to the food to make it liquid. Then the fly sucks it up.

FOG A cloud that forms close to the ground is called fog. Fog is formed when warm, moist air passes over cool land or water, or when cool air comes down over warm water or moist land. The water vapor in the air turns into tiny drops of water, so light they float in the air. That is why fog feels damp. After a clear warm day, heat from the land escapes into the sky and as the air cools a thin fog called mist may form.

See also CLOUD; WEATHER.

FOOD Our bodies need energy to live and grow. This energy comes from the foods we eat. The three most important substances in food are called nutrients. They are carbohydrates, fats and proteins.

Carbohydrates are food 'fuels'. They give us energy to work, move and keep warm. Sugar and starch are carbohydrates. We eat carbohydrates in bread, potatoes, rice, candy and cake. Cream, butter and the fat in meat provide us with fats. These are also good fuels. But if we eat too many carbohydrates or fats, our bodies store what they cannot use. Then we get fat. Proteins build the body's cells and are vital to good health. Protein-rich foods are eggs, lean meat, cheese, fish and beans. Our bodies also need minerals for strong bones and teeth, and vitamins.

Bacteria can turn foods bad. To preserve foods, they are canned, bottled, smoked, salted, pickled, frozen or dried. This stops bacteria from attacking them.

See also BACTERIA; FARMING; HUMAN BODY; VITAMIN.

FOOTBALL is one of America's most popular sports. The game, as we play it today, was actually invented by Harvard University and is based on the Canadian game of rugby football.

Football is played in two 30 minute periods, each of which is divided into two 15 minute quarters. A 15 minute interval separates the two halves, but because the official clock is frequently stopped to allow for fouls or time out, the game can often last for two or three hours.

The football field, called a *gridiron,* is 120 yards (109 meters) long, including end zones and 160 feet (49 meters) wide. The object of each team is to gain possession of the ball and score touch downs by moving toward the opponent's goal. The ball may be advanced by passing, kicking or running with it.

Before the game begins, a coin is tossed by the referee, and "called" by the visiting team's captain. If the visiting captain calls the coin correctly, he can choose either the goal he wishes to defend, or the position he wishes to play—kicking or receiving. if he calls the coin incorrectly, the first choice is left to the home team.

Once the choices have been made, the ball is kicked into play from the offensive (kicking) team's 35 yard (32 meter) line, and the offensive team, through a series of forward and lateral passes, tries to advance the ball. In order to keep possession of the ball, the offensive team must advance 10 yards within 4 "tries" or *downs.* A successful 10 yard advance is called a *first down.* The team then has a chance at four more "tries" to make another first down.

In the meantime, the defensive team is hard at work trying to stop the offensive team's progress and get the ball for themselves. The offensive team can lose the ball if they fail to make a first down, fumble, throw a pass that is intercepted or kick the ball to the defensive team.

Play resumes at the *line of scrimmage,* or the point where the defensive team stopped the ball. Once the ball is stopped, the offensive team *huddles* to plan a course of action. The team then lines up, the center "snaps" the ball through his legs to one of the players and the game is back in motion.

If a team has not scored enough yardage in the first three downs, it may *punt.* This means that one of the players takes a direct snap from the center and kicks the ball toward the opposing team. A team scores a touchdown when it legally carries the ball or completes a pass over the opponent's goal line, or recovers a fumble or a free ball in the end zone. A touchdown is worth 6 points. When a team scores a touchdown it may try to score an extra point by drop-kicking the ball between the goal posts and above the cross bar. This try is called a *conversion*, and if it is successful, is worth one point.

FOREST Land that is covered with trees is called a forest. Today about a third of the Earth's land surface is covered by forests.

In cold lands, the forests are composed mainly of conifers such as pines and firs. The largest coniferous forests are in northern Europe, Canada and Siberia. Milder countries have forests of broad-leaved trees like oaks, elms, birches and maples. In the hot, wet lands close to the equator, there are tropical forests of trees such as ebony and mahogany. This wood is very hard. The coastal areas of South America, Africa and southeast Asia, hold swamp forests of mangroves.

In many countries forestry is an important industry. Power saws and tractors can quickly cut down and haul away the tallest trees. But in a well-run forest, new trees are planted to replace them.

Today we are learning how to look after the world's forests. They provide shelter for animals and also stop the soil

This fossil insect is preserved in amber. Amber forms from the sticky resin which oozes from pine trees. Insects which became stuck in the resin were fossilized forever when the resin hardened into amber.

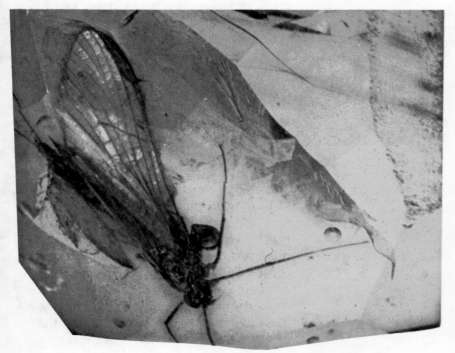

from being eroded (worn away). Trees put back oxygen into the air. And people who live in crowded cities want to enjoy the peace and beauty of the forest. In dry weather, the forest visitor must take special care. For a carelessly dropped match can start a forest fire, which can quickly destroy thousands of trees.

See also JUNGLE; TREE; WOOD.

FOSSIL Fossils are the hardened remains of dead animals and plants that lived thousands of years ago. They tell us what life was like before written records were kept.

Usually when an animal dies, its body decays. But sometimes it is preserved, or fossilized. Often only the hard parts of it, such as bones or a shell, are fossilized. A fossil may even be just the trace of a leaf or a footprint in the rock. But sometimes the whole body is preserved. Mammoths that died during the Ice Age and were buried in the snow have been found with all their skin and hair. The ice preserved them like a refrigerator.

Many fossils are the remains of sea creatures. A sea animal's body may be covered by sand and mud when it dies and sinks to the sea bed. The sand and mud help to preserve the animal's skeleton. Over millions of years, the sand and mud harden into rock. The skeleton buried in the mud also turns to hard stone. Sometimes the rocks that have been under the sea become dry land. As they are slowly worn away by rain and wind, the fossils inside them show up.

You can often see the pattern of leaves in coal. This is because coal is the fossilized remains of plants that grew millions of years ago in swamp forests. When the trees died, they sank in the mud and gradually hardened into coal.

FOX Foxes belong to the dog family. They hunt by night for rabbits, mice and voles. The female fox, or vixen, rears her cubs in an underground den.

Farmers dislike foxes, because they raid hen houses. In Britain the fox is hunted by foxhounds. But it usually gets away. Silver and blue Arctic foxes are bred on special farms for their fur. The little fennec fox lives in the desert.

The life cycle of the frog begins in the spring, when the females lay their eggs in ponds and streams. The eggs, or spawn, are covered with protective jelly. Each black dot grows into a tadpole. Tadpoles swim like fish and breathe through gills. But as they grow, they develop legs and their gills become lungs. Many are eaten by enemies, but some survive. After three months, the tadpoles have lost their tails and become baby frogs, able to hop about on land as well as swim in the water.

Eggs

Tadpoles

Adult

The cunning red fox normally hunts in fields and woodlands, but sometimes lives close to towns.

FRANCE is the largest country in western Europe. Its beautiful scenery includes forests, plains, valleys, high mountains and great rivers. The name France comes from the Franks, a people who once conquered France. In vineyards throughout France grapes are grown to make wine. Champagne, Burgundy and Bordeaux are areas famous

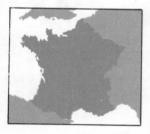

France is the largest country in Western Europe.

Facts and Figures
Area: 212,741 square miles
        551,000 square kilometers
Population: 43,000,000
Capital: Paris
Government: Republic
Money unit: French franc
Longest river: Loire, 634 miles
                1020 kilometers

The most famous French cathedral is Notre Dame in Paris. It stands on the Île de la Cité, a small island in the River Seine.

for their wines. France's many industries include mining and manufacturing.

Paris is the most important city in France. Many artists and writers have lived there. Paris is also a center of fashion.

The greatest French king was Louis XIV (1638–1715). But in 1789 the French people overthrew their king and set up a republic. This important event is is called the French Revolution. Later, the French emperor Napoleon conquered most of Europe.

World Wars I and II caused great suffering in France, for the country was invaded twice. But, led by President Charles de Gaulle (1890–1970), France grew strong again.

See also COUNTRIES OF THE WORLD; LOUIS XIV; NAPOLEON.

FROGS AND TOADS are amphibians. They can live on land. But must return to the water to lay their eggs.

Frogs and toads look rather alike. But frogs use their long back legs to hop. Toads crawl or run. They eat insects and worms, catching their prey with their long, sticky tongues. To protect themselves from enemies, some frogs and toads have poison glands. Others puff up with air to make themselves look bigger.

In spring frogs and toads travel to ponds and streams to breed. They lay eggs called spawn. The spawn looks like tiny black blobs in masses of jelly. The eggs hatch into tadpoles. Tadpoles swim like fish and breathe through gills. But soon they grow legs, lose their tails and develop lungs. Finally, they become tiny frogs or toads.

The midwife toad carries its eggs around on its back until they are ready to hatch. The Surinam toad keeps both eggs and tadpoles in pouches on its back.

See also AMPHIBIAN.

FRUIT We all recognize apples, bananas and oranges as fruits. But cucumbers, walnuts, pea pods, acorns and dandelion 'clocks' are also fruits.

The fruit is the part of a plant which protects the seed. It also helps to spread the seed, so that new plants can grow. Some fruits have wings (such as the sycamore) or light, fluffy heads (such as the dandelion) so that the seeds will blow away. Other fruits are sweet and juicy, so that animals will carry them away as food. Burrs are fruits which cling to the fur of passing animals. Many fruits split when ripe, letting their seeds fall to the ground.

Fruits with pits inside are called *drupes*. Plums, cherries and walnuts are drupes. Blackberries and raspberries are lots of tiny drupes clustered together. Inside a berry, the seeds are enclosed in soft pulp. Oranges, tomatoes, cucumbers and blackcurrants are all berries. In 'true' fruits, the fruit grows from the part of the flower called the *carpel*. 'False' fruits, such as apples and rose hips, are made from the swollen stem of the flower; the carpel forms the core.

Many fruits are good to eat and growing them is an important industry. The fruits we eat today have all been bred from wild plants. For example all modern apples are descended from the wild crab apple.

See also FLOWER; PLANT.

Fruits such as peaches and cherries, which have fleshy pulp around hard pits are called drupes. Raspberries and similar fruits consist of several little drupes. Tomatoes, grapes, gooseberries and oranges are berries. They are soft and fleshy, with many seeds. The actual fruit of an apple or pear is the core. Peas and nuts are dry fruits, with pods or skins to protect their seeds.

GALAXY Our Sun is part of a great family of stars. We call this family the Milky Way galaxy, or just the Galaxy. A galaxy is a group of stars which moves together through space. Many galaxies, including our own, look like great wheels which have spiral arms. Others have no arms. All of them spin around as they travel through space. Each galaxy contains about 100,000 million stars and no doubt many planets. Some stars are grouped together in giant *clusters*. The galaxies also contain great clouds of gas and dust. They are called *nebulae*. We can see many other galaxies from Earth. The Andromeda galaxy is a spiral galaxy much like our own.

GALILEO (1564–1642) was an Italian astronomer. In 1609 he became the first person to look at the heavens through a telescope. He saw the mountains on our Moon and the moons of the planet Jupiter. Galileo was skilled at mathematics and also carried out scientific experiments. He discovered how a pendulum swings. He also showed that things of different weights fall to the ground at the same rate.

GARDENS For thousands of years people have kept gardens. Most people like growing things. There are many different kinds of gardens. A flower garden, with its colors and perfumes,

The telescope used by the Italian astronomer Galileo. He believed, like Copernicus, that the Earth moved around the Sun. He was one of the first scientists to use the telescope (invented in 1608) to study the stars.

is beautiful to look at. A vegetable garden provides inexpensive, fresh food. Some gardens are arranged in neat patterns. Others have a more wild and natural look. Wherever people live, they make gardens. In a city, a garden may be a small back yard, a rooftop, or just a single window box.

Different plants need different kinds of soil. But all plants need water, light and air. When starting to make a garden, it is a good idea to find out which plants will grow best in sunny or shady spots.

GAS All the substances that make up our world can exist in one of three forms - as a solid, liquid or gas. Gases are different from the other two forms because they have no shape and completely fill anything they are put in.

The air we breathe is a gas, or rather a 'mixture of gases. It contains mainly oxygen and nitrogen. All living things need oxygen to live. We breathe in oxygen and breathe out another gas – carbon dioxide. Plants make their food from the carbon dioxide in the air.

Burning fuels produces carbon dioxide, too. It can also produce carbon monoxide, which is very poisonous. There is carbon monoxide in car exhaust fumes. There are many more poisonous gases, including chlorine and hydrogen sulphide, which has the smell of bad eggs.

Some gases are valuable as fuels, including natural gas and coal gas. Natural gas comes from the ground. Coal gas is made from coal. It contains carbon monoxide and hydrogen. So does water gas, made from steam and coke. Hydrogen is a very good fuel. It is also the lightest of all gases.

See also OXYGEN.

GEMS AND JEWELRY Sometimes in rocks you can find beautiful crystals that can be cut to show great brilliance and sparkle. They are called gems or gemstones. They can be set in gold, platinum and silver to form exquisite pieces of jewelry.

The finest gems are diamonds. Their brilliance, sparkle and hardness are unequaled. They are also very rare. Red rubies, green emeralds and blue

In the 1500s gardens were laid out in formal, geometrical patterns, with neat box hedges, shrubs, paths and flower beds. These gardens at a chateau in Villandry, France have been restored to their original design.

The gemstones used to make jewelery are cut from natural rocks and minerals. Flat surfaces known as facets are ground on to the stones, so that they reflect light in many directions. Many varieties of the mineral beryl are shown in the picture below. There is an emerald in its natural rock setting and one made up into a ring (center front) and a large aquamarine crystal (right back).

sapphires are also much sought after. Some gems are not crystals, but stones with a lovely play of color on their surface. They include opal and lapis lazuli. Pearls are neither crystals nor stones. They are fine gems that oysters produce in their shells.

GENETICS The science of genetics explains why living things look and behave as they do. All animals and plants reproduce themselves. One-celled animals, such as the amoeba, simply split in two. But more advanced animals have two sexes, male and female. Each individual produces sex cells. If a male and female sex cell join, the female cell grows into a new individual.

If both parents have two blue eye genes (b), all their children will have blue eyes. If one parent has two brown eye genes (B), and the other has two b genes, the children will all have brown eyes because the B gene is dominant. If one parent has a B gene and a recessive b gene, his own eyes will be brown. But if he marries a blue-eyed woman his children may have blue or brown eyes. If the same man married a woman with brown eyes but with a recessive b gene, he might still have some blue-eyed children.

Germany is divided into two countries.

East Germany

West Germany

Each parent passes on certain characteristics to its offspring. For example, we say someone has 'his father's eyes', or 'her mother's hair'. This process is called *heredity*.

Some inherited characteristics are stronger than others. They are 'dominant'. Weaker ones are 'recessive'. This was shown in the 1800s by a monk called Gregor Mendel. He experimented with peas, and wondered why, when he crossed a pink flowered pea with a white pea, the offspring was also pink. However, in the second generation, a quarter of the peas had white flowers. Pink was the 'dominant' characteristic. But the peas still contained a hidden 'instruction' to make white flowers as well.

Heredity works in an amazing way. Inside every cell are tiny *chromosomes*, largely made of a chemical called DNA. Different parts of each chromosome carry different 'coded messages'. Each part is called a *gene*. The genes carry all the information needed to make a new plant or animal. They decide its sex and also what characteristics it inherits from its parents.

Genetic changes, and also changes in the environment (surroundings) affect the evolution of living things. The cross-breeding of cattle to give more beef or milk to the farmer shows how genetics can be used to help Man.

See also CELL; REPRODUCTION.

GENGHIS KHAN (1167–1227) was one of the most feared men in history. Born Temujin, son of a Mongol prince, he became known as Genghis Khan, meaning 'conqueror of the world'. The Mongols came from central Asia. They were tough horsemen, and wherever Genghis Khan led his Mongol army, terrible tales were told of his cruelty and ferocity. He conquered many tribes in China, Russia, Afghanistan and Persia and so won an enormous empire for the Mongols.

GERMANY Two countries in Europe are called Germany. Until 1945 each was part of a single country.

Only northern Germany has a sea coast, on the North and Baltic Seas. Here the land is mostly flat. Central Germany is hilly and wooded, and in the south are high mountains and thick forests. The Black Forest and the winding valley of the River Rhine are very beautiful.

Germany has fertile soil and a mild climate. Farmers grow cereals, potatoes and sugar beet, and make grapes into wine. They raise cattle and pigs. Sausage is a favorite German food.

Germany has plenty of coal, iron ore, timber and hydro-electric power. So industry is important. There are many factories, especially in the area called the Ruhr.

German history goes back to the time of the Romans. But for hundreds of years Germany was split up into many small states. Eventually they joined together, led by the strongest state, Prussia. In the 1800s Germany built up a strong army, and this led to World War I (1914–1918), in which Germany was defeated. In the 1930s the Nazi dictator Adolf Hitler gained power. During World War II (1939–1945), much of Germany was destroyed. After the war, the Russians controlled the eastern part (now East Germany), while the western allies held the rest (West Germany). Berlin, the old capital, was also divided.

Both Germanies have built up new, modern industries. But East Germany is not so rich and the people have less freedom.

Facts and Figures
Area: West Germany, 96,139 square miles
        (249,000 square kilometers)
        East Germany, 41,506 square miles
        (107,500 square kilometers)
Population: West Germany, 62,000,000
              East Germany, 17,200,000
Capitals: West Germany, Bonn
            East Germany, East Berlin
Government: West Germany,
              Federal Republic
              East Germany,
              Communist Republic
Money Unit: Mark
Longest river: Rhine, 820 miles (1319 km)
Highest mountain: Zugspitze, 10,719 feet
                    (3267 meters)

GHOST A ghost is said by some people to be the spirit of a dead person. For some reason it cannot rest, but must haunt the living. Many old houses are supposed to have ghosts.

People have believed in ghosts for

thousands of years, and told stories about them. A typical ghost in a story appears and then disappears suddenly; it walks about at night, groaning or clanking chains, seeking revenge for some ancient wrong.

Few people say they have actually seen a ghost. Most say they do not believe in ghosts. But ghost stories are still as popular as ever.

The Moselle Valley in West Germany is famous for its fine wines. The grapes are grown on terraced fields on the slopes of the river valley.

The giraffe can reach the topmost branches and strip off leaves with its long tongue.

This beautiful wine glass was made in Venice. From the 1200s Venice made the finest glass in the world. The glass blowers called their glass 'crystal'.

For 1500 years men have shaped molten glass by blowing and twisting it on the end of a tube. In the Middle Ages the lost Roman secrets of glass-making were rediscovered in Italy.

GIRAFFE With its long legs and even longer neck, the giraffe can reach the topmost leaves in the trees. Even a new born giraffe is as tall as a man.

Giraffes live in Africa. They can run swiftly and kick powerfully to escape their enemies. When a giraffe drinks, it has to spread its legs wide in order to lower its head. It cannot bend its neck.

GLACIER A glacier is a slow-moving river of ice. From an icecap or high snow field, it flows down the slopes of mountains. Lower down, where the air is warmer, the glacier melts. In the Arctic, chunks of ice split off glaciers and float away in the sea as icebergs.

Glaciers push stones and boulders along with them. They scrape the soil from the land, smooth the hills and scour out valleys. The rocky mounds piled up by glaciers are called moraines.

During the Ice Ages glaciers spread across the Northern Hemisphere. Boulders carried with the ice can still be seen, even though the glaciers melted long ago.

See also ICE AGE; ICEBERG.

GLAND Glands are organs inside the body. They make chemicals which control many of the body's activities.

The *endocrine* glands pass their chemicals straight into the bloodstream. These chemicals, called hormones, carry 'messages' to various parts of the body. The endocrine glands control the body's growth. The ovaries in women and the testes in men are sex glands or gonads.

The *exocrine* glands release their chemicals through tubes, or ducts. Some of them produce the juices which digest food, and also tears, sweat and saliva. The pancreas produces a hormone called insulin, which controls the amount of sugar in the blood.

GLASS is a useful material. It is transparent, easy to shape, and cheap to make. It can be made as flat sheets for windows, or into curved lenses for cameras, microscopes and other instruments. It can be blown into bottles. Glass is also very easy to clean, because no common chemicals attack it.

Glass is cheap to produce because it is made from some of the cheapest materials you can think of – sand, limestone and soda ash. Sand and limestone are two of the commonest minerals in the Earth's crust. Soda ash is produced cheaply from salt water. These three ingredients are mixed together and heated in a very hot furnace. They melt and become glass. Special ingredients may be added to make heat-proof glass or colored glass.

GLIDER A glider is an aircraft without an engine. It stays in the air by riding on air currents. A glider pilot tries to carry the glider upward. Then he glides downward in the direction in which he wants to go until he finds another upward air current. Gliders may be launched into the air in several ways. They can be towed into the air by a car, an airplane or even a boat.

GOAT The goat was one of the earliest animals to be tamed by Man. Its milk, meat, wool and skin have been useful to people for thousands of years.

The goat is tougher than its relative the sheep. It can live in dry, rocky country. It climbs well and can eat almost anything. Herds of hungry goats have turned good pastures into deserts. Wild goats live on high mountain crags.

Goats are tough animals and can live on poor pasture.

GOLD is a heavy, yellow metal. It has been used for thousands of years to make jewelry and ornaments because it is beautiful to look at and does not lose its shine. It is also easy to shape. It can be drawn into fine wire or beaten into thin sheets without snapping. Gold is precious because it is scarce. It is found in the Earth as a metal. Sometimes large lumps of gold, or nuggets are mined in the rocks. But usually gold is found as fine dust, often in river beds.

GOVERNMENT People living together in a group have to agree on what jobs must be done and who should do them. Usually one person becomes the leader, or ruler. This is how the group is 'governed'. Today governments rule nations. Without a government there would be no schools or hospitals, no police force or postal service.

Government was needed as soon as people began living in groups. In a primitive tribe the best hunter or strongest warrior might become the ruler or chief. At first the ruler was chosen by the tribe. But then it became the custom that the ruler's son always took his place. The government then remained in the same family. This is 'hereditary rule', and in this way kings were created.

In ancient times some kings were so powerful that people thought they were gods and could therefore do no wrong. So the idea grew that kings had special rights and powers. This encouraged bad kings to rule cruelly and selfishly, and so become *tyrants*.

To help make sensible laws, good kings took advice from councils of wise men. In time these councils grew almost as powerful as the king. Sometimes they acted selfishly too. The ancient Greeks were the first to try a form of government called *democracy* or 'rule by the people'.

This was the beginning of *democracy* as we know it today. This is also the basis of thought on which the American system of government is founded. The American system of government is called a *republic*. In a republic, the power of the government rests in the citizens who vote on the issues. American citizens exercise their law

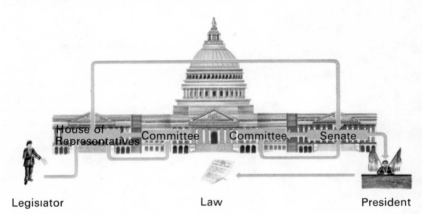

Legislator   Law   President

making power through their elected representatives—their Senators and Congressmen.

Monarchy is another form of government. In a monarchy, the head of state is a king, queen or emperor. If the head of state has full law making power, the government is called an *absolute monarchy*.

In the United States Congress passes all the laws. A bill is first voted on in the House of Representatives, before going to the Senate. It is also examined in detail by committees. Finally it is approved by the President and then becomes law.

The government of Great Britain is a *constitutional monarchy*. This means that though the Queen reigns, she does not rule. Her powers are limited by the government. The country is ruled by a government of ministers who are elected by the people. The head of the government is the Prime Minister. In a dictatorship, only one person, the dictator, has any power over the people.

In the United States the President is head of state and head of the government. He also commands the armed forces. Presidents are elected every four years. The United States parliament, called the Congress, is divided into the House of Representatives and the Senate. In a democracy more than one political party is allowed. But in Communist countries, only the Communist Party takes part in the government.

See also COMMUNISM; DEMOCRACY.

GRASS is the most important of all plants. Cereals are grasses that are also valuable foods. Many farm animals eat grass, fresh in summer and dried as hay in winter. Sugar cane is a kind of grass.

Most grasses are slender, with hollow stems and pointed leaves. The plants keep growing even when the leaves are cut. In fact, the more a lawn is mowed, the thicker it grows as the grass sends out side shoots.

See also BAMBOO; CEREALS.

GRASSHOPPER On warm summer days you may hear grasshoppers chirping in the long grass, though it is hard to spot them.

Grasshoppers hop with their strong back legs. Male grasshoppers 'sing' by rubbing their back legs across their wings. This attracts females and wards off other males.

Crickets are like grasshoppers. They prefer to live in trees, or in houses, or even underground.

See also LOCUST.

GRAVITY Throw a ball into the air and it will fall back to the ground. This is because the Earth pulls it back. The Earth's pull is called gravity. Gravity is one of the basic forces in the universe. Magnetism is another. Isaac Newton

A mountain grasshopper. Grasshoppers eat plants and some kinds are pests. Although they have wings, grasshoppers spend most of their time on the ground or in long grass.

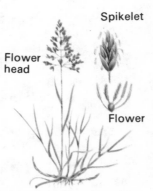

All grasses have thin, wiry roots, which hold the soil together, and slender stems. The flowers are arranged in groups called spikelets on a pyramid-shaped head. The wind shakes the flowers and carries away the pollen.

Spikelet

Flower head

Flower

first stated the laws of gravity. He said that every object in the universe has an attraction for every other object.

Gravity is what keeps all the heavenly bodies in their paths through the heavens. It keeps the Moon moving in a circle

around the Earth. It keeps the Earth moving around the Sun. If there were no gravity, the Moon and Earth would fly off into space.

The Moon is much smaller than the Earth and has a weaker pull. If you lived on the Moon, you could easily jump 6 feet (2 meters) high. But the Moon's gravity does affect the Earth. It pulls the oceans and causes the tides.

See also: MOON

GREAT LAKES The five great lakes, Superior, Huron, Michigan, Erie and Ontario, are located in North America along the United States and Canadian border. At one time, these lakes were mostly landlocked. But today, a series of canals connects the Great Lakes with the St. Lawrence Seaway. The St. Lawrence Seaway provides ships with easy access to the Atlantic Ocean.

Lake Superior is the largest of the Great Lakes. Lake Ontario is the smallest. Four of the five Great Lakes are under the joint control of the U.S. and Canada. Only Lake Michigan is completely within the United States.

The Great Lakes were formed thousands of years ago when glaciers moving from the north, settled in the northern valleys. As the ice receded, lakes were formed. The Great Lakes are open to navigation only seven to eight months a year. Storms and ice flows stop shipping all winter.

GREECE, ANCIENT

The ancient Greeks built one of the greatest of all civilizations. It began some 4000 years ago when wandering tribes from central Europe came to the land that we now call Greece. One of these tribes was known as the 'Graikos' or Greeks. At first they lived simply in small farming villages. They built wooden houses, used horses and carts for transport, and grew wheat in their fields.

But over the centuries, Greek civilization developed as the people learned better ways of doing things. Craftsmen made beautiful gold ornaments and bronze weapons. The Greeks developed art, music and poetry. Their kings lived in magnificent palaces, which had bathrooms with running water. About 2500 years ago the Greeks of Athens set up a new form of government. It was called *democracy*, meaning 'rule by the people'. All the citizens had a right to say how they were to be ruled. This was an important new idea.

Athens was only one of a number of city states in Greece. The states often quarreled. Athens' great rival was called Sparta, and the two states were very different. Sparta was a military state, ruled by all-powerful kings. Its people were soldiers, and the Spartans had no use for art, philosophy or comfortable homes. Boys and girls were taken from their parents at the age of seven and sent to special schools to make them tough and strong. If a Spartan baby was weak and sickly, its parents would leave it on a mountainside to die.

Life in Athens was more relaxed. The Athenians built fine temples and public buildings. Their homes were furnished with comfortable couches and chairs of wood and leather, and on the floors were beautiful mosaics. The people wore tunics called 'chitons' and the wealthy women had fine ornaments and jewels. For entertainment, the Athenians played music on flutes and lyres or they went to the theater. There they watched plays by Sophocles and Aristophanes. Some of these plays are still performed today. However, not everyone was rich and free. Many people in Greece were slaves.

The Greeks were great athletes. They loved running, javelin and discus throwing and wrestling. The first Olympic Games, named after Mount Olympus, home of the Greek gods, took place in 776 BC. The Greeks had many gods, but the greatest was Zeus, king of the gods.

The beauty of life in Athens can be seen from the ruins which still remain. But although the Athenians were not so strict as their neighbors, the Spartans, they were not soft or weak. Their army and navy were strong, and they won many battles. They defeated the Spartans and threw off invasions by huge Persian armies. The Athenians loved to hear stories of great Greek heroes and their deeds. The greatest of these stories are told by the poet Homer in two long poems, called the *Iliad* and the *Odyssey*.

The age of the city states ended in Greece in 338 BC. Then, King Philip of Macedonia brought all of Greece under his rule. His son Alexander the Great conquered a huge empire. But after Alexander died, no Greek ruler was strong enough to hold on to the empire. Greece became weak and in 146 BC, it was conquered by the Romans. The Romans did not value freedom and democracy as highly as the Greeks had done. But they borrowed many Greek ideas, particularly about art. These ideas have survived many centuries, and have influenced people ever since. The way we live and think today owes a great deal to the civilization of ancient Greece.

The ancient Greeks built splendid open-air theaters. The audience sat in rows on the hillside, while the actors, singers and dancers performed on the flat stage or orchestra below.

How guns developed: (from top to bottom) matchlock; flintlock; percussion lock; needle gun. The matchlock (1400) was fired by a smoldering match or fuse. The flintlock (1600) struck a spark to fire the powder, while the percussion cap (1815) had a chemical 'fulminate' which exploded when struck. The breech-loading Dreyse needle gun (1848) fired when a pin struck the percussion cap at the base of the bullet.

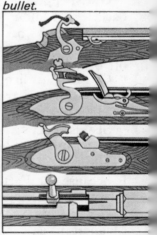

GUN Guns are weapons which fire bullets or shells. Small arms, sometimes called firearms or hand guns, include pistols, revolvers, shotguns, rifles and machine guns. The big guns used by armies are called artillery pieces. They include field guns, howitzers and mortars.

All guns work in roughly the same way. A gun has a long, hollow, metal *barrel*. The *bore* of a gun is the width of the hole in the barrel. One end of the barrel, the *breech*, is closed; the other end, the *muzzle*, is open. When the gun is fired, an explosive charge inside a *cartridge* sends a bullet down the barrel and out of the muzzle with great force. Most guns have spiral grooves, known as 'rifling' inside the barrel. These spin the bullet and make it go farther.

The earliest guns were like small cannons, and were first used in the 1300s. They were loaded by pushing gunpowder down the barrel and they fired a solid ball. Often the whole cannon blew up. The first hand guns, or muskets, were heavy and clumsy. After one shot, they had to be reloaded. In the 1800s the breech-loading gun was invented. This could fire more quickly. The repeater rifle and the revolver (such as the famous Colt 45) replaced the musket. From these guns were developed the quick-firing automatic weapons used today.

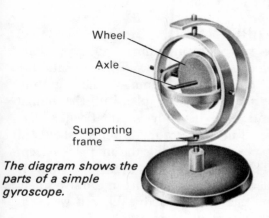

The diagram shows the parts of a simple gyroscope.

GYROSCOPE A gyroscope is a device that contains a wheel spinning rapidly on an axle. A toy gyroscope can be made to do amazing tricks and seems to defy gravity. For example, it can pivot at right angles on a stand supported only at one end. If it is properly mounted, a spinning gyroscope will remain pointing in the same direction, no matter how the supporting frame turns around it. This is the principle behind the gyrocompass, which planes and ships use to find their way through the air or across the seas.

HEART About 70 times every minute your heart beats. The beating you can feel is the throb of a pump at work, for that is all the heart is. It is a bag of extra strong muscle that pumps blood around the body. The blood carries oxygen which every cell of our bodies needs. The oxygen must be taken from the lungs and delivered to the cells while waste products must be collected from the cells and taken back to the lungs. The blood does the carrying and the heart does the pumping. So strong is its action that it easily forces blood up from our feet to our lungs.

The pump is divided into four parts, a left and right auricle above a left and right ventricle. The two sides of the pump work quite independently. Blood fresh from the lungs enters the left auricle and is forced down through a valve into the left ventricle. From there it is forced into the body's main artery, the aorta, and out of the heart ready to flow around the body. On the other side 'stale' blood from the body enters the right auricle, passes into the right ventricle and is forced out towards the lungs where it will dump its carbon dioxide and pick up vital oxygen.

HEAT is a form of energy that we can feel but not see. It is given out, together with light, when things burn. It is also given out when electricity passes through a coil of fine wire, as in an electric fire or a light bulb. Heat is also produced in the Sun and the stars when atoms combine together, and when atoms are split in nuclear power stations on Earth. You can make heat yourself by friction. If you rub your hand quickly up and down a piece of material, it will soon get hot. We describe how hot a thing is by its temperature, which we measure with a thermometer. When we heat something, it generally gets bigger. We say it expands. Metals expand most. They are also the best conductors (carriers) of heat.

See also THERMOMETER.

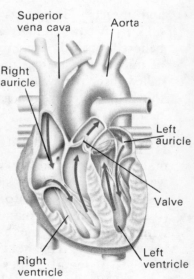

In this diagram, the arrows show how blood is pumped through the heart. At the top blood flows in from the head and arms and out to the body. At the sides blood flows in from and out to the lungs. At the bottom blood flows in from the lower part of the body and out again. The body's main artery is the aorta.

HEDGEHOG

When a hedgehog is frightened, it rolls itself into a prickly ball. But it usually ambles along hedgerows at night, snuffling for snails, slugs and insects. Hedgehogs do not suck milk from cows' udders as people once believed, but will visit gardens for a dish of milk. They belong to the mammals called insectivores, but eat almost anything. In winter hedgehogs hibernate in a nest of leaves.

HELICOPTER

A helicopter is a machine than can fly forward, upward, downward, and sideways. This is because it has a rotor, or rotating (turning) wing. Airplanes have fixed wings and their engines can drive them forward only. The helicopter's rotor consists of metal blades mounted on top of the body. Turned by the engine, the rotor twists itself into the air to lift the helicopter upward. When flying forward, the rotor blades are angled so that they push the air backward, just like you push the water backward when you are swimming. On its own, the spinning rotor would make the whole helicopter spin. But this is prevented by the movement of a small upright rotor situated on the tail.

HERALDRY

During the Middle Ages it was difficult to tell if a knight in armor was a friend or an enemy. So knights put *crests* on their helmets and painted designs called *devices* on their shields and on the cloth surcoats they wore over their armor.

Each knight had his own *coat of arms*, which became his family badge or emblem. Many families still have coats

A hedgehog and its young. When they are babies, hedgehogs have soft spines.

Some of the herbs used to flavor food are shown below.

Mint

Thyme

Sage

Garlic   Parsley

Left: A helicopter lands on an aircraft carrier at sea. Navies use helicopters to hunt submarines and for rescue work.

The coat of arms of a medieval knight bore elaborate symbols.

of arms. The study of coats of arms is called heraldry, and the people who control and design them are known as heralds.

HERBS

All plants with soft, rather than woody, stems are called herbs by botanists. But other people, especially cooks, use the name for certain highly-scented plants used to add flavor to food. Common herbs used in cooking are mint, parsley, garlic, sage, thyme and chives.

Years ago people grew herbs to use as medicines, and a few are still used for this purpose today. Herbs grow best in light soil. Most of them come from warm Mediterranean countries so they need plenty of sun.

HIBERNATION

In winter when food is scarce, many animals go into a long deep sleep. This is called hibernation.

During late summer and autumn, while food is still plentiful, the animal eats until its body is fat. Then it digs itself into the ground or finds a sheltered place to sleep. While the animal is asleep, its heartbeat and its breathing slow. It uses so little energy that it can live solely on the fat in its body. When it wakes in the spring, it is very thin.

Mammals which hibernate include dormice, bats and hedgehogs. Reptiles, such as snakes and tortoises, and amphibians, such as frogs and toads, also hibernate. Some animals, including certain bears and squirrels, spend much of the winter asleep. But on warm days they wake and eat. So they do not really hibernate.

HIMALAYAS The Himalayas are the highest mountains in the world. They rise like a massive wall between India and the rest of Asia. The highest peak is Mount Everest, 29,030 feet (8848 meters), the world's highest mountain.

'Himalaya' means 'home of the snows'. Huge glaciers and snowfields feed mighty rivers, such as the Ganges and Indus, which flow down from the mountains. No railways or big roads cross the mountains. For the few people that live in the Himalayas, such as the Sherpa people of Nepal, life is a constant battle with the wind, snow and cold.

HIPPOPOTAMUS In the rivers of Africa lives the huge hippopotamus. Its name means 'river horse' but it is actually related to the pig.

Despite their gaping jaws and tusks, hippos eat only plant food. They spend the day in the water, floating or walking along the river bottom, and come ashore at night. They love to wallow in mud. Hippos can be dangerous if annoyed, and the males fight savagely during the breeding season.

Animals in hibernation live on their fat as they sleep through the winter. The woodchuck, hedgehog and dormouse sleep soundly until spring. But bears and squirrels wake up on warmer days to look for food. In cold countries, cold-blooded animals such as snakes, toads, lizards and tortoises also hibernate. They crawl into sheltered places in the rocks or bury themselves underground. Bats and butterflies often choose old buildings as places to sleep in.

Hippos are suspicious of strangers. They often lie almost submerged in rivers, with just their eyes and nostrils showing above the water. At night they come ashore to look for food.

HISTORY When people talk of 'history' they mean events which happened in the past. Historians are mostly interested in people and events concerned with government and wars, because these things affect whole nations. But history is also concerned with ordinary people, and the way they live. Common household objects uncovered by archaeologists tell us just as much about the past as accounts of the lives and deeds of famous people.

Science, medicine, art, religion and architecture all have histories of their own. History is revealed in many ways: by digging for it, by reading about it in old books and manuscripts, by listening to people talking about things they remember, by recording events on tape and film. What is news today will be history tomorrow.

Butterfly

Bat

Snake

Toad

Dormouse

Lizard

Squirrel

Hedgehog

Bear

Woodchuck

WORLD HISTORY

	AFRICA	ASIA	EUROPE	AMERICA	AUSTRALASIA
2000BC	3100 Upper and Lower Egypt united 2700–2500 Pyramids of Giza built, Golden Age of art in Egypt 2050–1800 Middle Kingdom under Theban rulers	3000 Civilization of Sumeria 2400 Indus Valley civilization	3000 Neolithic Age in Europe. Minoan civilization develops in Crete 2000 Bronze Age in north Europe 1900s–1200s Trojan civilization flourishes		
1500BC	1570 The New Kingdom of Egypt 1490–1436 Egyptian Empire at peak of power 1200s Hebrews leave Egypt	1792–1750 Empire of Hammurabi in Babylonia 1650 Hittite Empire begins 1600 Israelites go to Egypt 1500s Aryan invasion of India. Start of Shang dynasty in China 1115 Start of Assyrian Empire 1020s Chou dynasty starts in China 1000 David king of Israel	1600 Myceneans invade southern Greece 1450 Minoan civilization at peak in Crete 1150s Dorians put end to much of Aegean civilization 800 Greek colonization in Mediterranean 753 Traditional foundation of Rome		
1000BC	1000 Negro colonization of Kush (Ethiopia) 814 Foundation of Carthage 670 Assyrians conquer Egypt 525 Persians conquer Egypt			1300–500 Olmecs in Mexico, the first American civilization	
500BC	500 Nok civilization founded in Nigeria 332 Alexander the Great conquers Egypt 306 Ptolemy I founds new dynasty in Egypt 30 Death of Antony and Cleopatra. Rome conquers Egypt	551 Birth of Confucius 530s Buddha preaching 559–530 Empire of Cyrus the Great in Persia 326 Invasion of India by Alexander the Great 221–207 Chin dynasty in China. Great Wall completed 200s Rule of Asoka, greatest of Maurya emperors in India	551 Democracy established in Athens 500s and 400s Peak of Etruscan power 461–431 Golden Age of Athens 200s Rome conquers Etruscans and defeats Carthage 146–130 Rome conquers Greece 44 Julius Caesar assassinated 27 Augustus becomes first Roman emperor	800–AD200 Peak of Olmec civilization	
0	100 Kingdom of Ethiopia founded	206–AD221 Han dynasty in China, huge empire created 300 Yamato clan rise to power in Japan 320–535 Rule of Guptas, a Golden Age in India	43 Roman occupation of Britain 330 Byzantium (Constantinople) becomes capital of Roman Empire 395 East and West Roman Empires split. Start of Byzantium Empire 476 End of Roman Empire in Western Europe	300s–800s Peak of Mayan civilization 400 Inca civilization well developed	
500AD	800s Civilization of Ghana	589–618 Sui dynasty rebuilt China after almost 400 years war 618–1279 Tang and Sung dynasties in China 1192 Yoritomo first shogun in Japan	711 Muslims invade Spain 732 Christians stop Muslim invaders at Tours 800 Charlemagne crowned Holy Roman Emperor 1066 Normans defeat Anglo-Saxons at Hastings	900s–1200 Mayan culture of Chichén Itzá	750? The first Maoris arrive in New Zealand
1000AD	1000 Kingdoms of Oyo and Ife in west Africa 1174–1193 Saladin rules in Syria and Egypt 1300s Mali Empire in west Africa 1400s and 1500s European settlements on west coast	1275–1292 Marco Polo in China 1300 Ottoman Turkish state founded 1279–1368 Yuan dynasty in China 1368 Ming dynasty founded	1100–1300 The Crusades 1240–1480 Mongols control Russia 1450s Start of Renaissance 1453 Ottoman Turks take Constantinople. End of Byzantine Empire	1492 Columbus reaches America 1400–1532 Peak of Inca civilization	
1500AD	1500s Songhai Empire replaced Mali Empire	1526 Foundation of Mogul Empire in India	1517 Reformation begins in Germany 1547 Ivan IV crowned first Tsar of Russia	1500s Spanish conquer Maya, Inca and Aztec	
1600AD		1639 All foreigners except Dutch expelled from Japan 1644 Manchu dynasty succeeds Ming dynasty in China	1618–1648 Thirty Years War 1642–51 English Civil War	1607 Colony founded in Virginia 1620 Pilgrim fathers sail to America in the 'Mayflower'	1642 Abel Tasman discovers New Zealand
1700AD	1700s–1900s European colonies being established in Africa	1757 British East India Company became leading power in India 1799 French invade South Vietnam	1750 Start of Industrial Revolution in England 1756–1763 Seven Years War 1789–1799 French Revolution	1776 American Declaration of Independence 1789 George Washington becomes first American president	1770 Captain James Cook discovers east coast of Australia and claims it for Britain 1788 First convicts transported from Britain to Australia
1800AD	1869 Opening of Suez Canal 1899–1902 Boer War	1853 Japan persuaded to open their ports to foreign trade 1858 Indian mutiny, British Government took over rule in India 1867 Shoguns stripped of power in Japan 1885 Indian National Congress party founded	1815 Napoleon defeated at Waterloo 1851 The Great Exhibition 1861 Unification of Italy 1870 Unification of Germany 1870–1 Franco-German War	1861–65 American Civil War 1890 United States stretches from east to west coast of America	1840 Maoris signed Treaty of Waitangi, giving Great Britain sovereignty over New Zealand 1845–72 Settlers fought Maoris in Maori Wars in New Zealand 1852 Britain granted New Zealand a constitution
1900AD	1914 All Africa except Libya and Ethiopia colonized by European nations 1950s–1970 Most European colonies became independent countries	1912 Republic of China established 1937–1945 Sino-Japanese war 1947 India and Pakistan gain independence. Democratic constitution in Japan 1949 China taken over by Communists under Mao Tse Tung	1914–18 World War I 1936–39 Spanish Civil War 1917 Russian Revolution 1931 The Great Depression 1939–45 World War II 1956 Hungarian Revolution 1968 Uprising in Czechoslovakia	1929 Wall Street Crash 1945 United Nations set up 1959 Hawaii becomes 50th state of USA 1969 America's first men on moon	1901 Australian states unite to form the Commonwealth within the British Empire. The first federal parliament opened 1907 New Zealand became a dominion within the British Empire

HOBBY A hobby is an activity that you enjoy doing in your spare time. Some ideas for hobbies include stamp collecting, canoeing, handicrafts, model ship building and even bird watching and star gazing.

A hobby starts because you have a special interest in something. Hobbies can be carried into adulthood. President Roosevelt, for instance, never lost his love for stamp collecting. And many grown women still look for new dolls to add to their collections.

Very often hobbies can teach you many things you might not otherwise know. In stamp collecting, for instance, you can't help but learn something about the history and culture of different countries. Or, if your hobby is quilting or handicrafts, you are bound to learn about how different styles of stitchery or pottery reflect the times when they were popular. Often, rare collections become valuable and can be sold for a lot of money.

HORSE For thousands of years Man has valued the horse for its strength, speed and reliability. It has helped him work, transportation and sport.

The first horse was an animal no larger than a small dog. It is known as *Eohippus* or the 'dawn horse'. It had four toes on its front feet and three toes on its back feet. It lived in forests and grazed on the trees. Later horses lived on the grassy plains. They had to run swiftly to escape their enemies. Gradually over millions of years, the horse lost all its toes except one. Today, the horse runs on tip toe and is one of the fastest of all animals.

The Eskimo snow house, or igloo, is quickly built and makes a warm shelter.

In Asia, riverside huts of bamboo are built on 'stilts'.

Rows of sturdy brick-built houses can be seen in Dutch towns.

A New Forest pony stands guard over her foal.

In the wild, horses eat grass and live in herds. The mares (females) and their foals are led by the strongest stallion (male). Today, there are only a few wild horses left, living in Mongolia. The mustang is a half-wild horse that lives in America.

No one knows when horses were first tamed. Their first use was to pull war chariots, and cavalry played an important part in wars until early in this century. Horses were the fastest form of transport until the 1800s, when the steam locomotive and automobile replaced them. Also, their strength made horses invaluable on farms where they could pull wagons and plows.

Many different types of horses have been bred. Among the largest are the Shire and Clydesdale breeds. The Shetland pony is one of the smallest. The fastest of all horses are the Thoroughbreds, which are used for racing. Thoroughbreds are descended from Arabian horses.

See also EVOLUTION; ZEBRA.

HOSPITAL Some early hospitals were run by monks. They cared for sick people as well as they could. But people did not know what caused disease. So the sick were not always treated properly. Later, hospitals were set up by governments. But as late as the 1800s many hospitals were dark and dirty.

A hospital today is clean and bright. Inside are wards and sun rooms for the patients, laboratories, 'theaters' where surgeons carry out operations, and all kinds of equipment. As well as doctors and nurses, there are technicians, radiologists (who study X-rays), pharmacists (who prepare drugs), social workers, ambulance drivers and other staff who help run the hospital.

See also MEDICINE.

HOUSE In prehistoric times men used to live in caves. Then they began building simple huts from mud, straw and leaves. Even today many people in hot climates, in Africa, South-East Asia, and South America, still live in huts like this.

Better dwellings are made in hot climates by building houses out of mud bricks, dried in the sun. They are called adobe houses. In most countries, though, house bricks are made from clay. They are baked hard in furnaces (kilns) and joined together with mortar (a mixture of cement, lime, sand and water). Bricks were first widely used in the 1500s.

In countries rich in timber, such as Canada and Scandinavia, many houses are built of wood. Where local stone is available, as in the English Cotswolds, builders use that for making houses. In the cold Arctic, Eskimos build their igloos from blocks of snow.

Several materials may be used to roof houses. In hot countries huts are often roofed with palm leaves or dried grasses. Closely laid straw, or thatch, also makes a good waterproof roof even in wetter climates. But most roofs are made from tiles or slates, laid on a wooden framework. Most houses have sloping roofs to let the rain drain off. But, in hot, dry climates many houses have flat roofs.

In Borneo a whole village may live in one big dwelling called a long-house. But in most countries houses are occupied by a single family or a family group. Even so, many families are often housed under the same roof. They may live in 'town' or 'row' houses which are joined side by side. In apartment houses, many different families live under the same roof.

In some towns, very tall 'high rise' apartments are built. Here there is one entrance to the building. But each apartment has its own separate entrance. With high rise apartments, many families can live above a small area of land.

HOVERCRAFT A hovercraft is often called an air-cushion vehicle because it glides above the ground or water on a cushion of air. The cushion of air is created by a huge fan, which forces air beneath the craft. The air is held there by flaps or skirts around the sides. Backward-facing propellers on top of the craft, propel it forwards and steer the craft. The propellers are powered by engines like those of an airplane. In England, some hovercraft operate as car ferries across the English Channel. Each hovercraft can carry 34 cars and 175 passengers.

HUMAN BEINGS Creatures have lived on the Earth for millions of years. But people exactly like us have lived for only a few thousand years. We belong to a group of mammals called the primates. Our scientific name is *Homo sapiens*, which means 'thinking man'.

Scientists believe that human beings evolved (developed) from small primitive mammals like today's tarsiers and lemurs. Our 'family tree' then divided into two groups: man-like creatures (hominids) and ape-like creatures (pongids). Fossil remains of our primitive ancestors have been found in Africa and Asia. These early man-like creatures walked on two legs, and their skulls and teeth were quite like our own. But their brains were much smaller, about the same size as an ape's. After these 'ape-men', however, came creatures much more like modern human beings. They had bigger brains and they could use tools. Having a bigger brain made it possible for primitive man to develop until *Homo sapiens* appeared perhaps about 100,000 years ago.

The human brain gave human beings the power to hunt, kill, capture and tame other animals. Human beings developed skills far greater than those of any other creature. Dolphins can talk to each other, using 'click' sounds. Apes can use simple tools, such as sticks, to reach fruit. Ants and bees live in well-organized communities. But none of these animals can use skills on such a scale as humans can.

The great changes which humans have made on the Earth are all due to our greater brain power. This made it possible for us to control the environ-

Skeletons of a man (left) and a gorilla. The gorilla walks mainly on all fours, while the man stands upright.

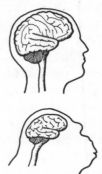

Compare the brain of a man (top) and a gorilla. Their heads are roughly the same size, but the man's brain is much larger. The human brain also has many more 'wrinkles' on its surface. It is these which give us greater brain power.

The large SR-N4 hovercraft has four engines and weighs 165 tons. It carries passengers and cars across the English Channel and can travel at 80 miles (130 km) an hour.

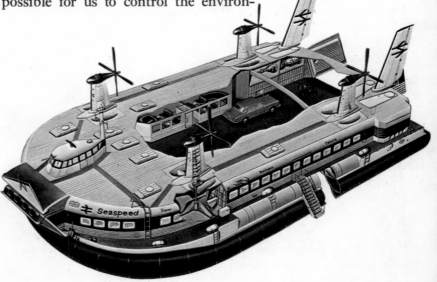

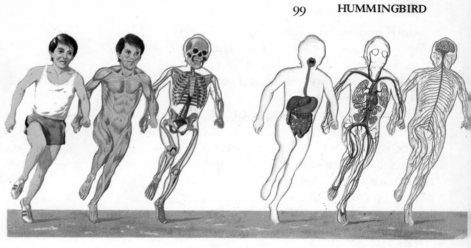

ment in which we live. Primitive men learned to make fire and to use it for warmth and cooking. Modern men learned to grow food (instead of hunting for it), and to make metal tools. They settled in villages and towns, and used language and writing to store and pass on the knowledge they had gained. In this way, civilization developed. Today, humans, and their machines, dominate the Earth.

HUMAN BODY Our bodies are made of millions of tiny cells which are grouped together into separate tissues and organs. On the outside of our body is skin. This protects us from heat, cold, injury and germs. Inside we have a skeleton. Without our skeleton, our bodies would be quite floppy. Our bones give us our shape and allow us, with the help of our muscles, to move about. They also protect the soft parts inside us. The skull protects the brain, the ribs protect the lungs and the spine (backbone) protects the rope of nerves that runs down our backs and is linked to all parts of the body. The brain controls almost all we do. Some nerves bring it signals from the senses. Other nerves send signals from the brain to the muscles.

Our bodies need oxygen and food. We get the oxygen from the air when we breathe. The air goes to our lungs via the windpipe. In the lungs, oxygen from the air passes through the lung walls into the blood. The blood carries the oxygen to every cell of the body. It also carries digested food, which is burned by the oxygen, like fuel in an automobile, to give us energy.

Our food begins its journey in our mouths. First it is crushed, then churned and 'treated' with chemicals in parts of the digestive tract which consists of esophagus, stomach, small intestine and large intestine.

The blood which forms such an elaborate transport system is made in some of our bones. It is pumped around the body by the heart, with arteries taking fresh blood from the lungs and veins carrying 'stale' blood to them.

The body produces lots of waste. Some of this is excreted through the skin when we sweat, some (carbon dioxide) when we breathe out. Other waste is removed via the bowels and the bladder.

The only organs which are different in a man and a woman are the reproductive organs. A woman has a vagina and ovaries which contain ova (eggs). A man has a penis, and testes which contain sperm. The fertilization of a female egg cell by a male sperm cell produces one new cell which has, within its microscopic size, all the makings of a complete new human body.

See also BLOOD; BRAIN; BREATHING; CELL; EAR; EYE; GLAND; HEART; NERVOUS SYSTEM; REPRODUCTION; SKELETON; SKIN; TEETH.

HUMMINGBIRD Hummingbirds are the smallest birds in the world. Most kinds live in the forests of South America.

Hummingbirds are marvelous fliers. They can hover in mid air and even fly backwards. Their wings beat so fast they make a humming noise. With their long beaks and tongues, hummingbirds suck nectar from flowers. Some also catch insects.

The human body has several important systems which all work together. Shown here (from left to right) are the muscles, the bones or skeleton, the digestive system, the blood system and the nervous system.

A brightly colored hummingbird hovers in front of a hibiscus flower. It rolls its tongue into a tube to suck up nectar from the flower.

HURRICANE Violent tropical storms called hurricanes start over the sea. Moist air is sucked up to a spiraling cloud. Howling winds circle the storm area and heavy rain occurs.

Hurricane winds reach up to 198 miles (320 kilometers) an hour. Yet at the center of the storm, it is quite calm. Winds blow the hurricane harmlessly across the sea. But when it hits the coast, it causes great damage. Over land the hurricane then dies down, because it has no moisture to feed on.

Hurricanes are tracked by radar and by satellites, so that people can be warned. In the Pacific Ocean hurricanes are called typhoons.

HYENA When lions make a kill, they cannot eat all the meat. The hyenas gather to finish the meal, cracking even the largest bones with their powerful jaws.

Hyenas live in Africa and Asia. They are useful scavengers, but also hunt their own prey. The strange howl of the laughing hyena sounds almost like weird human laughter.

See also SCAVENGER.

The spotted hyena is the largest member of the hyena family. It lives on the plains of Africa.

ICE When the temperature drops to freezing point, 0°C, or 32°F, pure water freezes and turns into ice. Ice is lighter than water, which is why water freezes only on top. It also takes up more space than water. That is why water pipes often burst in the winter. The water freezes into ice and splits the pipes or pipe joints. Snow is made up of ice crystals of many beautiful shapes.

In the freezing Arctic waters off the coast of Greenland, huge icebergs float amid the sheets of pack ice. These icebergs break off glaciers and float south until they melt in warmer seas. The biggest icebergs may be over 246 feet (75 meters) high.

ICE AGE The Ice Ages were times of intense cold. Sheets of ice spread southwards from the North Pole, covering much of Europe, North America and Asia. The most recent Ice Age ended about 11,000 years ago. Glaciers (rivers of ice) carried soil and rocks along with them like huge bulldozers. They scraped the land clear of soil and smoothed hills and valleys. The Great Lakes in North America were made by ice scooping out the ground. So were the fiords of Norway and New Zealand.

During the Great Ice Age many plants and animals were killed by the cold. Others, such as the mammoth and the woolly rhinoceros, grew thick coats to keep warm. Human beings had to find other ways of keeping warm. So they took to the shelter of caves and made clothes from the skins of animals. In time the ice sheets melted and the weather grew warm again. But it is not certain that in the future there will never be another Ice Age.

See also CAVE MEN.

ICEBERG In the cold polar seas drift 'islands' of ice called icebergs. They are formed from masses of ice which break off the end of a glacier or ice sheet and float off into the sea.

The Incas were fine craftsmen. This gold ceremonial knife is decorated with turquoise.

An iceberg can weigh millions of tons. But only the tip of the iceberg shows above water. About eight times as much is hidden beneath the surface.

In the north Atlantic Ocean ships keep a look out for icebergs floating south from the Arctic. In 1912 the liner *Titanic* hit an iceberg and sank on her first voyage.

See also GLACIER.

INCA Hundreds of years ago the Incas ruled an empire in the Andes Mountains. Its heart lay in the South American country we now call Peru. All the people living in the mountain valleys had to work for the Incas. In return, the Incas made sure that everyone had a home and enough to eat.

The Incas believed that their king was the son of the Sun god. He was always obeyed. They built great stone temples and worshipped the Sun. They had good roads, but no horses or wheeled carts. Fast runners carried messages from one city to the next.

The Incas became very rich. This was their downfall. In 1532 came Spanish explorers seeking gold. They had horses and guns and they captured the Inca king, Atahualpa. They forced the Incas to fill a room with gold treasures as a ransom for their king's release. But then they killed him and made themselves rulers of Peru. The Peruvians were so used to obeying orders, that they made little effort to fight back.

INDIA is a large country in Asia. It has more people than any other country in the world except China. India is shaped like a triangle, with sea on two sides. In the north it is cut off from the rest of Asia by the Himalaya mountains. Great rivers, such as the Brahmaputra and Ganges flow across the plains south of these mountains.

India is cut off from its Asian neighbors by sea and by the Himalayas.

The Taj Mahal (right) was built as a tomb by an Indian emperor.

Parts of India are dry and hot. It is cooler in the mountains, but most people live in the fertile river valleys. India gets most of its rain during the monsoon season. If the rains fail, crops die and famine threatens the lives of millions.

India's wild animals include lions, tigers, leopards, elephants, rhinoceroses, deer, wild cattle, monkeys and snakes. Most of them live in the forests and jungles.

Many Indians are poor farmers, who live in small villages. Others live in crowded cities like Calcutta. Industry is developing in India. There are steel-works, mines, chemical and textile factories and engineering works. India

Most Indians follow the Hindu religion. But there are also Buddhists, Sikhs, Muslims and Christians. The people are divided into social groups called castes, and speak 14 major languages.

Civilization began 4500 years ago in the area that includes India. Invaders brought new ideas about art, literature, architecture and religion. One of the greatest Indian rulers was the Mogul Emperor Akbar (1542–1605). From the late 1700s until 1947 most of India was ruled by Britain. Then it became independent. The Muslims in India set up their own country called Pakistan.

Facts and Figures
Area: 1,261,775 square miles
      (3,268,000 square kilometers)
Population: 600,000,000
Capital: New Delhi
Government: Republic
Money unit: Rupee
Longest River: Brahmaputra,
      1800 miles
      (2896 kilometers)
Highest mountain: Nanda Devi
      25,648 feet
      (7817 meters)

INDUSTRIAL REVOLUTION Until the 1700s most people in Europe worked on the land. They grew their own food and made cloth and other goods by hand in their own homes. There were no factories and few large towns. The Industrial Revolution changed all this. It began in England, where men invented machines powered by steam engines.

The new machines made it possible to make goods very cheaply in factories. Instead of making cloth at home, people went to work in large mills where wool and cotton were spun and woven on machines. One spinning machine could do the work of eight hand spinners.

Life in the factories and mills was hard and dangerous. Workers were sometimes killed or crippled by unsafe machines. They worked 13 hours a day for low wages. Children had to work as well, and were even sent down the mines to drag coal tubs along. Towns grew quickly as workers came in from the countryside. Most lived in badly built slum houses. Gloomy factories with smoky chimneys sprang up everywhere.

After 1840 laws were made to improve conditions for the workers, especially women and children. Factory owners were forced to fence in dangerous machinery. Trade unions were started to look after the workers' interests.

INSECT Insects are by far the most numerous members of the animal kingdom. They are found in every part of the world.

There are hundreds of thousands of different kinds of insects. But they are all built on a similar plan. The body is divided into three sections. An insect's *head* has eyes, jaws and antennae, or feelers. The middle part, or *thorax*, carries three pairs of jointed legs and sometimes two pairs of wings as well. The end part is called the *abdomen*.

Most insects reproduce by laying eggs. Instead of bones, they have a hard case covering the outside of their bodies. As the insect grows, it has to shed this case and grow another. Blood flows around the outside of the insect's internal organs. It breathes through its skin by means of tiny tubes called spiracles.

There are three main groups of insects. In the first group are primitive, wingless insects such as the little silverfish, which you sometimes see in the kitchen. When it hatches, the baby silverfish looks like a miniature adult. It molts, or sheds its skin, as many as 50 times before it is fully grown.

Insects belonging to the second group molt less often. The young are born

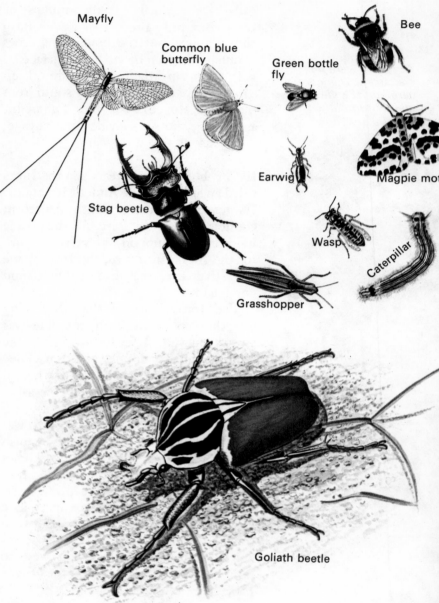

Mayfly

Common blue butterfly

Bee

Green bottle fly

Earwig

Magpie mot

Stag beetle

Wasp

Caterpillar

Grasshopper

Goliath beetle

looking much the same as their parents and eat similar food. But some changes do take place as they grow. For example, young grasshoppers develop wings.

The most advanced insects belong to the third group. They pass through separate stages of development, from egg to adult. At each stage, the insect looks different and has a different way of life. Butterflies lay eggs. But the eggs do not hatch into butterflies. Instead, they hatch into larvae called caterpillars, which do not look at all like butterflies and eat different food. A caterpillar grows and turns into a pupa or chrysalis. Finally, the adult butterfly emerges, perfectly formed, from the pupa. This process of change is known as 'metamorphosis'.

Insects of different kinds are found all over the world. They range in size from tiny fleas to goliath beetles as big as a human hand.

4 Adult

3

Pupa

1 Egg

2

Larva

The most advanced insects have a four-stage growth cycle or 'metamorphosis'. The adult lays eggs, which hatch into larvae. Each larva turns into a pupa or chrysalis, and finally another fully-formed insect emerges.

Human beings dislike some insects, because they are harmful. Insects such as the mosquito and the tsetse fly carry diseases. Flies, bugs, fleas and cockroaches are other insect pests. The locust and the colorado beetle are insects which cause great damage to crops.

But care must be taken not to kill the many insects which are useful. Without the work of bees and other flying insects, flowers would not be pollinated and fruit trees would not bear fruit. The honey bee is kept for its honey and wax, and the silkworm for its silk. Insects help to make the soil fertile by eating dead matter. Some insects actually help by eating insect pests—the ladybug preys on harmful aphids and is welcomed by gardeners.

The most interesting insects are those which live in highly organized communities. The best known insects which do this are ants, bees and termites. Thousands of these insects may live in a single colony. Each one has its own job to do, and cannot live on its own.

See also ANT; BEE; BEETLE; BUTTER-FLIES AND MOTHS; CAMOUFLAGE; FLY; GRASSHOPPER; LOCUST; MOSQUITO; PARA-SITE; SCAVENGER; TERMITE; WASP.

INVENTIONS Throughout history people have created new things. Most of these new products, or inventions, have given us an easier and better life. We can all enjoy the machines and equipment of our modern life, such as cars and airplanes, radio and television, papers and books, sewing machines and record players, ball-point pens and cameras, zippers and safety pins.

Not all inventions come about in the same way. Many inventors see a need for something and set about to produce it. This gives rise to the saying 'necessity is the mother of invention'. The English weaver James Hargreaves saw the need for a machine to spin cotton quicker, and he invented the spinning jenny.

Other inventors just seem to invent for the love of it. Thomas A. Edison was such a man. In his lifetime he registered, or patented, more than 1000 inventions. He invented the light bulb and phonograph.

Inventions are often the product of

INVENTIONS AND INVENTORS

Invention	Date	Inventor
Movable type	1450	J. Gutenberg (G)
Telescope	1609	Galileo (I)
Steam engine	1712	T. Newcomen (B)
Lightning conductor	1760	B. Franklin (US)
Spinning jenny	1764	J. Hargreaves (B)
Hot-air balloon	1783	Montgolfier bros (F)
Cotton gin	1793	E. Whitney (US)
Electric battery	1800	A. Volta (I)
Glider	1804	G. Cayley (B)
Steam locomotive	1804	R. Trevithick (B)
Printing press	1810	F. Konig (G)
Miner's safety lamp	1815	H. Davy (B)
Stethoscope	1819	R. Laënnec (F)
Revolver	1836	S. Colt (US)
Telegraph	1836	S. Morse (US)
Sewing machine	1845	E. Howe (US)
Dynamite	1866	A. Nobel (S)
Typewriter	1867	C. Sholes (US)
Telephone	1876	A. Bell (US)
Phonograph	1877	T. Edison (US)
Electric lamp	1879	T. Edison (US)
Steam turbine	1884	C. Parsons (B)
Gasoline engine	1885	K. Benz, G. Daimler (G)
Air-filled tire	1888	J. Dunlop (B)
Diesel engine	1892	R. Diesel (G)
Radio	1895	G. Marconi (I)
Radio valve	1904	J. Fleming (B)
Jet engine	1930	F. Whittle (B)
Digital computer	1944	H. Aiken (US)
Polaroid camera	1947	E. Land (US)
Hovercraft	1955	C. Cockerell (B)

(B=Britain; F=France; G=Germany; I=Italy; S=Sweden; US=United States).

Wheel 3000 BC

Gunpowder AD 1000

Steam Engine 1700s

Match 1827 Safety-pin 1849

Telephone 1876

Radio 1895 Television 1920s

Laser 1960

many people. The airplane was first flown by the Wright brothers, but they did not invent most of its parts. They drew upon the work of others who had gone before. The German engineers Daimler and Benz built the first successful cars by extending other people's ideas and adding some of their own. The same goes for television, too, which the Scotsman John Logie Baird first demonstrated.

See also BELL, A.; EDISON, T.; MARCONI, G.

Ireland is one of the British Isles. It is a country split in two as a result of its troubled history.

IRELAND is one of the British Isles. Northern Ireland is part of the United Kingdom. Southern Ireland is a republic.

Ireland is mainly a farming country. It has fertile soil and a mild, moist climate. The center of Ireland is flat, but there are mountains near the coast.

There are many rivers, lakes called 'loughs' and bogs made of rotted plant material called peat, which can be dried and burned as fuel.

Some Irish people still speak an ancient language called Gaelic. But most speak English. In the republic most people are Roman Catholics; in Northern Ireland most are Protestants.

Ireland has had a troubled history. From the 1500s it was ruled by England. Many Irish people were poor and thousands emigrated to England and the United States. In 1921 26 of the 32 Irish counties set up an independent country, which became the Republic of Ireland in 1949. Many people in the south want the six northern counties to become part of the republic. In Northern Ireland quarrels between Protestants and Catholics have led to fighting, bombings, murders and riots.

Facts and Figures
Area: Republic
        27,027 square miles
        (70,000 square kilometers)
    Northern Ireland
        5,452 square miles
        (14,120 square kilometers)
Population: Republic, 3,100,000
             Northern Ireland, 1,545,000
Capitals: Republic, Dublin
           Northern Ireland, Belfast
Government: The Republic is independent,
             Northern Ireland is part of the
             United Kingdom.
Money unit: Pound
Longest River: Shannon
        230 miles
        (370 kilometers)
Highest Mountain: Carrantuohill,
        3,416 feet
        (1,041 meters)

IRON AND STEEL Steel is our most important metal. It would be difficult to imagine life without steel because we use it for so many things. Most cars, ships and machines used in industry are made of steel. Steel girders and rods form the frames of skyscrapers and give strength to concrete dams and roads. No other metal that is so strong is so cheap.

Steel is not a pure metal. It is an alloy, made up mainly of iron, together with small amounts of carbon and one or two metals besides iron. Iron by itself is quite soft and weak. But adding the other ingredients makes it hard and strong. Steel is like iron in other ways. It is

magnetic, and it rusts easily. But by adding metals such as chromium and nickel, we can make a steel that does not rust. It is called stainless steel.

Iron is found in the form of a mineral, or ore, in the ground. Crude iron is made in a blast furnace by heating iron ore with coke and limestone. It is called a blast furnace because hot air is blasted through it to make the coke burn fiercely. Steel is made by purifying the crude iron in other furnaces.

ISLAND An island is a piece of land with water all round it. The biggest island (not counting the continents) is Greenland.

Some islands are bits of land masses which have been cut off by water. This may happen when land sinks or the sea rises. The British Isles were formed by such changes. Another kind of island rises out of the sea. These islands are actually the peaks of underwater volcanoes. Many South Pacific islands are of this type; so is Japan.

Islands are also made by tiny coral animals and plants. They may build a ring of reefs called an atoll, with a lagoon or lake in the middle.

ITALY On the map Italy looks like a boot sticking out into the Mediterranean Sea. The islands of Sardinia and Sicily are also part of Italy. In the north the Alps form a mountain wall between Italy and the rest of Europe.

Southern Italy is warm and fairly dry. In the north it is cooler, with more rain. Both agriculture and industry are important. Italy is famous for its wine and for 'pasta'–foods such as spaghetti, macaroni and ravioli. Most of the factories are in northern Italy.

Most Italians are Roman Catholics. The center of the Catholic Church is the Vatican, a tiny independent state in the middle of Rome.

Italy has many old and beautiful buildings. A lot of them are in Rome, because 2000 years ago the Romans ruled Italy. Later separate city states grew up. The greatest were Genoa, Florence and Venice. Art and learning flourished, especially after the Renaissance, which began in the 1400s.

The Italian city of Florence (or Firenze) was a center of art and learning during the Renaissance. It has many art treasures and beautiful buildings.

Italy has a long coastline washed by the warm Mediterranean. In the north are the high Alps.

Because Italy was divided, it was often ruled by foreign countries. Not until 1861 was Italy united as an independent kingdom. In the 1920s Italy came under the fascist dictator Mussolini. Italy fought on the side of Germany during World War II. After the war Italy became a republic .

Dressed in their kimonos, a Japanese family sits down to a meal at home. Family life is very important in Japan.

Facts and Figures
Area: 115,830 square miles
(300,000 square kilometers)
Population: 55,600,000
Capital: Rome
Money unit: Lira
Longest river: Po, 405 miles
(652 kilometers)
Highest Mountain: Monte Rosa
15,204 feet, (4,634 meters)

JAPAN The islands which make up the country of Japan lie off the northeast coast of Asia. The largest islands are Honshu, Hokkaido, Kyushu and Shikoku.

The islands are the tops of underwater mountains. Earthquakes are common and there are volcanoes and hot springs. Japan has heavy rainfall and a cool climate. Its short but fast-flowing rivers are used to produce hydro-electric power. There are few large wild animals, but many trees.

The Japanese came from mainland Asia perhaps 3000 years ago. On the islands lived the white-skinned, hairy Ainu people. There are few of them left now. Most Japanese live in cities. Rice, fish and vegetables are the main foods. There are many factories making all kinds of goods from cars and ships to radios and zip fasteners.

Ancient Japan was ruled by warrior lords. Until the 1850s Japan had little contact with the world outside. But then its rulers decided to learn western ways. Modern cities and factories were built, and trade with Europe and America started. Japan became powerful, and its rulers became warlike. In World War II Japan joined Germany and Italy, and Japanese forces conquered much of Asia. But in 1945 Japan surrendered.

After the war life changed even more rapidly for the Japanese. Today, crowded cities, busy factories and modern roads and railways contrast with ancient temples and peaceful gardens. Japan's Emperor

The islands which make up Japan lie off the northeast coast of Asia.

As the jellyfish floats on the surface, its stinging tentacles hang down in the sea, ready to hold and paralyze its prey.

no longer has any power. There is an elected parliament and a government led by a prime minister.

Facts and Figures
Area: 142,857 square miles
(370,000 square kilometers)
Population: 105,000,000
Capital: Tokyo
Governemtn: Constitutional monarchy
Money unit: Yen
Longest river: Shinano
225 miles
(362 kilometers)
Highest mountain: Fujiyama
12,390 feet,(3,776 meters)

JELLYFISH A jellyfish looks like a transparent umbrella floating in the sea. The body of this sea animal is mostly water. If it is stranded on the beach, a jellyfish dies.

Jellyfish swim by squirting out water from their 'umbrellas'. They catch other sea animals with stinging tentacles which hang beneath their bodies. Some jellyfish, such as the Portuguese man-of-war, can hurt bathers.

JESUS CHRIST was the founder of Christianity. Christians believe that he was the son of God. He was born in Palestine, when the Jews were ruled harshly by their Roman conquerors. Some Jews wanted to fight the Romans. Others were waiting for a savior, the Messiah, to rescue them. Ancient prophets had spoken of such a man.

But Jesus was only a carpenter's son, from a small town called Bethlehem. He taught people to trust in God, to lead good peaceful lives and promised eternal life in heaven. He performed miracles, healing the sick and making blind men see again. Jesus' followers said he was the Messiah. But others feared he was just a troublemaker. The Romans thought so too. Jesus was arrested and executed on the Cross. But his followers went on teaching others what he had taught them, even though the Romans tried to stop them. Many of these early Christians died for their belief in Jesus.

JOAN OF ARC (1412?–1431), a simple peasant girl, is the greatest heroine in French history. In 1429, France was at war with England, because the English king was trying to become king of France too. Joan believed she heard heavenly voices telling her to save France. Dressed in armor, and with her hair cut short she led the French army to victory and saw Charles VII, the true king, crowned King of France. But the English caught her, and in 1431 they burned Joan as a witch.

JULIUS CAESAR (100?–44 BC), was one of the greatest leaders of ancient Rome. His armies conquered many lands, making the Roman Empire larger and more powerful. He invaded Britain, and he also fell in love with Cleopatra, the Queen of Egypt. At home, Caesar built aqueducts to bring drinking water to Rome, and was a firm ruler. By 45 BC he had been made dictator for life. This meant he could rule just as he wished. A group of Romans feared he would make himself king, so they murdered him.

JUNGLE In part of the tropics the weather is hot and rainy. Here, plants grow quickly. There are thick forests, parts of which are still unexplored. A tropical forest is often called 'jungle', although a better name is 'rain forest'.

Jungle is an Indian word, meaning 'wild place'. In forest clearings, where trees have fallen or been cut down, thick undergrowth quickly springs up. There are long grasses and tangled bushes, but few big trees.

In a rain forest there is little undergrowth. The tall trees make a roof of leaves, which shut out the sunlight. So on the forest floor it is damp and gloomy. Because it is dark, few plants can grow among the dead trees and rotting leaves. But there are fungi (which can live without light), ferns and creepers. Giant creepers, called lianas, wind themselves around the tree trunks and hang down from the branches. All the plants in the forest must struggle to reach the sunlight.

A tropical rain forest has three layers, like the stories of a tall building. At the bottom are shrubs, ferns, lianas and young trees. Higher up, the crowns of the trees interlock to form the canopy, or roof, shutting out the light. At the top, the tallest trees emerge in places above the canopy.

When they are born, baby kangaroos or 'joeys' are tiny and quite helpless. For six months they never leave their mother's pouch.

Forest animals live on the ground and also in the trees. In the jungles of Asia live tigers, wild boars, deer and buffalo. In the huge Amazon forests of South America there are jaguars, tapirs, sloths, monkeys and large snakes called anacondas. Apes, such as the African gorilla and chimpanzee, and the Asian gibbon and orangutan, are forest dwellers. There are also many big, colorful butterflies and birds which live among the branches.

Near the coast, the forest often changes to mangrove swamp. Some mangrove trees have long curved roots which anchor them in the soft mud. Rivers are used instead of roads by the few people who live in rain forests. In special game reserves, rare animals such as the gorilla and the Asian rhinoceros, are safe from hunters. However, the forest trees are valuable for timber. And in Africa, Asia and South America forests are being cut down to make way for new roads and farms. This is destroying the animals and plants which live in the rain forests.

KANGAROO Kangaroos live in Australia. They are the largest of the marsupials, the animals which carry their young in pouches.

Kangaroos eat grass and leaves. They travel about in groups called mobs, led by an old male known as a boomer. With their powerful hind legs and using their long tails to balance them, kangaroos can leap long distances.

Gray kangaroos are the biggest. Wallabies are small kangaroos.

See also MARSUPIAL.

KINGS AND QUEENS In the past most countries were ruled by 'monarchs': kings (men) or queens (women). Usually the king's eldest son succeeded him, which meant that the same royal family might reign for hundreds of years. Some kings were so powerful that everyone feared them.

Today, though, most kings and queens have little real power. Some countries which have kings and queens include: Sweden, Saudi Arabia and Great Britain. In Great Britain for instance, the power of the Queen is limited. Parliament rules.

Two of history's famous kings include King Tutankhamen of Egypt who began a 10 year reign at the age of 10; and the French King Louis XIV. The overthrow of Louis XIV's government led to the beginning of the French Revolution. In the late 1800's, Queen Victoria ruled England. During her reign, Britain reached the height of its power and prosperity. That period of time is referred to as the Victorian Age.

KITE Kites were the first 'flying machines'. The Chinese made kites from bamboo and thin paper perhaps 2000 years ago. In the 1800s experiments with large man-carrying kites helped develop the first airplanes.

It is quite easy to make a kite, using thin strips of wood and strong paper or plastic. Some kites need a 'tail' to balance them. There are several different kite shapes to choose from.

KIWI The kiwi is the national bird of New Zealand. It cannot fly, but it waddles about the shady forest floor, searching for worms and insects to eat.

The kiwi has hair-like feathers, no tail, strong claws and a long bill. It is the only bird that has nostrils at the tip of its bill. The kiwi uses its nostrils to smell its food.

KNIGHTHOOD In Europe during the Middle Ages, knights were the strongest and highest class of warrior. Though there are many tales of battles between the knights, they were not as bloody as one might think. For the knight always tried to capture his opponent rather than kill him. Captured opponents meant money. For the enemy would often pay large sums of money (ransom) to get their warrior back.

Knights lived by a set of rules and customs called the *Code of Chivalry*. According to the code, enemies were to be treated as honored guests and attacks were to be announced in advance. These rules were made for the knight's own advantage. For a knight never knew when he himself might be captured or attacked. And he certainly did not want to be treated harshly or

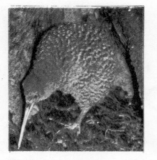
Kiwis hide by day and hunt for food after dark.

The reef knot is a good one for joining ropes.

A slip knot tightens when the rope is pulled.

Sailors often use two half hitches.

Sheet bends fasten thin ropes to thick ones.

The koala has strong claws and can climb a tree in a series of jumps, clinging on to the trunk.

caught without his armor!

Eventually, the Code of Chivalry came to include being generous to the poor and protecting women and children.

Before he could become a knight, a young boy had to serve as a page and squire. As time went on, many knights became *mercenaries*, or hired soldiers who played an important part in the wars of the Middle Ages.

KNOT Everyone needs to be able to tie a knot at some time. Sailors, builders and mountaineers have special knots which are important for their different activities. Most of the knots we use were first made by sailors.

To tie two lengths of string or rope together, a *reef knot* is best. A *bowline* or 'slip knot' makes a loop at the end of a rope. A *hitch* is a knot used to fasten a rope to a post or ring. A knot used for joining ropes is called a *bend*.

KOALA Although it looks like a small bear, the koala is really a marsupial. It lives in Australia.

Koalas are good climbers. They clamber about in eucalyptus trees, feeding on the leaves. When the baby koala is big enough to leave its mother's pouch, it rides on her back.

Koalas were once shot for their fur. But now these harmless little animals are protected.

See also MARSUPIAL.

LAKE A lake is a large area of still water surrounded by land. Many lakes were formed during the Ice Ages by glaciers scooping out hollows in the land. When the ice melted, the hollows filled with water. Some lakes are man-made. They are created when dams are built across rivers.

Some lakes are so big that they are called seas. The Caspian Sea in Asia is the largest lake in the world. Its water is salty. Even saltier is the Dead Sea in the Middle East. The largest fresh water lake is Lake Superior. It is one of the five Great Lakes of North America.

In time many lakes dry up. This is because rivers flowing into them deposit mud and sand on the bottom, while 'overflow' rivers flowing out drain off more and more water.

In a ruby laser light is concentrated on to a ruby crystal, producing a brilliant, high-powered beam. When focused through a strong lens, the laser beam can cut through the hardest metals and even through a diamond.

LANGUAGE When we speak, we are using language. Language is a collection of 'sound signs' or words. We use it to communicate with one another. There are more than 2800 different languages in the world and many more *dialects* or local variations. The language spoken by the largest number of people is Chinese. Next comes English, which is spoken in more countries than any other language.

English belongs to the Indo-European language family. Its closest relatives are German, Dutch and the Scandinavian languages. Another group in the Indo-European family includes the Romance languages, such as French and Italian.

Languages die when people stop speaking them. Latin is a dead language. It was once spoken by the Romans. Although no one speaks it today people are still interested in Latin, because many English words came from it.

All languages change. People make up new words and 'borrow' words from other languages. Invaders add more new words. That is why English often has two words with similar meanings, such as 'help' (from Anglo-Saxon) and 'aid' (from French). There are many other examples. 'Knife' is a Viking word, 'drama' comes from Greek, 'carnival' from Italian, 'coffee' from Turkish. In this way language grows richer.

LASER A laser is an instrument that produces a thin beam of very pure light. The beam from some lasers is so powerful that it can blast a hole through metal or even be bounced off the Moon. Other lasers are not so powerful. These are used in surgery to remove diseased body tissues, and also to repair tissues in the eye. One of the most exciting new uses of lasers is in communications. Laser beams can send television signals and telephone messages. Sending telephone calls by laser may soon replace our present telephone system in which we send electric signals along copper wires.

LEAD is one of the heaviest metals. It is soft and easy to shape and does not rust. It was once used on roofs and windows to keep the rain out, but it is now too expensive to be used in this way.

Lead is mixed with other metals to make useful alloys, such as pewter, which contains lead and tin. The metal used for printer's type contains lead. Solder used for joining electrical wires and pipes also contains lead. And lead is also used in some car batteries.

LEATHER is a very useful material made from the skin of animals. Over three-quarters of all leather is used to make shoes. But clothing, saddles, footballs and suitcases can also be made of it. Most leather comes from the hides of cattle. Pig skin and goat skin are also widely used. The animal skins have to be treated to make them soft and to stop them from rotting. This treatment is called tanning.

LEECH Leeches are related to earthworms. Some leeches feed on dead animals. Others are parasites.

Many leeches live in water, but some live in trees in hot countries. A leech attaches itself to a passing animal and sucks the animal's blood until its body is swollen. Then it drops off.

In the past, doctors thought some illnesses were caused by having too much blood. So they used leeches to 'bleed' the patient.

LEONARDO DA VINCI (1452–1519) was a great Italian artist, scientist and inventor. He was interested in drawing accurately and knowing how everything he drew worked. Leonardo became fascinated by the way in which the human body, machines, and the universe worked. He invented designs for tanks, a sort of helicopter, a parachute and diving gear. He also designed buildings and built canals and harbors. Although Leonardo painted few pictures, his *Last Supper* and *Mona Lisa* are among the best paintings in the world.

LEOPARD AND JAGUAR Two of the most handsome big cats are the spotted leopard and jaguar. They are smaller than lions and tigers. But they are very strong and fierce.

The leopard lives in Africa and Asia. It is an expert tree climber and sometimes lies in wait for its prey in a tree. And it will drag a half-eaten antelope into the branches out of reach of hyenas. Most leopards are golden with black spots, but some are black all over. Snow leopards live in the mountains of Asia.

Jaguars live in the forests of South America. They are good swimmers, and catch fish as well as deer and tapirs.

LIBERTY, STATUE OF. The Statue of Liberty is a monument which was presented to the American people by the people of France on July 4, 1884. It is a memorial to American independence and a symbol of friendship between the two countries. The 305 foot statue is molded out of copper. It stands on Liberty Island at the entrance to New York Harbor—the gateway to the New World.

The leech's flat body becomes fat and swollen with blood as it feeds. Its sucker mouth has sharp teeth.

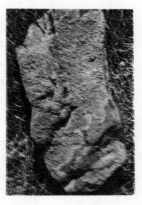

In time lichens will break down rock into soil.

The leopard of Africa and Asia and the South American jaguar look similar. But the jaguar is more heavily built, and its skin is patterned with black 'rosettes' rather than spots. Black leopards and jaguars are sometimes seen, but are rare.

LIBRARY A library is a collection of books. Most schools have libraries and there are public libraries in many towns. People can borrow books from the library and return them after they have read them.

The first libraries were started more than 4000 years ago. They contained clay tablets and papyrus scrolls. The most famous library in the ancient world was at Alexandria (Egypt). In the Middle Ages books were so precious that libraries chained them to bars to stop people from stealing them. Today, the world's biggest libraries, including the British Museum in London, the Library of Congress in Washington D.C., the Bibliothèque Nationale in Paris and the Leningrad Library, contain over 6 million books.

LICHEN You often see a grey crust on rocks and tree trunks. It is made of tiny plants called lichens.

A lichen is really two plants in one. One part is a fungus. The other part is a green plant called an alga. The fungus cannot make its own food. Instead it takes in water and minerals for the alga. The alga uses the water and sunlight to make food for itself and the fungus.

LIGHT The Sun is a huge furnace that gives out vast amounts of energy as heat and light. Its light is one of the most important things to us on Earth. It enables us to see by day. We see things because objects reflect light into our eyes. Sunlight also gives green plants the energy to make their food. And all

Jaguar

Leopard

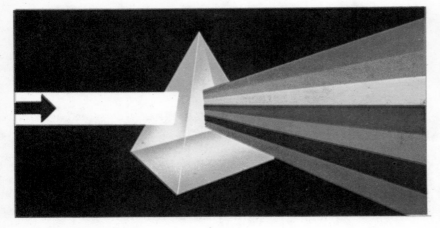

animals, including ourselves, rely on plant food to live.

Light is a way in which things give off energy. A laser gives off a very energetic beam of light that can cut metal. Ordinary light is not powerful but when it falls on certain materials (solar cells) electricity is produced.

Light travels in straight lines – you cannot shine a light around a corner. But you can reflect the light beam around a corner with a mirror. Light also bends when it passes from air into glass or water. This is called *refraction*. A pencil half-in a glass of water looks bent because of refraction. The bending of light by curved pieces of glass, or lenses, makes it possible to magnify objects, as in the microscope and telescope. When light is bent by a wedge of glass (prism), it splits up into bands of color.

LIGHTHOUSE For hundreds of years sailors have used some form of lighthouse to warn them that they are approaching land or dangerous rocks or sandbanks. Lighthouses are built on harbors, headlands and rocks off the shore. One is 985 feet (300 meters) tall and its light can be seen for more than 19 miles (30 kilometers). Each lighthouse flashes in a special way so that sailors can recognize it. The flashes are produced by a glass lens that turns slowly around a powerful lamp. In places where lighthouses cannot be built, lightships, or floating lighthouses are used instead.

LIGHTNING is a gigantic electric spark that zig-zags between the clouds in

When white light (such as sunlight) shines through a shaped piece of glass called a prism, the rays are bent, or refracted. The light splits into the seven colors of the rainbow, which make up the spectrum.

The lighthouse tower must be strong to withstand wind and waves. On top is the powerful lamp.

a thunderstorm. It also travels down to the ground, where it can cause great damage. It can split trees like matchwood and set fire to buildings. Tall buildings have to be protected from lightning by a lightning rod. This is a steel rod attached to a wire that goes into the ground. It provides a harmless path for the electricity in the lightning to follow.

LINCOLN, Abraham (1809-1865) was one of the most famous Presidents of the United States. He was a poor boy, born in a log cabin. Yet he rose to become President in 1860. Lincoln hated slavery. When the states of the South (which kept slaves) tried to break away from the North, civil war broke out. Lincoln led the North to victory, and slavery was abolished. Lincoln was assassinated by John Wilkes Booth.

LION The lion is called 'the king of beasts'. With the tiger, it is the largest member of the cat family. Lions are fierce hunters. But when well fed, they spend most of the time sleeping or basking in the sun on the grassy plains.

Lions live in groups called prides. Only the males have manes. The females, called lionesses, do most of the hunting.

Lions feed mainly on antelopes and zebras. They creep up on their prey and kill it after a short chase. An old or sick lion may become a man-eater.

Lions once lived in Europe. Now wild lions are found only in parts of Africa and in a special reserve in India.

The lioness has no mane. Although she usually makes the kill, the male lion always eats first. The young cubs have to wait until last.

Above: Locusts breed in vast numbers. But they have many enemies, including birds, other insects and man.

The Gila monster is a poisonous lizard which lives in the deserts of the southwest United States.

The people of the high Andes have used llamas as pack animals for hundreds of years.

The tail of the Norway lobster is eaten as scampi.

LIZARD Lizards are reptiles. Most lizards have four legs, but some are legless. The slow worm is a legless lizard. Unlike snakes, lizards have moveable eyelids and ears which can be seen.

Most lizards live in warm climates. Most kinds lay eggs, although some produce live young. Lizards feed on insects, small mammals or plants.

The largest lizard is the Komodo dragon. The Gila monster is poisonous. Interesting lizards include the chameleon, which changes color, and the gecko, which has special pads on its feet which help it to walk upside down on ceilings. Flying lizards actually glide, using folds of skin as wings. Most lizards prefer dry land, but the marine iguana is a good swimmer.

If a lizard is grabbed by its tail, the tail usually breaks off. This gives the lizard a chance to run away. Later a new tail grows in place of the lost one.

See also CHAMELEON; DINOSAUR; REPTILE.

LLAMA The llama looks like a small woolly camel without a hump. It lives in the high Andes mountains of South America.

Llamas are useful because they can carry loads along narrow mountain tracks. They also provide people with meat, wool, skins for making leather and fat for candles. When a llama is bad-tempered (which is quite often) it spits.

The guanaco, alpaca and vicuna are other South American relatives of the camel.

LOBSTER Lobsters are animals with crusty shells. They belong to a group called crustaceans.

Lobsters live in the sea and walk about on the seabed. They use their long antennae to find food, and their strong pincers to catch it. Lobsters eat shellfish and dead sea animals.

If a lobster loses a leg or a claw, it grows another one. It molts, or sheds its skin as it grows. The lobster hides in the rocks until its new shell has hardened.

See also CRAB; SHRIMPS AND PRAWNS.

LOCK Many different kinds of locks are used on doors and drawers to prevent them being opened by the wrong people. The simplest kind is unlocked by a key which is shaped to move the bolt that is stopping the door or drawer from opening. Combination locks are different and much more difficult to open. They do not have a keyhole. Instead, they have a dial which you move so many times to the left and right. When the correct combination of turns is dialed, the locking bolt can be freed. Safes and vaults have this kind of lock. Many bank vaults have time locks. They are combination locks connected to a clock and can only be opened at certain times.

LOCUST Locusts are one of the most harmful insect pests. In hot countries huge swarms of these grasshoppers darken the sky. When the swarms land they eat every green plant in sight. One swarm, by the Red Sea in the Middle East, was said to cover about 1,158 square miles (3,000 square kilometers) of land.

Young locusts, or hoppers, have no wings. When food is scarce they group together and migrate. At first, they hop. When their wings grow, they fly, forming large swarms in the sky.

Poisonous chemical sprays are used to kill locusts. Even so a plague of locusts is still a serious disaster for farmers.

See also GRASSHOPPER.

LOUIS XIV (1638–1715) reigned longer than any other king of France. He became king before he was 5 years old. He made himself master of France and fought many battles against other countries. To show off his wealth and power, Louis built a magnificent palace at Versailles, near Paris. Here, the French nobles gathered to attend the king's court. Louis was known as the 'Sun King'. But his wars and extravagance made France weaker, not stronger.

Lever

Inclined plane

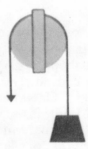

Wheel and axle

Pulley

Wedge

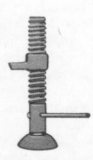

Jackscrew

LUTHER, Martin (1483–1546) At the time of Martin Luther most Christian churches in Europe belonged to the Roman Catholic Church. Luther was a monk. He thought the Church had moved too far away from the teachings of the Bible. And he protested that churchmen were cheating people by selling them pardons for their sins. The Pope, who was head of the Catholic Church, asked Luther to change his views. Luther refused and was excommunicated (cast out of the Church). But many Christians agreed with Luther and they set up 'Protestant' churches of their own. Luther had started a great religious movement. It is known as the Reformation.

MACHINES, SIMPLE Machines are devices that put energy to work. Much of what we do in daily life depends on them. Most machines are complicated devices. But they are all based on six types of machines: the lever; the inclined plane; the wheel and axle; the pulley; the wedge; and the screw (see illustrations).

By using these simple machines as a starting point, engineers have made new and better machines which can do a vast range of things. All machines, whether the simple lever or a giant crane, make it possible for people to do things that they otherwise could not.

MAGIC Primitive people were afraid of nature, because they did not understand what caused such things as storms or disease. Many thought that the forces of nature were controlled by good and evil spirits. They believed that magic gave them power over these spirits. Each tribe had a witch doctor or medicine man, who used spells and magic ceremonies to influence spirits and other 'supernatural' beings. In this way, he could make it rain, or cure sickness, or bring victory in battle. He also claimed to see into the future.

The cave paintings done by Stone Age men may have had a magic meaning, giving the hunters power to kill animals for food. Different peoples from all over the world have told stories about witches, wizards and magicians. This shows how

strongly people have believed in magic. Some magic was good, or 'white'; but other magic was bad, or 'black'. Superstition and fortune-telling are kinds of magic; so is wearing a charm or having a mascot to bring good luck.

Sometimes pagan priests and witch doctors used tricks to make people believe they had magic powers. But the clever tricks of stage magicians and conjurors today really have nothing to do with magic.

See also FAIRY TALES; MYTHS AND LEGENDS.

MAGNET Magnets are pieces of metal that can pick up objects. They are usually made of iron or steel and they have a power we call *magnetism*. The magnetism is most powerful at the ends of the magnet. If you hang a bar magnet from thread, it always points its ends towards the Earth's North and South magnetic poles. So we call the two ends its north and south poles. The magnet always points North-South because the Earth itself acts like a giant magnet. And one magnet affects another.

Magnetism is closely related to electricity. When electricity passes through a coil of wire, the coil acts like a magnet. Magnets made in this way are called *electromagnets*. There are electromagnets in telephone receivers, electric bells, electric motors and generators. Generators work because the movement of a wire in a magnetic field sets up an electric current in it.

MAMMAL Mammals are the most advanced animals. They are vertebrates (animals with backbones) and they are warm-blooded. They can control the temperature of their bodies by sweating or panting when it is hot and shivering when it is cold. Because of this, mammals can live in hot and cold climates. They have leathery or furry skins.

Almost all mammals, including human beings, give birth to live young. The female feeds the young with milk from her body, and cares for them until they can look after themselves.

Two primitive mammals, the platypus and the echidna, lay eggs. Marsupials are also mammals. Their young are born undeveloped and stay in the female's pouch until they are old enough to leave it.

Mammals range in size from tiny shrews to huge whales. Most mammals are land animals. But dolphins and whales spend all their lives in the sea, and seals are more at home in water than on land. Bats are the only mammals that can fly.

About 200 million years ago, dinosaurs ruled the Earth. The first mammals were small reptile-like animals. But they survived when the dinosaurs died out. The mammals were more intelligent. And they were able to adapt their way of life to changing conditions.

MAMMOTH The mammoth was a hairy elephant. It lived during the Ice Age but is now extinct.

Mammoths had long woolly hair and a thick layer of fat to keep out the cold. They scraped away the snow with their tusks to get at the plants underneath. Prehistoric men hunted mammoths for food and drew pictures of them inside caves. In Siberia mammoths have been found preserved in the ice.

See also ELEPHANT; FOSSIL; PRE-HISTORIC ANIMALS.

MAP A map is a drawing which shows all or part of the Earth's surface. It can show how cities, roads, railways, rivers, mountains and other features are arranged on the land.

A flat map cannot be really accurate because the Earth is round. Maps are drawn by various methods called *projections*. Some make parts of the Earth appear larger than they actually are.

Maps are drawn to scale. For example, a distance of 3.9 inches (10 centimeters) on the map, may represent about one-half mile (1 kilometer) on the ground. A map drawn to this scale can show very small details. Larger scale maps show countries, continents or the earth.

Political maps show countries, and often cities, roads and railways, Physical maps show mountains, rivers and other land features. Contour lines join places which are the same height above sea level Special maps show how much rain falls, how hot or cold it is, or what kind of plants grow. Sea maps called charts tell ships'

navigators where there are safe channels, rocks and lighthouses, and give the depth of the water.

Most maps are criss-crossed by lines. Running east and west parallel to the equator are lines called parallels of latitude. Running north and south and passing through the poles are lines called *meridians of longitude*. These lines fix the position of a place on the map. They are measured in degrees (up to 180), minutes and seconds. The equator is 0° latitude. Greenwich, in Britain, is longitude 0°. Latitude is written first. New York, for example, is at 40°45″ N (45 degrees 45 minutes north of the equator); 74°0″ W (74 degrees 0 minutes west of Greenwich).

Early maps were not very accurate. Modern maps are made from measurements made by surveyors and with the help of photographs taken from aircraft and space satellites.

MAPLE SYRUP comes from the sap of maple trees. At the beginning of the sugaring season, a small hole is bored into the tree, and the sap drained out. In large sugarhouses the sap is strained and boiled into syrup. It takes an average of 35 gallons of sap to make 1 gallon of syrup.

MARCONI, GUGLIELMO (1847-1937) was the Italian inventor of wireless telegraphy, or what we now call the radio. Marconi had always been interested in science. In 1894 he read about the work of a German scientist, Heinrich Hein who had produced a new kind of electrical wave by means of electric sparks.

Marconi thought that if messages could be sent over these electrical waves, they would be useful at sea. Within 5 years, he was able to send a message of dots and dashes from England across the English Channel to France. His dream, however, was to send a message across the Atlantic Ocean. He accomplished this on December 12, 1901. And a few years later, the usefulness of the wireless was proven at sea. Marconi won the Nobel Prize for his invention of the wireless.

MARSUPIAL Marsupials are primitive

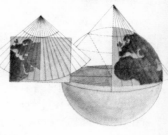

Conical projections (top) are used to make the maps in most atlases. Lines of latitude and longitude are curved. In the Mollweide projection (bottom) the grid, or graticule, is drawn to a definite plan. Here the scale is true at every point on the map, but land areas appear distorted.

The wallaby is a small relative of the kangaroo. Like all marsupials, the wallaby carries its young in a pouch. A new-born wallaby is completely helpless.

mammals. Most marsupials live in Australia and New Guinea, but one, the opossum, lives in the Americas.

A marsupial is born tiny and undeveloped. It crawls into its mother's pouch, where it sucks milk and is safe until it is big enough to leave the pouch.

Australia's marsupials have adapted to many ways of life. There are grass-eaters (kangaroos), flesh-eaters (Tasmanian devils), tree-climbers (koalas), burrowers (wombats), and even marsupial mice, shrews and moles.

See also KANGAROO; KOALA.

MATHEMATICS

When we subtract, divide or multiply we do arithmetic. This is one branch of mathematics, a science that deals with numbers and shapes. The other main branches of mathematics are algebra and geometry. Arithmetic deals with figures; algebra deals with figures and symbols; geometry deals with shapes. Other branches deal with angles, curves and changing quantities.

MEASUREMENT

How long is your desk? How heavy are you? How much water is in the bottle? We find the answers to these questions by measurement. We measure things using a device or instrument marked with a scale of numbers. To measure length we use a ruler. For weight, we use scales. For volume, we use a measuring cup.

Although the numbers on the various scales may be the same, they mean different things. A number on a ruler for instance, would measure inches or feet. A number on a measuring cup or scale, however, would measure ounces or pounds. This system of weighing objects is called *avoirdupois weight*. In most countries of the world, though, the *metric system* is used. Some units of measurement in the metric system include grams and kilograms to measure weight; and centimeters, meters and kilometers to measure distance or the length of an object.

MEDICINE

Since very early times people have searched for medicines to heal wounds and cure diseases. The first

GREAT ADVANCES IN MEDICINE		
Discovery	**Discoverer**	**Date**
Microscope	Zacharias Janssen	1590
Blood Circulation	William Harvey	1628
Vaccination	Edward Jenner	1796
Anaesthetic	William Morton	1846
Antiseptic surgery	Joseph Lister	1865
Germs cause disease	Louis Pasteur	1877
Psychoanalysis	Sigmund Freud	1895
X-rays	Wilhelm Roentgen	1895
Radium	Pierre & Marie Curie	1898
Penicillin	Alexander Fleming	1928

drugs came from berries and herbs which had healing powers. Magic was also thought to be important. For the person who knew about medicines was usually the priest or the witch-doctor.

The Greek doctor Hippocrates, who lived about 2500 years ago, is often called the 'Father of Medicine'. The ancient Greeks and Romans knew what the inside of the human body looked like. But they did not know how the different parts worked, or what made them go wrong. Until the Middle Ages doctors thought that there were four liquids called 'humors' inside the body, and that if these liquids weren't mixed properly, people became ill. They also believed disease was caused by 'bad air' and witchcraft.

Medicine made little progress until the 1600s, when doctors began studying anatomy (the parts of the body). By cutting up dead bodies, they began to find out how the body works. But since no one knew about germs, doctors did not bother very much about cleanliness. Many patients died because hospitals were dirty places.

Over the next 200 years progress in medicine was slow. But in the 1700s *vaccination* was discovered as a way of preventing disease, and later *antiseptics* were developed to kill harmful germs. *Anaesthetics* were used to stop people from feeling pain during operations. In the 1900s the discovery of X-rays meant that doctors could examine the insides of their patients to find out what was wrong. Powerful new drugs called *antibiotics* were also discovered.

These and other discoveries have helped make the modern hospital very different from the hospitals of 100 years ago. Engineers have built machines such

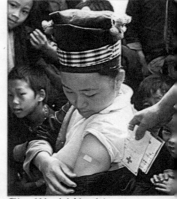

The World Health Organization and the Red Cross send medical help to people in poor countries.

The heart-lung machine has saved many lives. It can take over the work of the heart, and is used by doctors when carrying out heart surgery.

as 'heart and lung' machines to help doctors. Surgeons can 'transplant' kidneys and other organs from one person to another. Today doctors study diseases of the mind as well as diseases of the body.

See also DISEASE; DRUGS.

MEDITERRANEAN SEA The
Mediterranean is almost surrounded by the continents of Europe, Asia and Africa. It has a narrow outlet to the Atlantic Ocean through the straits of Gibraltar. The Adriatic and Aegean seas are part of the Mediterranean.

Mediterranean means 'middle of the Earth' in Latin, for the sea was the center of the ancient world. It played an important part in trade and the spread of learning.

After 1869, when the Suez Canal was opened, ships could sail from the Mediterranean into the Red Sea and the Indian Ocean to the Far East. Today, with its warm climate and many beautiful islands, the Mediterranean is a favorite spot for vacations.

METALS In the Earth's crust there are
more than 90 chemical elements. The most important group of elements are the metals. There are over 60 different metals. They are very different from the other elements.

Metals pass on, or conduct, electricity and heat well. Most non-metals do not. Many metals have a silvery, shiny surface. They are tough and strong, but can be bent and hammered without breaking. Mercury is an unusual metal because it is a liquid. Uranium is a metal that is radioactive–it gives off dangerous rays.

A few metals, such as gold, silver and platinum, can actually be found in the ground in the form of a metal. But most metals are found in minerals called ores. They are chemically joined to other elements, and must be separated out before they can be used. For example, iron is often found joined to oxygen in iron oxide, an ore.

There are several different ways of taking, or extracting, a metal from its ore. Iron is extracted by smelting, a process in which the ore is heated in a furnace with coke. Aluminum is extracted from its ore, bauxite, by means of electricity. The metal is obtained when the ore is melted and electricity is passed through it.

There are many different ways of shaping metals. Molten metals are shaped by molding, or casting. Hot metal can be shaped by forging (hammering) and rolling. It can be extruded, or forced through holes. Cold metal can be pressed or cut into shape by machines. It can be joined by welding. In welding, molten metal is used to make a join that hardens when it cools.

See also ALUMINUM; COPPER; GOLD; MINING; SILVER.

METEOR On some nights you may see
bright streaks in the sky. Though they look like falling stars, these glowing trails are actually made by meteors, lumps of rock or metal. As they shoot through the upper part of the Earth's atmosphere they burn up in a flash of light. Some of the bigger lumps reach the ground. These meteorites, as they are called, can make huge holes, or craters, in the earth.

To purify zinc blend, the finely ground ore is treated in a flotation tank. Any impurities stay at the bottom, while air bubbles carry the pure ore to the surface, where it is skimmed off.

MICHELANGELO (1475–1564) was
born in Florence during the Italian Renaissance. His full name was Michelangelo Buonarroti. He was a great sculptor, architect, painter and poet. Michelangelo carved figures from giant marble blocks. Among his most famous

Aluminum is produced from its ore, bauxite, by means of electricity. The bauxite is melted and electricity is passed through it to obtain the metal.

statues are *Pietà* and *David*. Between 1508 and 1512 he painted the ceiling of the Sistine Chapel in the Vatican. He adorned it with hundreds of figures depicting the Creation of the World according to the Book of Genesis. Most of the time he worked lying on his back on scaffolding high above the floor.

See also RENAISSANCE.

MICROSCOPE A microscope is an instrument that makes small objects look bigger. With a microscope we can see things that are invisible to the naked eye. We call these things microscopic. Pond water, for example, swarms with all kinds of microscopic plants and animals. To see them you need a microscope that magnifies about 20 times. If you have a microscope that magnifies several hundred times, you can see the cells in blood.

Ordinary microscopes magnify by bending light rays with glass lenses. The bent rays make an image which is bigger than the original object. The simplest of these microscopes is the magnifying glass. Electron microscopes are much more powerful than ordinary microscopes, and can magnify things hundreds of thousands of times. They magnify by bending beams of electrons, rather than light rays.

MIDDLE AGES When the Roman Empire fell in AD 476, the many different tribes in Europe formerly ruled by the Romans were left to look after themselves. It took about 1000 years for strong nations to grow out of this confusion. In between lay what historians have called the Middle Ages. They were not very safe times to live in.

In the early Middle Ages, without Roman armies to protect it, Europe was overrun by barbarians. Fierce tribes such as the Goths and Vandals sacked and burned towns and drove the people away. Later, in the 800s and 900s, the Viking raiders from Scandinavia attacked and plundered many coastal towns. Soon the ancient art and learning of Rome was forgotten, except by monks.

To defend themselves, people banded together under the protection of strong leaders, or Kings. The poor peasants worked on the great estates, or manors, of rich nobles and Knights. They became vassals – that is, they had to work or give up some of their crops in return for the protection of the nobleman, the lord of the manor. The nobles in turn became the vassals of the king. In return for the king's protection, they promised to supply soldiers in time of war. Serving as a soldier was therefore another of the peasant's duties. This arrangement is known as the feudal system.

Life in the Middle Ages was often harsh and cruel. The peasants had to obey the lord of the manor. Anyone who broke the law was severely punished. The Church was rich and powerful. And anyone who questioned the Church's teachings was punished harshly too. Most people lived in dark, smoky huts. They had barely enough to eat, especially in winter. Then most of the farm animals had to be killed, because there was nothing for them to eat. People knew little about hygiene or medicine. Sometimes terrible plagues swept the land, and killed many thousands of people.

But slowly knowledge grew. Beautiful cathedrals were built. Art and poetry developed. Universities and schools were founded. Gradually government became more settled, and trade flourished. With the voyages of discovery in the 1400s and the Renaissance, or 'rebirth of learning', the Middle Ages came to an end.

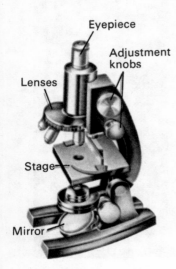

Eyepiece

Adjustment knobs

Lenses

Stage

Mirror

A standard optical microscope. It has a base, a tube containing the lenses, and a body to hold the tube. Objects to be studied under the microscope are put on glass slides.

Far right: This illuminated picture is from a Book of Hours made in the 15th century for the Duke of Berry, brother of the King of France. It is for the month of July and shows peasants reaping corn and shearing sheep. In the background is the castle of Poitiers, which was the Duke's home. Rare and valuable books like these give us a fascinating picture of life in the Middle Ages.

MIDDLE EAST The desert lands of south-west Asia and north-east Africa are often called the Middle East. This area includes Turkey, Syria, Lebanon, Jordan, Israel, Iraq, Iran, Egypt and the whole of Arabia. Most of the people are Muslim Arabs. Many are poor, but oilfields underground have made some Middle East countries rich.

In 1948 the Jews founded the state of Israel in what had been British-ruled Palestine. The Arabs would not accept this. There have been four wars between Israel and the Arab countries, in 1948, 1956, 1967 and 1973.

MIGRATION Many swallows spend the summer in Europe. But in the autumn they fly south to the warmth of Africa. This journey is called migration.

Many animals migrate to find food or to breed. Caribou move south to escape the Arctic winter. African antelope migrate during the dry season to find water and fresh grass.

Some birds fly very long distances. The Arctic tern flies from the Arctic winter to the Antarctic summer, and back again. The monarch butterfly travels south across North America. A few cross the Atlantic Ocean.

Frogs, toads and newts spend most of their time on land. But they return to ponds and streams to lay their eggs. Salmon return from the sea to breed in the same rivers where they hatched.

Perhaps the strangest migration is that of the lemming. Every few years thousands of these little rodents cross Scandinavia. When they reach the sea, many drown. The lemmings migrate when there is not enough food around. Some scientists think that in the past, when the seas were narrower, the lemmings were able to swim to land where there was more food.

See also EEL.

MILK is one of our most valuable foods. It contains fats, sugar (carbohydrate), proteins, minerals and vitamins. It gives us energy, builds our bodies and keeps us healthy. Mammals feed their young with milk produced in their bodies.

The milk people use comes from cows, and also from sheep, goats and camels.

Coal-mining underground is hard and dangerous. Steel props support the roof as the miners take coal from the seam with coal-cutting machines.

Four examples of the long journeys made by migrating birds. From top to bottom: the swallow, Arctic tern, wheatear and bobolink. The Arctic tern makes the longest migration of all, flying from the Arctic to the Antarctic and back again.

Other foods, such as butter, cream and cheese, are made from milk. Farms which keep cows for their milk are called dairy farms.

MINING means taking minerals from the ground. It is one of our most important industries and supplies many other industries with their raw materials. The ores from which we make metals are the main minerals mined. Many millions of tons of iron ore are mined every year to be made into steel. Coal mining is very important too.

Sometimes mineral deposits can be dug out from the surface. Other deposits lie just below the surface. The soil is first stripped off, then explosives break up the deposits. Power shovels load the mineral into trucks. This is called open-cast mining. If sand, gravel or rock are mined in this way, it is called quarrying.

Often the mineral deposits are buried deep in the ground. Miners have to travel down shafts and in trains along tunnels to reach them. In many mines miners work on several levels and the tunnels stretch for hundreds of miles. Most minerals are blasted loose from the rock. But coal can be cut by machines because it is quite soft.

MIRAGE If you look at a road on a hot day, you can sometimes see what appears to be a puddle on it. When you get nearer, the 'puddle' disappears. This is a mirage. A mirage is caused by light rays from the sky being reflected from layers of hot air just above the ground. Thirsty travellers often see mirages of a lake.

MOHAMMED (570?–632) The Arab prophet Mohammed founded the religion of Islam. He taught people to stop worshiping idols and follow the 'true God', called Allah. In 622 Mohammed's enemies drove him out of his birthplace, Mecca. He fled to the city of Medina, and converted many people to the new religion. Then he defeated his enemies in battle, captured Mecca and destroyed the false idols. Mohammed's teachings are written down in the Muslim holy book, the Koran. By the time Mohammed died, Islam had spread throughout Arabia.

MOLE Moles live underground almost all their lives. They dig tunnels in the earth at great speed with the long, broad claws in their strong front feet. Moles are not blind, but their eyes are weak. They use their ears, noses and delicate touch organs on their bodies to find their way out.

Moles dig to find food. They eat worms. Sometimes they store worms in underground store rooms. Moles do not drink; they get all the moisture they need from their food.

Moles push earth from their tunnels to make molehills.

MOLLUSK Mollusks are soft-bodied animals. To protect themselves, many mollusks have shells.

Some mollusks, like the mussel, stay inside their shells and hardly ever move. Others, such as the cockle, use their single foot to move around. Snails and slugs crawl very slowly.

The largest and most active mollusks are the octopus, which has no shell, and the squid, which has its shell inside its body.

See also OCTOPUS; OYSTER; SEASHORE; SHELLS; SLUG; SNAIL.

MONASTERY A monastery is the home of a religious community. The monks who live in the monastery take religious vows promising not to marry, not to possess money, and to do whatever work they are asked to do. They spend the day working, studying or in prayer. The long tunic many monks wear is known as a *habit*.

The first Christian monasteries were started about 200 years after the death of Christ. By the Middle Ages there were several important 'orders' of monks and friars (friar means brother).

Some monks work outside the monastery as missionaries and teachers. Others remain in the monastery and lead very strict lives. Women who choose the religious life are called nuns and live in a convent.

There are also monks in the Buddhist religion. They shave their heads, wear yellow robes and live by begging.

MONEY When people first began to trade, they did not use money to buy things. Instead they exchanged goods. A hunter might exchange some furs for a new spear. This method of buying and selling is called *barter*.

When people settled in towns, trade became more complicated. The barter system was too clumsy. So *token goods*, such as cattle or shells, were used. This was the beginning of the money system. About 2500 years ago, small pieces of metal, or coins, came into use. Because everyone accepted that gold and silver were precious, the first coins were made of these metals.

This worked very well until the Middle

The oyster is a valuable mollusk. This pearl oyster has been cut open to show its precious jewel inside.

The 'heads' side of a coin is called the obverse.

The reverse, or 'tails', side may show the value of the coin and the date that it was issued. This one shows it is worth 100 Italian lira. The words, or 'legend', stamped on a coin, stand out in relief.

People used to clip pieces off gold and silver coins. To stop this, the edges were 'milled', or 'grained'.

...ges when merchants grew tired of ...arrying heavy bags of gold around with ...hem. They began to exchange pieces of ...aper, promising payment for goods ...ought. They set up banks, in which to ...eep their gold safe. The banks began to ...ssue paper money, or bank notes, and ...eople gradually accepted that these had ...he same value as gold.

Today, the government controls how ...much money is made by minting coins ...nd printing notes. The money we use is ...oken money: that is, modern coins are ...nade of cheap metals and have little ...alue in themselves. Coins and notes ...ave a value marked on them. But the ...eal value of money is the amount of ...oods it will buy. Because coins are heavy ...nd awkward to use, they are used only ...or small payments.

See also BANK.

MONGOOSE The mongoose of Africa ...nd Asia looks like a large weasel. It is ... brave fighter, and will kill and eat ...oisonous snakes. When it fights a snake ...s dangerous as the cobra, the mongoose ...ounces so quickly that the snake cannot ...trike with its fangs. Mongooses also eat ...irds' eggs, insects, lizards and small ...nammals.

The mongoose avoids the cobra's fangs and pounces when the snake tires.

MONKEY Monkeys are smaller ...relatives of the apes. Both apes and ...monkeys belong to the group of animals ...called primates.

Old World monkeys live in Africa and ...Asia. New World monkeys live in Central ...and South America. New World monkeys ...have *prehensile* tails, which can grasp ... a branch like an extra hand. Old World ...monkeys cannot use their tails like this.

Monkeys are lively, intelligent animals. ...They use their hands and feet to hold ...things. Most monkeys live in groups. ...They eat fruit and other parts of plants, ...insects, small mammals and birds' eggs. ...New World monkeys climb about in the ...trees. But some Old World monkeys,

including baboons, stay on the ground.

Old World monkeys include the long-nosed proboscis monkey, the rhesus monkeys, guenons and macaques. The rock ape of Gibraltar is the only European monkey. In the forests of South America live the noisy howler monkeys, the sad-faced capuchins, the long-legged spider monkeys and the little squirrel monkeys and marmosets.

See also APE; BABOON.

MOON The Moon is our next-door neighbor in space. It travels around the Earth once every month. The word *month* means 'one moon-th'. We know more about the Moon than we know about any other heavenly body except the Earth. Astronomers have studied the Moon for hundreds of years. And now men from Earth have actually been there. They have walked on the Moon, and brought back soil and rocks to scientists on Earth.

The Moon is a ball of rock, about a quarter the *diameter* (width) of the Earth. It has no atmosphere. Because there is no air there is no weather on the Moon, and no sound. There is no water and no life of any kind. It is very hot in the sunlight, but icy cold in the shade.

Even with our eyes, we can see that the Moon's surface is not smooth. Some areas are dark, while others are light. The dark areas are great flat plains. They are called *maria*, or seas, because people once thought they were vast oceans. The light areas are highlands. They contain jagged peaks and mountain ranges.

Everywhere on the Moon there are pits, or craters. Some are small; others are as large as 143 miles (230 km) across. Most craters were formed when large lumps of rock hurtled into the Moon from outer space. The whole surface is covered with loose rocks and a thick layer of fine dust.

The Moon can be seen from Earth on most clear nights of the year. The Moon shines because it reflects light from the Sun. The shape of the Moon appears to change during a month. First it is a thin crescent, or C-shape. It gradually gets bigger until we can see the whole disk. Then it gets smaller until it finally disappears. The Moon does not change

Golden spider monkey

Long-nosed proboscis monkey

Black howler monkey

Squirrel monkey

its shape, of course. What does change is the area we can see which is lit by the Sun. This area changes because of the Moon's movement around the Earth every month. We call these changes the phases of the Moon.

MOSQUITO The mosquito is a fly with a small body and long legs. Some mosquitoes spread diseases, including malaria. The male is harmless. But the female mosquito feeds on the blood of animals, including human beings. The insect pours a juice into the wound to stop the blood clotting, or hardening. This is when diseases are passed on.

Mosquitoes lay their eggs in water. The larvae hang by their tails from the surface. In warm countries, where mosquitoes are most dangerous, the eggs and larvae are destroyed with chemicals.

See also DISEASE.

MOSS Mosses are simple plants. They do not have flowers, but reproduce by sending out tiny offshoots. Spores, or cells, grow on these shoots. When the spores are ripe, they are blown away by the wind. New moss plants develop from the spores which land in places where they can grow.

Most mosses like damp, sheltered spots. But they also grow on walls, rocks and bare sand. Bog moss, or sphagnum, forms thick, spongy layers of peat.

MOVIES In the early 1900s in cities across America, a new form of entertainment appeared as people began to pay a nickel to see a "flicker" at their local "nickelodeon." So began the American movie industry. The name "nickelodeon" came from the nickel price of admission.

The first movies were nothing like the sight and sound extravaganzas our theaters show today. In fact, they were often no more than travelogues or replays of sports events. They had no plot or story line, and were of course, silent. The only sound was the feverish playing of the pianist which kept pace with the action and suspense of the film.

Gradually, due to improvement in technology and the movie industry's need to compete with its new rival, television, movies became longer, more exciting and more varied.

Subtitles were added in 1912, sound in 1927. Color came into widespread use in the early 1930's. The first full-length "epic" was *Birth of A Nation*. This movie made history for two reasons: first because it dealt with the Civil War and Reconstruction, a topic people had very strong feelings about; secondly, because it developed and improved many new camera techniques.

During the 1930s and 1940s, which many people called the Golden Age of the American film, movies became extremely popular. Often, movie theaters would have stage shows, quiz games and prize drawings, to make a full evening's fun.

Many different types of movies were also produced. They include animated cartoons made famous by Walt Disney; and documentaries which present factual, historical, political or social events in an informative style.

Over the years, many new technological advances appeared. Three dimensional films, which enabled the viewer to see three-sided figures with the use of special eyeglasses became a favorite of horror movie producers. Cinemascope was a projection system which used a giant wall-to-wall curved screen. Stereophonic sound used several loud speakers around the theater and gave the audience the feeling that it was surrounded by sound and action.

See also: ANIMATED CARTOONS.

Above: The Moon shows 'phases' as it moves across the Earth. It takes 29½ days to complete these phases, as more or less of its surface is lit by the Sun. First it waxes (from crescent, or new, moon to full moon) and then wanes (from full back to crescent).

One of the first, and greatest, film 'stars' was the comedian Charlie Chaplin.

MOUNTAIN Mountains are masses of rock which rise above the surrounding land. People usually think of a mountain as rising at least 20,000 feet (about 600 meters).

Mountains are usually grouped together in ranges, chains or massifs. Some mountains are the cones of volcanoes. But most are formed by folding and sideways movements of the crust, or outer skin, of the Earth. These movements push up the rocks to build mountains. Mountain building takes millions of years. It is still going on today in parts of the Earth. The rocks are worn away by rain, wind, ice and snow to form jagged peaks and sheer walls.

The world's highest mountains are the Himalayas in Asia. Other high mountains are the Andes in South America, the Rockies in North America and the Alps in Europe. There are also many mountains under the sea.

See also ALPS; ANDES; HIMALAYAS; ROCKY MOUNTAINS.

Some Of The World's Highest Mountains		
Africa		
Kilimanjaro	19,342 feet	
	5,895 meters	
Antarctica		
Vinson Massif	16,861 feet	
	5,139 meters	
Asia		
Everest	29,030 feet	
	8,848 meters	
Australasia		
Djaja	16,536 feet	
	5,040 meters	
Europe		
Elbrus	18,481 feet	
	5,633 meters	
Mont Blanc	15,772 feet	
	4,807 meters	
Matterhorn	14,692 feet	
	4,478 meters	
North America		
McKinley	20,322 feet	
	6,194 meters	
South America		
Aconcagua	22,836 feet	
	6,960 meters	

MOUSE The house mouse has been a common pest for thousands of years. It is a small rodent, with teeth designed for gnawing. It spoils food and leaves unsightly droppings.

Mice are active at night. They use their keen sense of smell to find food; they also have sharp hearing. Mice have many enemies, but they breed in great numbers.

White mice can be kept as pets. The wood mouse, field mouse, harvest mouse and dormouse are mice which live in the countryside.

See also RAT.

Tree-line

Snow-line

MOZART, Wolfgang Amadeus (1756–1791) Many people think the Austrian composer Mozart was the greatest musical genius the world has known. He began writing music at the age of five. Two years later his father took him to play at concerts in the great cities of Europe. Mozart wrote music for the church, beautiful operas, and 41 symphonies for the orchestra. He worked hard but earned little money and died very poor at the age of 35.

MUSEUM A museum is a building which houses a collection of objects that people can look at. The objects may be of artistic, historical, scientific or technological nature. But the function of a museum extends beyond just displaying objects. Many museums carry on educational programs, organize field trips and clubs and publish educational material.

One of the first institutions to be called a museum was founded in Alexandria, Egypt in the 3rd Century B.C. Its purpose was to collect information that could be of interest to scholars. The museum had a collection of art and objects including elephant tusks, hides of unusual animals and instruments of the day which were used in surgery and astronomy.

MUSHROOM On an autumn morning, you may find that little umbrella-shaped plants have sprung up on the grass over-

On a mountain, different plants grow in zones at various heights. On the lower slopes are deciduous trees, higher up, conifers. Above the tree-line are shrubs, alpine flowers, and then lichens and mosses. Snow covers the highest peaks.

Mice have many enemies. They rely on their sharp ears and quivering whiskers to warn them of danger. They find their food mainly by its smell.

night. They are mushrooms, plants that belong to the fungus group.

Fungi are not green. They contain no chlorophyll, so they cannot use sunlight to make their food, like other plants. Instead they feed on dead and decaying plant and animal matter. Some fungi are parasites. They feed on living plants and are harmful to crops.

The mushroom has no flowers or seeds. It reproduces by means of cells called spores, which are on the underside of the 'umbrella'. The spores are blown away by the wind. When a spore falls to earth in a damp place, it puts out tiny branching threads to find food underground. Then it pushes up its stalk. On top of the stalk is the umbrella, containing more spores.

The meadow mushroom is good to eat. But some other fungi, called toadstools, are poisonous. Some of the poisonous fungi look like mushrooms, so take care not to pick them by mistake.

MUSIC is a set of sounds arranged in a way that is pleasant to hear. It has *rhythm* (a beat) and usually *melody* (a tune). Many people make music to show their feelings. When they are happy, they whistle or sing. Sadness, too, can often be best expressed in music.

Music can be heard in natural sounds, such as bird songs. Many sounds have their own rhythm. Think of a hammer banging a nail, or even your own heart beating. These rhythms can be copied by people beating with a stick on a stone, or on a drum. Music is made up of *notes* that may be long or short, loud or soft, high or low.

Musical instruments have been made for thousands of years. There are three main groups of instruments. *Wind instruments* are played by blowing down a hollow wooden or metal tube with holes cut in it. By covering some holes with the fingers, different notes are produced. Wind instruments include flutes, clarinets, oboes, bassoons, trumpets and horns. *Stringed instruments* have strings stretched across a hollow box. The

strings are bowed, as in a violin, or plucked, as in a guitar, to make different notes. Short strings make high notes and long strings make low notes. Stringed instruments include violins, violas, cellos, basses, guitars, banjos, lutes and mandolins. Instruments such as drums, cymbals and bells, which are hit with hammers or sticks, are called *percussion instruments*. A large group of people playing instruments together form an orchestra.

At first the music had a simple melody and rhythm. But it gradually grew more complicated. Two or three tunes were played together. This made a richer sound and was called *counterpoint*. But it was too difficult to remember without writing it down. People who make up music and write it down are called *composers*. Two great composers of counterpoint were Bach and Handel. Much great music has been written for orchestras by composers such as Haydn, Mozart, Beethoven and Brahms. They wrote *symphonies* (long pieces of music for orchestras) and *chamber music* (for smaller groups of instruments). They also wrote music for choirs to sing. Some composers have written operas, which are musical plays in which all the words are sung.

People often call this kind of music 'classical' music. But there are many other kinds of music, including folk songs, jazz and pop music. Modern music is very different from the music of the 1800s. It has difficult rhythms and sounds, and sometimes requires electronic instruments as well as wind, stringed and percussion instruments.

See also BACH; BEETHOVEN; MOZART; OPERA; TCHAIKOVSKY.

Music can be made in many different ways. Most of us can enjoy the stirring music of J. S. Bach (top), the fine singing of an opera star like Maria Callas (center) and the tunes of pop groups such as the Beatles (bottom).

These pictures of the poisonous death cap show how a fungus grows. When it is ripe, its gills release millions of spores. Then the fungus decays.

Harp

SOME FAMOUS COMPOSERS

Antonio Vivaldi, Italian (1678?–1741)
Johann Sebastian Bach, German (1685–1750)
George Frederick Handel, German, naturalized British (1685–1759)
Joseph Haydn, Austrian (1732–1809)
Wolfgang Amadeus Mozart, Austrian (1756–1791)
Ludwig van Beethoven, German (1770–1827)
Gioacchino Rossini, Italian (1792–1868)
Franz Schubert, Austrian (1797–1828)
Hector Berlioz, French (1803–1869)
Felix Mendelssohn, German (1809–1847)
Frédéric Chopin, Polish (1810–1849)
Robert Schumann, German (1810–1856)
Franz Liszt, Hungarian (1811–1886)
Giuseppe Verdi, Italian (1813–1901)
Richard Wagner, German (1813–1883)
Anton Bruckner, Austrian (1824–1896)
Johannes Brahms, German (1833–1897)
Peter Ilich Tchaikovsky, Russian (1840–1893)
Anton Dvořák, Czech (1841–1904)
Edvard Grieg, Norwegian (1843–1907)
Edward Elgar, British (1857–1934)
Giacomo Puccini, Italian (1858–1924)
Gustav Mahler, Austrian (1860–1911)
Claude Debussy, French (1862–1918)
Jean Sibelius, Finnish (1865–1957)
Sergei Rachmaninov, Russian (1873–1943)
Igor Stravinsky, Russian (1882–1971)
Aaron Copland, American (1900–   )
Dmitri Shostakovich, Russian (1906–1975)
Benjamin Britten, British (1913–1976)

Pieces to listen to

Bach	Well Tempered Clavier
	Air on the G String
	Jesu Joy of Man's Desiring
	Brandenburg Concertos
Beethoven	Ode to Joy, Emperor Concerto
	Eroica Symphony
	6th Symphony
Berlioz	Symphony Fantastique
Bizet	Carmen Overture
Brahms	Hungarian Dances
Britten	Let's Make an Opera
	Simple Symphony
	Young Person's Guide to the Orchestra
Chopin	Selection for *Les Sylphides*
	Ballade No 2
Dvořák	New World Symphony
Elgar	Enigma Variations
	Pomp and Circumstance
Gershwin	Rhapsody in Blue
Grieg	Peer Gynt Suite
	Piano Concerto
Handel	Water Music
Haydn	Clock Symphony
Mendelssohn	Hebrides Overture
Mozart	Eine Kleine Nachtmusik
	Magic Flute
Prokofiev	Peter and the Wolf
Rossini	William Tell Overture
	Thieving Magpie Overture
Saint-Saëns	Carnival of the Animals
Sibelius	Karelia Suite, Finlandia
Smetana	Vltava
Tchaikovsky	The Nutcracker Suite
	1812 Overture, Swan Lake
Verdi	Grand March from Aïda
Wagner	Ride of the Valkyries

Clarinet

Double bass

Cello

Violin

Trumpet

Horn

Kettle drum

Triangle

Cymbals

Bass drum

MYTHS AND LEGENDS Stories told long ago, and passed down from generation to generation, are known as myths and legends. No one knows who first told them or how much truth they contain.

Primitive people made up stories to explain the mysteries of nature. Some myths, called 'creation myths', tell how the world was made. Others are about the gods who rule the world. For example, to explain how the Sun rises and sets each day, the Greeks told how the Sun god Apollo drove across the sky in a golden chariot.

Ancient myths often included magic and religion. And many exciting myths tell of brave heroes who have adventures in strange lands, and fight battles against enemies and monsters.

Some of the best known myths are those told in ancient Greece. They are about the gods the Greeks believed in: Zeus, the king of the gods; Hades, god of the underworld; Poseidon, god of the sea; and many others, most of whom were believed to live on Mount Olympus. Other Greek stories are about heroes and wars. The greatest of these are told by the poet Homer in two long poems, the *Iliad* and the *Odyssey*. The *Iliad* is about the war between the Greeks and the Trojans, while the *Odyssey* tells of the adventures of Odysseus (Ulysses) on his way home from the war.

The people of northern Europe also told many stories about their gods. The chief Norse god was Odin or Woden, and he led a rather quarrelsome family, including Thor (god of thunder), Freya (goddess of love), Balder (god of sunlight), Tiw (god of war) and Loki (god of fire). From these gods come the English names for four days of the week: Tuesday (from Tiw), Wednesday (from Woden), Thursday (from Thor), and Friday (from Freya). Norse tales are full of monsters, giants, trolls and elves. According to Norse myths, the first man was made from an ash tree, and the world will end in a terrible battle between the gods and their enemies.

There are myths and legends from every part of the world, especially America, India, China and Egypt. The Celtic people of Europe told many tales about fairies and warrior heroes. The most famous legendary hero of Europe is King Arthur. Arthur may have been a real king. But the stories about him and his Knights of the Round Table contain bits of legends and fairy tales, as well as half-forgotten history. This is how most legends are made. Another famous example is the legend of Robin Hood.

NAPOLEON BONAPARTE (1769–1821)

was France's greatest general. He was born on the island of Corsica. After the French Revolution in 1789, Napoleon conquered much of Europe. In 1804 he made himself Emperor of France. But in 1812 his army had to retreat from Russia, and in 1815 the British and Prussians beat the French at the battle of Waterloo. Napoleon was exiled, and died in prison on the lonely island of St Helena.

NERVOUS SYSTEM

The human body is a wonderful machine. All its parts have their own jobs to do. The brain gives the 'orders'. The 'messengers' are the nerves.

The nervous system is a complicated network of nerves. Important messages are sent along the spinal cord. From here the nerves branch off to every part of the body. As well as carrying orders from the brain, they also send back signals from the eyes, ears and other senses. These tell the brain what is happening outside the body, as well as inside.

There are millions of cells in the nervous system. The fastest messages they carry are called *reflexes*. A reflex tells the muscles to pull our fingers away from a hot iron, often even before the brain has had time to feel the heat.

See also BRAIN; CELL; HUMAN BODY.

Below: According to the ancient Romans, Neptune was the god of the seas and rivers. If he was angered, Neptune sent floods and storms, and also made the earth shake.
Right: The legend of St George tells how a brave knight fought and slew a terrible dragon which ravaged the land. St George became the patron saint of England.

NEST

Birds build nests in which to lay their eggs and rear their young. Usually the nest is well hidden and out of reach of enemies.

Some birds have very simple nests – just holes in the ground or messy piles of twigs. But many birds take great trouble, weaving nests from twigs and grasses and lining them with feathers, moss and hair. Some nests are completely enclosed, with just a small entrance hole. House martins build mud nests under the eaves of houses. Woodpeckers nest in holes in trees.

Rabbits and mice make underground nests for their young. And the sickleback, a fish, builds an underwater nest for its eggs.

NEWSPAPER

The first printed newpapers, which appeared about 300 years ago, were like pamphlets and were not published every day. Today, daily newspapers have large pages to cover the news and comment on world events.

The editor decides what is to appear in the newspaper. The sports editor, news editor, and features editor are in charge of different parts of the newspaper. Reporters bring in and write the news, and copy editors prepare it for printing. Advertisements help pay for the newspaper.

Newspapers are sometimes referred to

Some birds' nests, from top to bottom: The golden oriole makes a hanging nest; the tailor bird weaves a nest between leaves; the long-tailed tit's mossy nest is almost enclosed; while the American robin's nest is a cup of mud, twigs and grass.

as 'the press'. In some countries the government controls what the newspapers can print.

NEWT Like their relatives, frogs and toads, newts are amphibians. They can live on land, but return to water to lay their eggs.

Newts have lungs, but they also breathe through their skins. They eat insects and worms. In winter, newts hibernate. When spring comes, they travel to ponds and ditches to breed. They lay eggs which hatch into tadpoles. Most of the tadpoles turn into newts by the autumn.

See also AMPHIBIAN; FROGS AND TOADS.

NEWTON, Isaac (1642–1727) was one of the greatest scientists and mathematicians the world has known. He was the first person to explain the force of gravity, which holds the universe together. He also did many experiments with light. Newton split up light into a spectrum, or band of color. He also built the first reflecting telescope. Newton was born in England. He studied mathematics and science at Cambridge University in England.

See also COLOR; GRAVITY; LIGHT; TELESCOPE.

NEW ZEALAND Two long narrow islands, the North Island and South Island, and a few smaller islands, make up the country of New Zealand. It lies in the south Pacific Ocean, far from other lands.

New Zealand has high mountains, volcanoes, hot springs, fast-flowing rivers and glaciers. Low land rims much of the coast. This is where most towns and cities are. The climate is mild, with good rainfall.

The grasslands are ideal for sheep and cattle farming. New Zealand is famous for its butter, cheese and meat, and also for its fruit. Minerals are scarce. But water power and energy from the hot springs are used to make electricity, and there are supplies of coal, oil and natural gas.

There were no people in New Zealand until the Maoris sailed there in canoes from Polynesia perhaps 1000 years ago.

About 300 years ago, the Dutch discovered and named New Zealand. But the country was mainly settled by people from Britain. Today New Zealand lives by trade with other nations.

See also KIWI.

NILE The Nile is the longest river in the world. It flows north from the lakes of central Africa into the Mediterranean Sea. At Khartoum in the Sudan the White Nile is joined by the Blue Nile, which rises in the mountains of Ethiopia.

Without the Nile, few people could have lived in the desert along its banks. Every spring, the river flooded and made the soil fertile. By the Nile the ancient Egyptians built a great civilization. Today, man-made barriers, such as the Aswan Dam, control the Nile's flow, providing water for crops and for making electricity.

NOBEL PRIZE Every year six Nobel prizes may be awarded, for outstanding work in chemistry, physics, medicine, literature, economics and the cause of peace. Two or three people may share a prize, and the prize winners may come from any part of the world. To win a Nobel prize is a very great honor.

The money for the prizes was given by a Swedish chemist called Alfred Nobel. He invented dynamite, a powerful explosive, and became a rich man. But he was saddened to see his invention used for war and destruction. The prizes were first awarded in 1901, five years after Alfred Nobel's death.

Newts are amphibians. They spend part of their lives in water, and part on dry land.

A view of Wellington by night. This city is the capital of New Zealand. It stands on the shores of a large bay, which forms a fine natural harbor.

Facts and Figures
Area: 103,861 square miles
        269 square kilometers
Population: 3,100,000
Capital: Wellington
Government: Parliamentary state
Money Unit: Dollar
Longest River: Waikato,
        270 miles (434 kilometers)
Highest Mountain: Mt. Cook,
        12,350 feet (3764 meters)

New Zealand's national bird is the kiwi. Both the North Island and the South Island are mountainous. In the north, around Rotorua, is a volcanic region, with geysers, hot springs and mud pools.

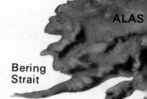

ALAS

Bering
Strait

NORTH AMERICA is the third largest of the Earth's continents. It stretches from the cold wastes of Alaska in the north to the hot deserts of Mexico and the tropical forests of Central America in the south. Canada and the United States of America cover most of North America. The continent's many islands include the Caribbean Islands and Greenland.

North America covers about a sixth of the Earth's land surface. A narrow isthmus, or neck of land in Central America, joins it to South America. Down the western side of North America run the rugged Rocky Mountains, and there are lower mountain chains in the east. In the center of the continent are wide grasslands called prairies. The Canadian Shield, a wild region of lakes and forests in northern Canada, has valuable minerals, such as coal and oil. In the south of the continent are coastal plains, swampy in places. The longest river in North America is the Mississippi, which joins another long river, the Missouri. The Great Lakes are the largest fresh water lakes in the world. The thundering Niagara Falls plunges deep between two of the Great Lakes.

North America has a wide range of climates. In most of the Arctic lands of the north it is too cold for trees to grow. Farther south are huge forests, first of conifers and then of broad-leaved trees. The central plains have less rainfall, so instead of forests, there are grasslands. In the southwest there are hot deserts, and in the hot, moist isthmus of Panama there are tropical forests.

Many of the wild animals of North America look like those of Europe and Asia. The bison, caribou, moose, wolf and bear all have European relatives. This is because North America was once joined to Asia by a land bridge crossing what is now the Bering Strait between Alaska and Russia. The first people in North America also came from Asia. They were the American Indians, who crossed the land bridge about 30,000 years ago. Most were farmers, but some moved out onto the plains to hunt bison. In Central America the Aztec and Maya peoples built fine stone pyramids crowned by temples.

North America is a continent of great contrasts. It has some of the world's largest cities, such as New York. But there are huge areas with hardly any people at all. The United States is the richest large country in the world. But in Central America the countries are small and poor.

Crops grown in North America include wheat, fruit, vegetables and cotton. Forestry and furs are important in the north, and fishing is a major industry. Canada and the United States are great industrial countries, with plentiful raw materials and many factories.

People have made great changes to the land in North America. They have cut down forests to build homes and farms. They have dammed the rivers to make electricity. The prairies have been turned into enormous wheatfields, or used to graze millions of sheep and cattle. All this has happened in the last 300 years.

Viking seafarers probably reached North America about 1000 years ago. But Europeans did not begin to settle there until the 1600s, after the voyages of Columbus and other explorers. Europeans called North America the 'New World' and set up colonies in the eastern coastal lands. Gradually people moved west into new territory. English settlers founded the colonies which eventually became the United States of America. British and French colonists founded Canada, while the Spanish ruled Mexico and Central America until the countries became independent. In the 1800s people from many parts of Europe came to North America. The black people are descended from slaves who were brought to North America from Africa.

See also AMERICAN COLONIES; AMERICAN INDIAN; AZTEC; CANADA; COUNTRIES OF THE WORLD; ROCKY MOUNTAINS; UNITED STATES OF AMERICA.

NUCLEAR POWER Under certain conditions uranium atoms can be made to split. When they do so, large amounts of energy are released as heat and light. The splitting of the atom, or rather its nucleus, is called nuclear fission.

Scientists can now control the fission of uranium and use the energy it releases to produce nuclear power. In

North America extends from the Arctic Circle in the north almost to the Equator in the south. A vast mountain chain runs down the western side of the continent. The largest part of this chain is the Rocky Mountain range which runs from Alaska to northern Mexico. To the east of the Rockies are vast plains where wheat and cattle farms are found.
Hot deserts occupy part of the southwest, and there are flat marshy plains in the southeast. In the northeast, between Canada and the United States are the famous Great Lakes and Niagara Falls.

CANADA

ROCKIES

Hudson
Bay

Canadian Shield

Prairies

Great Lakes

Grand
Canyon

The
Great
Plains

Appalachians

Atlantic
Ocean

MEXICO

WEST
INDIES

Pacific
Ocean

Caribbean
Sea

CENTRAL
AMERICA

NORTH AMERICA

Panama
Canal

Four kinds of nut:
(from top to bottom)
hazelnut, peanut or
groundnut, acorn and
coconut. Coconuts and
peanuts grow in warm
countries. Acorns are
the nuts of oak trees and
hazelnuts of hazel trees.

Hazelnut

Peanut

Acorn

Coconut

At its outer edge, the
continental shelf
plunges steeply down to
the ocean floor or abyss.
This is a flat plain
crossed by ridges and
trenches. Rising from it
are mountains and
volcanoes, some of
which break the surface
as islands.

furnaces, called reactors, great heat is produced when the nucleus of the atom splits. This heat is used to boil water. In nuclear power stations the steam from the boiling water is used to drive the turbines generating electricity. Nuclear power is also used to drive some ships.

In atomic bombs nuclear power is used in a destructive way. In these bombs no attempt is made to control a nuclear reactor and all the energy is released in a short time, causing a terrifying explosion.

See also ATOM.

NUT Some trees bear fruits called nuts. Inside the tough shell of the nut is a seed. Many animals crack or gnaw at nuts to get at the seed inside.

Ripe nuts fall to earth in autumn. The seed sends a new shoot pushing through the shell; and a new tree begins its life.

Sweet chestnuts, walnuts, almonds and coconuts are good to eat. So is the peanut, which is not really a true nut. Some nuts contain oil which can be processed to use in cooking.

OCEANS About 70% of the Earth's surface is covered by water. The large areas of water which separate the continents are called oceans. The water is salty. Smaller areas of salt water are called seas.

There are five oceans. The biggest and deepest is the Pacific Ocean, which separates America and Asia. Next come the Atlantic Ocean and the Indian Ocean. The Antarctic and Arctic Oceans surround the poles. They are mostly covered with ice.

Around most coasts a shelf of land runs out under the sea. This is the *continental shelf*. It lies up to 5,090 feet, (180 meters) deep, and may stretch for hundreds of miles. Beyond the continental shelf, the ocean floor drops steeply. It flattens out again at a depth of about 11,976 feet, (3,650 meters). The bottom of the ocean is called the abyss. It is a flat plain, crossed by ridges, high mountains and deep trenches, like the surface of the land. The deepest trench is the Mariana Trench in the Pacific.

Life on Earth began in the oceans. Today, sea creatures range in size from enormous whales to tiny drifting animals, too small to be seen without a microscope. There are many plants, including huge seaweeds. Most of the animals and plants live in the upper layers of water or on the continental shelf. This is because sunlight, which the plants need to make food, cannot penetrate deeper than about 493 feet, (150 meters). But in the cold, dark depths of the oceans live strange deep-sea fishes that feed on each other.

The oceans are never still. The rise and fall of the tides, which takes place roughly every 12 hours, is caused by the gravitational pull of the Earth and the Moon. The surface of the water is moved by waves, caused by the wind. In a storm, waves can reach heights of 99 feet. The most destructive waves are called *tsunamis*, which is Japanese for 'great waves'. They are caused by undersea earthquakes and volcanoes. Below much of the surface of the oceans run currents of cold or warm water. Often these are rich in food, so fish (and fishermen) gather near them. Currents also affect

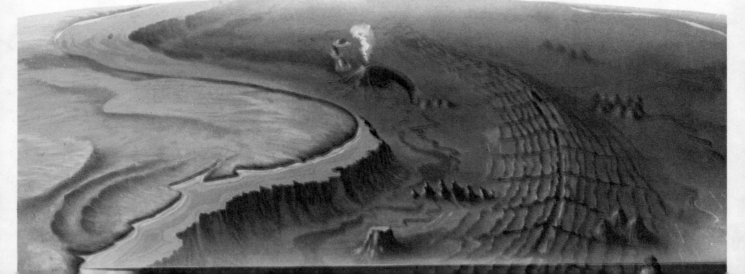

the climate of the land. For example, the warm Gulf Stream, a current which flows across the Atlantic Ocean from the Gulf of Mexico, keeps parts of western Europe mild and ice-free in winter.

Many people's lives depend on the oceans. Fish is an important human food. Beneath the ocean floor are deposits of oil, natural gas and other minerals. The tides have been harnessed to make electricity, and salt sea water can be turned into fresh water for drinking. Ships carry trade across most of the world's oceans and seas.

See also ATLANTIC OCEAN; PACIFIC OCEAN.

OCTOPUS The octopus lives on the sea bed. It is a mollusk but has no shell. It has a soft body and eight coiling arms, or tentacles, which it uses to pull itself along. Suckers lining its tentacles help it to catch crabs and other animals for food.

Octopuses can change color to match their surroundings. This hides them from enemies. But if they are frightened

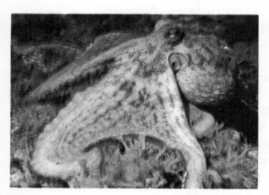

they have another escape. They squirt out an inky fluid which hides them as they swim away.

OIL is a greasy substance. Mineral oil is found in rocks under the ground. Another name for it is petroleum, which means 'rock-oil'.

The story of oil began millions of years ago, when tiny creatures and plants lived in the seas. When they died, they fell to the bottom and became covered with sand. After many years their bodies changed into drops of oil. The drops gradually joined together to form underground pools trapped in the rocks.

Oil men drill into the Earth's crust to find these pools. Then they pipe the

Ostriches live in dry sandy areas. They will eat almost anything, including sand to help their digestion.

Left: The octopus has a large brain and is quite intelligent.

Below: An oil derrick. A big oilfield has many of these towers, each drilling down to the oil below. Most oil is found in the Middle East and Russia. Recently, rich deposits have been found beneath the North Sea.

oil from the oil wells to factories called refineries. There the oil is split up, or refined. The pure oil can then be made into useful products. Its most important use is for fuel: gasoline for automobiles; kerosene for aircraft; and diesel oil for ships and trains. Oil is also used for heating; for greasing machinery to make it run smoothly; and to make paint and detergents.

OLYMPIC GAMES The ancient Greeks were very fond of running, wrestling and other sports. Their best athletes took part in the Olympic Games, which were named after Mount Olympus, the home of the Greek gods. The first prize was an olive wreath.

This idea was taken up again in 1896, when the first modern Olympics were held at Athens. The Games are now held every four years, each time in a different country, and many nations take part in the different sports. The winners receive medals of gold, silver and bronze.

OPERA An opera is a play in which the actors sing the words of the story. The first operas were written in Italy in the 1600s. The actors recited the story to music. Later, complete songs called arias were added.

Many operas tell sad stories, but some are gay and have happy endings. Famous composers of operas include Monteverdi, Mozart, Verdi, Puccini and Wagner.

OSTRICH The ostrich is the largest living bird. It has wings but cannot fly. Instead, it runs at great speed. Unlike other birds, the ostrich has only two toes.

Ostriches live in flocks on the dry African plains. They eat fruit, leaves and seeds and lay their eggs in the sand. In the past many ostriches were killed for their tail feathers, which were used to make fans, hats and to decorate clothing.

OTTER Otters belong to the weasel family. They are wonderful swimmers. They paddle the water with their webbed toes and use their strong tails as rudders. Their thick fur keeps out the wet and cold.

The river otter eats mostly fish and frogs. Its home is a hole in the river bank called a holt. The sea otter is larger and rarely comes on land. It eats crabs and shellfish.

OWL Owls are birds of prey. Their large eyes see well in the dark and they fly noiselessly on their broad wings. Hunting by night, they swoop down on small animals such as mice and voles, and carry them off in their strong claws. The owl rips flesh with its hooked beak but it cannot digest fur, skin and bones. It spits them out in the form of a pellet.

Some owls hoot, others let out an eerie screech.

OXYGEN is a gas in the air which all living things need. We take oxygen into our lungs when we breathe in. From our lungs, it is carried by the blood to every cell in our body. The oxygen is used to 'burn' our food and produce energy. Nothing can burn without oxygen. In fact burning is also called *oxidation*. In industry oxygen is used in the gas torches that cut and weld metals. It is also used in liquid form to burn the fuel in rockets.

OYSTER Oysters are mollusks that live on the sea bed. They are good to eat But they are even more highly valued for their pearls.

The oyster's soft body is protected by a hinged shell. If a grain of sand gets inside the shell, the oyster covers it with the same shiny material that lines the inside of its shell. This stops the sand irritating the oyster, and makes a pearl. That is why the shell lining is called mother-of-pearl.

See also MOLLUSK.

PACIFIC OCEAN The Pacific is the largest and deepest ocean in the world. It separates America from Asia. Steady winds blow across the ocean. They are called trade winds, because sailing ships used to rely on them. They blow from the northeast in the North Pacific and from the southeast in the South Pacific. The currents are affected by these winds. They circulate clockwise in the North Pacific and anti-clockwise in the south.

There are many beautiful tropical

islands in the Pacific. Most are the tips of underwater volcanoes, some crowned by coral atolls. The word *Pacific* means 'peaceful'. But the ocean is not always calm. Sometimes earthquakes shake the ocean floor and cause terrible waves called *tsunamis*.

PAINTING No one knows when people first began painting. The oldest known paintings were made by Stone Age men in caves thousands of years ago. They mostly show hunters chasing animals. The primitive men who drew them may have thought that the pictures would magically bring them good hunting.

Much later, people started to decorate their homes and temples with paintings. The Egyptians and Greeks loved painted vases and pottery. They also painted scenes of everyday life on the walls. Wall paintings made in wet plaster are known as *frescoes*. The Chinese invented a system of picture-writing and made beautiful pictures on silk and plaster.

During the Middle Ages in Europe most paintings were done for churches. So painters mostly painted stories from the Bible. Their pictures were formal and traditional. But then Italian painters, such as Giotto, Fra Angelico and Botticelli, began to paint in a more natural way. Their Bible characters looked like real people. In the 1400s Florence and Venice became great centers of the Renaissance—the 'rebirth' of learning. Florence was the home of three of the greatest artists of all time: Michelangelo, Leonardo da Vinci and Raphael.

During the Renaissance painters often

The female otter makes a den in a hole near the river bank. There she has her young. Baby otters do not have to be taught to swim, but sometimes need a push from their mother to get them into the water.

Rembrandt painted this picture of himself as an old man around 1660.

Raphael painted many pictures of the Madonna and Child. Much of his best work was done in Florence.

The 'Virgin of the Rocks' by Leonardo da Vinci is one of the finest Italian masterpieces.

At first Henri Matisse and his friends were called 'wild beasts' because people did not like their work. But by 1948 people had come to admire paintings like his 'Large Red Room'.

FAMOUS PAINTERS

Giotto, Italian (c. 1266–1337) – Religious frescoes showing 'real' people

Jan van Eyck, Flemish (c. 1387–1440) – Religious paintings and portraits in oils

Fra Angelico, Italian (c. 1387–1455) – Religious frescoes full of light and color

Masaccio, Italian (1401–c. 1428) – Studied perspective, light and anatomy

Sandro Botticelli, Italian (c. 1444–1510) – Painted religious and classical pictures

Leonardo da Vinci, Italian (1452–1519) – Sculptor, scientist and painter of human figures and landscapes

Albrecht Dürer, German (1471–1528) – Woodcuts and engravings

Michelangelo Buonarroti, Italian (1475–1564) – Also an architect and sculptor

Titian, Italian (c. 1477–1576) – Portraits and classical subjects

Raphael, Italian (1483–1520) – Religious frescoes

Pieter Breughel, Flemish (c. 1525–69) – Scenes of country life

El Greco, Spanish (c. 1541–1614) – Religious paintings

Peter Paul Rubens, Flemish (1577–1640) – Religious scenes, portraits and landscapes

Velazquez, Spanish (1599–1660) – Portraits

Rembrandt von Ryn, Dutch (1606–69) Religious subjects and portraits

Thomas Gainsborough, English (1727–88) – Portraits

Francisco Goya, Spanish (1746–1828) – Portraits

J. M. W. Turner, English (1775–1851) – Landscapes

John Constable, English (1776–1837) – Landscapes

Edouard Manet, French (1832–83) – Landscapes

Claude Monet, French (1840–1926) – Impressionist

Pierre Renoir, French (1841–1919) – Impressionist

Paul Cezanne, French (1839–1906) – Landscapes and 'still life' paintings

Paul Gauguin, French (1848–1903) – Landscapes and people, especially in the South Seas

Vincent van Gogh, Dutch (1853–90) – Landscapes

Henri Matisse, French (1869–1954)

Pablo Picasso, Spanish (1881–1973) – Painted in many styles, including 'Cubist'

Salvador Dali, Spanish (born 1904) – Surrealist painter

Above left: 'Le Repas' by Paul Gauguin shows a family in Tahiti sitting down to a meal. Gauguin left his home in France to paint the people of the South Sea islands.

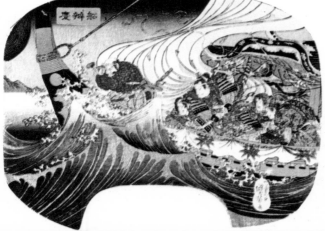

Left: In China and Japan artists painted on cloth, silk or board rather than on canvas. This print of a storm at sea is by the 19th-century Japanese painter Utagawa Kuniyoshi.

took scenes from history and Greek and Roman legends as their subjects. They also painted portraits of people from life, and realistic scenes from nature. Rubens, a Flemish painter, was the first great master of landscape painting. Dutch and Flemish painters were also fond of showing amusing scenes of country life.

Many painters worked for a rich patron, or master. Usually he was a nobleman or a rich merchant. Patrons liked to have their portraits painted. Rembrandt, a Dutch painter of the 1600s painted hundreds of portraits, including a number of himself.

During the 1700s many painters worked for fashionable society. They painted people in family groups, often against a background of a garden or a fine house. In England, Reynolds and Gainsborough were skilled portrait painters. Later, Constable painted beautiful landscapes. But styles of painting began to change once again as artists experimented with new ideas. An important change was called Impressionism. Impressionist painters loved to paint light and shadow, and ignore the details, which could be captured perfectly in a photograph. Painters tried to show things in a painting which a photograph could not show. They tried to express feelings and ideas. By the early 1900s some were making pictures as designs and shapes, rather than as copies of objects. This is called *abstract* painting. The greatest modern painter was Picasso.

PANAMA CANAL The Panama Canal is at the narrowest part of Panama, the Central American country that connects North and South America. This 51-mile (82 kilometer) waterway has brough the Atlantic and Pacific coastlines of the United States

The African gray parrot can imitate almost any sound. Male birds make the best talkers.

The first live panda was not seen outside China until 1937. Little is known of their habits in the wild, and pandas are difficult to breed in zoos.

closer by thousands of miles, and has changed the trade routes of the world. The United States began to build the Canal in 1904, under terms of an agreement which allowed the U.S. to occupy and control a zone 10 miles (16 kilometers) wide across the isthmus (a narrow strip of land). The first ship crossed the Panama Canal on August 15, 1914. In 1978 Panama and the U.S. signed a new treaty giving Panama control of the canal by 2,000.

PANDA One of the world's rarest animals is the giant panda. It looks like a furry black and white bear. But the panda is not really a bear at all.

Pandas live in bamboo forests in the mountains of China. They eat mostly bamboo shoots and leaves. Pandas do not breed easily in captivity, so few have been seen in zoos outside China.

A small cat-like animal, called the red panda, lives in the Himalaya Mountains.

PAPER Many years ago people used to write on clay tablets and parchment. Parchment was made from animal skins. The ancient Egyptians made a writing material called papyrus, from a kind of reed. Our word *paper* comes from 'papyrus'. Until recently grass plants were still used to make paper. But now we use wood fibers.

PARASITE A parasite lives in or on some larger living thing and feeds on it. It is an uninvited guest. And the animal or plant on which it lives is called a host.

Some animal parasites, such as tapeworms, live in the stomachs of their hosts. Others, such as fleas and lice, cling to the skin of their hosts and suck their blood.

Parasites often harm their hosts by taking too much food, or by causing diseases. Some mosquitoes, not only suck blood from their victims but infect them with malaria.

PARROT A pet parrot may live up to 50 years and learn to 'talk'. Actually, the bird only imitates sounds. It cannot understand the words it says.

In the wild, parrots live in forests in Australia and other warm countries.

They flock together high in the trees. The different kinds include the parakeet, the cockatoo and the macaw. They all eat fruit, buds and nuts.

PEACOCK Anyone who has seen a peacock displaying his feathers knows why we say 'As proud as a peacock'. The male bird has a long train of colorful feathers. When raised, they spread out like a quivering fan.

The peacock struts about, showing off in front of the female. She is called a peahen, and looks dull compared with the male. Peacocks are often kept in parks and zoos. They have a harsh, screaming call.

PENGUIN Penguins are sea birds that live on coasts around the Antarctic.

Unable to fly, penguins use their wings as paddles and are excellent swimmers. They have webbed feet and streamlined bodies, with a layer of thick fat to keep out the cold. On land, penguins can only waddle clumsily. Often they find it easier to slide on their stomachs.

PENS AND PENCILS A pen is a writing tool that uses ink. In ancient times swamp reeds were used for pens. Early in the 7th century, people began to use goose quills (quills are the hollow parts of feathers). The word *pen* comes from *penna,* the Latin word for pen. When people sharpened their quills, they used small *penknives.* The first fountain pen, which had a barrel to hold ink and a cap to protect the point, was made in the United States in 1884. Ball-point pens were invented in South America in 1943.

Pencils are sticks of *graphite,* a soft, black form of carbon, surrounded by wood—which keeps the user's fingers from getting soiled.

PEOPLES OF THE WORLD There are more than 4 billion people in the world. A hundred years ago there were only about 1.2 billion. All these people live in more than 145 countries and speak almost 2800 different languages. There are many differences in the color of skin, eyes and hair, and in the shape of faces. And people have different customs, beliefs and ways of life.

No two people are exactly alike. But scientists arrange the peoples of the world into three main groups. People with white skins are called *Caucasoids*; people with yellow skins are called *Mongoloids*; and people with black skins are called *Negroids.*

The Caucasoids include most of the people living in Europe, America, India and Australia – more than half the world's population. Mongoloid peoples include the Chinese, Japanese, American Indians and Eskimos. Negroid peoples include the Negroes of Africa and some of the people of the Pacific islands.

People have occupied every part of the world except some of the very coldest, driest and steepest places. They have mixed together and intermarried. So people from one or more of the three groups now live in practically every country in the world.

PIG The pig is a very useful, intelligent animal. Its grunt is about the only part of it we do not use. We eat its meat as pork, ham, bacon and sausage; its skin can be made into leather; and its bristles go into brushes. Male pigs are called *boars*, and females *sows.*

The peacock's train spreads like a fan.

Emperor penguins with a chick.

The modern pig is bred for its meat.

Right: Negroid people have dark skins.

Below right: Mongoloid people have bronze skins and straight hair.

Below: Caucasoid people have pale skins, and curly or straight hair.

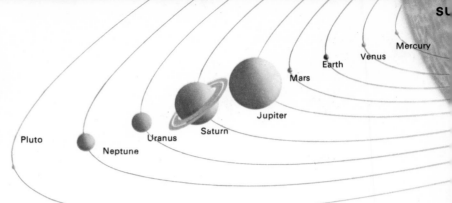

PIONEERS The first settlements in America were on the Atlantic Ocean. To the west was the frontier and, right from the start, people kept pushing westward: hunters, trappers, miners, farmers, soldiers, surveyors.

The first highways in America were rivers. Settlers paddled and poled up side rivers into the wilderness, carrying their household goods. Paths cut through forests were called *traces*.

In the 1840s and 1850s thousands of pioneers made the long trek west on the Overland Trail to Oregon and California. They traveled in groups of 30 or more covered wagons. On fine days a wagon train traveled 20 miles (32 kilometers).

Pioneers who settled in wooded areas would build houses out of logs. On the Great Plains, homes were made of deeply rooted grass, or *sod*.

Life was hard on the frontier so families had lots of children to help them work and carve a future out of the wilderness.

See also AMERICAN COLONIES.

PIRATE Until about 150 years ago sea voyagers had more to fear than sudden storms. They faced the added danger of pirates. These fierce bands of sea-robbers sailed the seas in fast, well-armed ships. When they saw a merchant ship, they chased and captured it. They stole its cargo and robbed the passengers. Sometimes they would kidnap rich people and hold them captive until a large 'ransom' of money was paid.

Pirates had a special black flag, the skull and crossbones or 'Jolly Roger'. Sometimes they pretended to sail a harmless merchant ship. Then, when they were ready to attack, they would fly the dreaded black flag.

The Barbary pirates lived on the coast of North Africa. They captured Christians and sold them as slaves. In the 1700s many pirate bands sailed the Caribbean Sea. They attacked ships carrying gold from South America to Spain.

As a result, pirates became very rich. But most were caught and hanged, and their island hideouts destroyed. By the 1800s ships could sail most seas without fear of a pirate raid.

PLANET Most stars appear to be fixed in the same place in the heavens. But some appear to wander in the night sky. Ancient peoples called these stars planets, meaning 'wanderers'. We know now that the planets are not stars at all. They are small bodies which circle around the Sun. Unlike stars, planets do not produce their own light. They shine because they reflect the Sun's light. There are nine planets circling the Sun: Mercury (the planet nearest the Sun), Venus, Earth, Mars, Jupiter, Saturn, Uranus, Neptune and Pluto. Astronomers believe there may be other planets beyond Pluto which have yet to be discovered. Jupiter is the largest planet, over 1000 times larger than the Earth. Mercury and Pluto are the smallest planets. But even smaller are the minor planets or asteroids, a collection of rocks that circles the Sun between Mars and Jupiter. The largest is 497 miles, (800 kilometers) wide.

The planets can be divided into two groups, *gaseous* and *rocky*. The Earth is the biggest of the rocky planets, which also include Mercury, Venus, Mars and Pluto. Pictures taken by spacecraft have shown what the first three planets are like. They have a rough surface covered with great pits, or craters, and strewn with rocks. We know little about Pluto because it is so far away. Unlike the Earth, Mercury has no atmosphere, or air, and Mars has only a little. But Venus has an atmosphere so thick and full of clouds that we cannot see through them.

The other planets are made up mainly of gases. The giant planet Jupiter, for example, contains mostly hydrogen. Much of it is in very cold liquid form. The other gaseous planets are probably similar. Saturn is particularly interesting because it is surrounded by rings of gas and dust.

This diagram shows the order of the nine planets in the solar system and their distances from the Sun. Jupiter and Saturn are by far the largest. Closest to the Earth are Venus and Mars.

The green leaves of plants contain chlorophyll. This, and energy from the Sun, makes photosynthesis possible. The plants take in carbon dioxide from the air and water from the soil to make sugars, and in turn give off oxygen.

Carbon dioxide

Sun

Oxygen

Water

The Earth is the only planet known on which life can exist. Mercury and Venus are too hot for life to exist. And the outer planets are too cold. It is just possible that some kind of life could exist on Mars. But there are other planets in the universe, circling around other suns. Perhaps life exists on them.

PLANT There are two main groups, or 'kingdoms' of living things on the Earth: the animals and the plants. Usually it is easy to tell the difference. Unlike most animals, most plants cannot move around. Plants have no nervous system. And green plants can make food from chemicals in the soil and air.

Plants do not only grow in the soil. They grow in the sea, in fresh water, in rocks, and even in the air. Some plants are so tiny they can be seen only through a microscope. Others grow to be huge trees or long seaweeds, larger than any animal. Plants also live longer than animals. Some trees are thousands of years old.

Most plants are green. The green color is caused by a substance called *chlorophyll*. This is used by the plant to make its food. The way it does this is called *photosynthesis*. The plant takes in water through its roots and carbon dioxide gas from the air through its leaves. Chlorophyll rearranges the ingredients of water and carbon dioxide to produce sugar and oxygen. But it can only do this in sunlight. So plants only make food during the day. The sugar made by photosynthesis is the 'fuel' the plant needs to grow. The unwanted oxygen is released through the plant's leaves. So, as it feeds, the plant gives back oxygen to the air. This oxygen is breathed in by animals. If the plants did not supply it, all the oxygen in the air would soon be used up.

Leaves and roots can tell us a lot about plants. Among flowering plants there are two sorts of leaves. *Monocotyledons*, such as lilies, bluebells, daffodils and grasses, have long straight leaves. Inside the leaf, veins act as breathing tubes. In the monocotyledons most of the veins run in the same direction. *Dicotyledons*, such as peas, roses and broad-leaved trees, have leaves in which the veins criss-cross to form a delicate network. When the leaf dies, you can sometimes see this network in the leaf 'skeleton'. Because broad leaves lose moisture quickly, plants in dry regions have thin, spiny leaves. The leaves of a cactus are no more than spines. These protect the thick, juicy stem from animals seeking water. And some plants, such as peas, use certain leaves as tendrils to help them climb. A small group of plants are carnivorous (flesh-eating); they use their leaves as traps to catch insects.

The plant kingdom includes several groups. The simplest plants of all are algae. Some algae are simply a single cell, which reproduces itself by splitting in two. Others, including seaweed, are much bigger. Fungi are plants which have no chlorophyll, so they are not green and cannot make their own food. Instead they feed on rotting or dead matter, from other plants or animals. Mosses and liverworts are another group. They live on land. But, like fungi, they have no proper roots, and no flowers. Ferns are more advanced. They have stems, leaves and roots. But they cannot make flowers and seeds.

Seed-bearing plants produce male and female cells. The cells join to form a fertile seed. When the seed is released, it grows into a new plant. Conifers are part of a group of plants that protect their seeds inside hard cones. But most seed-bearing plants have flowers, and protect their seeds inside cases called fruits.

See also CACTUS; FERN; GRASS; LICHEN; FUNGUS; MOSS; SEAWEED; TREE.

The plant kingdom is divided into groups: the Angiosperms or flowering plants (1), which include dicotyledons (such as broad-leaved trees and most flowers) and monocotyledons (such as lilies and grasses); Gymnosperms (2) (including conifers); ferns (3); mosses (4); fungi (5); and algae (6).

PLASTICS are manmade materials that have a wide variety of uses. They can be made into furniture and car bodies, buckets and bags, shoes and clothing, cutlery and dishware. There are many different kinds of plastics, all of which can be shaped easily. Many are shaped by blowing, squirting or pressing into molds. One type of plastic melts when it is heated. Another type is heat-proof.

Important plastics include nylon, polyethylene, PVC and polystyrene. All are made with chemicals obtained from oil. Some plastics are made from wood.

Nylon is a hard plastic. But it can also be drawn out into very fine threads, or fibers. These fibers are used to weave such things as stockings and lingerie. Polyethylene is a soft plastic used to make products that will bend. It is made from a gas called ethylene. 'Poly' means many, thus 'polyethylene' means that the basic unit, or molecule, of the plastic is made up of many units of ethylene joined together. Most other plastics are made up in this way.

PLAYS, or *dramas,* as we know them were first performed in ancient Greece. They were written as poetry, and poets competed against one another to win a prize for the best play. Often they wrote *tragedies*; plays with serious stories and often sad endings. But they also wrote *comedies*: plays with happy endings. The plays were performed by actors in theaters built so well that every member of the audience could hear. And often as many as 2000 people attended.

The Roman playwrights (writers of plays) copied many of the Greek ideas. But they had even stricter rules about how a play should be written and acted.

The earliest plays of modern times were acted stories from the Bible. They were called *miracle* and *mystery* plays. The craft guilds (such as the silversmiths) would put on a play each year. At first, actors performed in church, although later the story was acted out in the courtyard of an inn, or on carts wheeled through the streets. Later, people performed *morality* plays, in which the hero (main character) met a number of good and bad characters. The play contained a moral or lesson.

Some of the first indoor theaters were built in England in the 1500s. Companies of actors performed the plays of Shakespeare, Marlowe and Jonson. Often the playwright would act a part in his own play. There was little scenery, and actors wore the clothes of their own day. Boys took women's parts, as women were not allowed to be actors. Plays were also being written in France and Spain at this time.

Early American theater was heavily influenced by English drama and the Puritan movement. In the mid 1700s, Williamsburg Virginia, with its new playhouse and troupe of actors was the country's theater capital. The first important American play, *The Contrast,* was written by Royall Tyler. Other important plays included: *Fashion; or Life in New York;* and *Uncle Tom's Cabin.*

During the late ninteenth and early 20th centuries; the seat of American theater moved to New York. New York with its famed "theater row", Broadway, is still the most important city for American drama.

A costume design for a masque. This was a play with music and dances, popular at court in the early 1600s.

FAMOUS PLAYWRIGHTS

Aeschylus, Greek (*c.* 525–456 BC)
Sophocles, Greek (496–406 BC)
Euripedes, Greek (480–406 BC)
Aristophanes, Greek (*c.* 450–406 BC)
Terence, Roman (*c.* 195–159 BC)
Christopher Marlowe, English (1564–93)
William Shakespeare, English (1564–1616)
Ben Jonson, English (1572–1637)
Moliere, French (1622–73)
Jean Baptiste Racine, French (1639–99)
William Congreve, English (1670–1729)
Oliver Goldsmith, Anglo-Irish (1730–74)
Richard Brinsley Sheridan, Irish (1751–1816)
Henrik Ibsen, Norwegian (1828–1906)
August Strindberg, Swedish (1849–1912)
Oscar Wilde, Irish (1856–1900)
George Bernard Shaw, Irish (1856–1950)
Anton Chekhov, Russian (1860–1904)
Luigi Pirandello, Italian (1867–1936)
Eugene O'Neill, American (188–1953)
Jean Cocteau, French (1889–1963)
Bertolt Brecht, German (1898–1956)
Samuel Beckett, Irish (born 1906)
Tennessee Williams, American (born 1911)
Eugene Ionesco, French (born 1912)
Edward Albee, American (born 1928)
Harold Pinter, English (born 1930)

William Shakespeare. This is one of several portraits of him.

Sarah Bernhardt (1844–1932) was a French actress.

FAMOUS POETS

Homer, Greek (*c.* 9th century BC) – *The Iliad, The Odyssey*
Virgil, Roman (65–8 BC) – *The Aeneid*
Dante Alighieri, Italian (1265–1321) – *Divina Commedia*
Geoffrey Chaucer, English (*c.* 1340–1400) – *Canterbury Tales*
Pierre de Ronsard, French (1524–1585) – *Odes*
William Shakespeare, English (1564–1616) – Sonnets
John Donne, English (1572–1631) – Songs and Sonnets
John Milton, English (1608–74) – *Paradise Lost*
Jean de la Fontaine, French (1621–95) – *Fables*
Johann von Goethe, German (1749–1832) – *Faust*
William Blake, English (1757–1827) – *Songs of Innocence and Experience*
Robert Burns, Scottish (1759–1824) – *The Jolly Beggars, The Two Dogs*
William Wordsworth, English (1770–1850) – Lyrical Ballads, *The Prelude*
Samuel Taylor Coleridge, English (1772–1834) – *The Ancient Mariner*
George Byron, English (1788–1824) – *Don Juan*
Percy Bysshe Shelley, English (1792–1822) – *The Skylark, Adonais*
John Keats, English (1795–1821) – Odes
Victor Hugo, French (1802–1885) – Odes
Alfred Tennyson, English (1809–1892) – *In Memoriam, Morte d'Arthur*
W. B. Yeats, Irish (1865–1939) – Poems, 1895
Robert Frost, American (1874–1963) – Collected Poems, 1930
Rainer Maria Rilke, German (1875–1926) – Lyrics
T. S. Eliot, American (1888–1965) – *The Waste Land*
Dylan Thomas, Welsh (1914–1953) – Collected Poems, 1934–52 ·
Robert Lowell, American (born 1917) – *Lord Weary's Castle*

POETRY The oldest stories we know were first told as poetry. In a poem the words are often arranged to a musical beat or rhythm. This makes them easy to remember. So before people could record stories by writing them down, they sang them or 'recited' them as poems. Many of these early poems told of exciting battles or of wars between the gods. Some were remembered and told for many generations, and in time they were written down. The greatest of the ancient 'epic' poems, full of the deeds of brave heroes, are the *Iliad* and *Odyssey* of Homer, a Greek, and the *Aeneid* of the Roman poet Virgil.

A poem is even easier to remember if it is arranged in a pattern which rhymes. You can see this in the first two lines of *Humpty Dumpty*:

Humpty Dumpty sat on a *wall*
Humpty Dumpty had a great *fall*.

This 'nursery rhyme' is easy for even small children to remember. Nursery rhymes are often very old, and were passed down from parents to children, long before they were written in books.

There are different styles and forms of poetry. The lyric is usually a short description of the poet's own thoughts and feelings. The sonnet is fourteen

Geoffrey Chaucer was the first great English poet. He was also a civil servant and his jobs included collecting taxes on wool.

William Wordsworth (below) wrote poetry which described ordinary life in everyday language. This was the beginning of the Romantic Movement.

lines with a set rhyme scheme. An elegy is a sad poem, often about a dead friend, normally written in a regular rhythm, or 'meter.'

Poetry which is written in a meter is known as verse. But the rhythm does not have to be regular all the time. This would be dull. Blank verse has a rhythm, but it does not rhyme. Shakespeare used blank verse in his plays. Modern poets often prefer free verse, which does not have rhyme or a strict rhythm.

POISON A poison is a substance which attacks the body, and can cause sickness or death. Some poisons are dangerous when swallowed. Others damage the lungs, the skin, and the nervous system. Chemicals, drugs, gases, acids and bad food can all be poisonous.

Some medicines are poisonous if used wrongly. So it is important to follow the directions carefully when taking medicine. Poisons used to kill pests should be kept in a safe place.

Primitive tribes used poisoned arrows for hunting. Later poison gas was used in war. Poisonous snakes inject *venom* into their prey to kill it. There are poisonous plants too.

POLICE Our laws are the rules by which we all live. The police make sure the laws are kept. The first real police force was developed by Sir Robert Peel in London in 1829. By 1844, a similar system was developed in New York City, and was soon adopted by other cities. American policemen were nicknamed "cops" or "coppers." Some people believe the term comes from the eight-pointed copper star once worn by New York policemen; others think the name was composed from the first letters of the words "constable on patrol."

Today every country in the world has police. The main job of the police is to try to prevent crimes.

The police help people in many ways. They protect our freedom and property. The police forces of many countries work together through an organization called Interpol. But in some parts of the world there are secret police who arrest people who criticize the government.

POLLUTION In a big city, smoke from chimneys and fumes from cars make the air dirty and cause smog, a mixture of smoke and fog. The dirt makes life unpleasant for people and damages their health.

Sewage, waste from factories and oil from tankers are poured into rivers and oceans. The poisons they contain spoil beaches and kill fish and birds. Chemicals used to kill insect pests and weeds can also build up in the soil and harm animals. These are all forms of pollution.

Every day we throw away enormous amounts of garbage. Wood and paper decay. But plastic may never decay, so getting rid of it is a problem. Nuclear power stations produce radioactive waste, which is so poisonous it has to be sealed up and buried for hundreds of years.

Pollution can threaten our health, and even make it impossible for plants and animals to live. Scientists are trying to find ways of preventing pollution. We can all help by taking greater care of the world around us.

See also AIR POLLUTION; CONSERVATION.

POND LIFE Even a small pond is home to a remarkable number of animals and plants. Around the water's edge grow rushes and flowers. Birds nest among the tall reeds; and the moorhen and coot make their nests in the shallows.

Duckweed is a water plant which floats on the surface. Other pond weeds grow underwater, putting down roots into the mud. The plants provide food and shelter for pond animals and also give out oxygen which they need for breathing.

Tiny water animals include the amoeba and hydra. They can be seen best under a microscope. Such creatures, and the water fleas, or daphnia, are food for fish.

The surface of the water forms a kind of skin. On this skin lives an insect called the pond-skater. It skims across the surface without breaking the skin. The water boatman is a beetle that rows itself about upside down, using its long back legs as oars. It can dive to the bottom, but it must come to the surface for air. So must the fierce water beetle, and the water spider, which carries bubbles of air down to its underwater nest.

Some pond insects spend only part of their lives in the water. The larva or nymph of the dragonfly breathes through gills until it is ready to climb out of the water and emerge as an adult dragonfly. The mayfly, alder fly and caddis fly also spend part of their lives underwater. The caddis fly larva builds itself a tub-like home made of tiny pebbles or bits of plant stuck together.

Other pond creatures include water snails, leeches, freshwater shrimps, mussels, worms, crayfish and small fish such as sticklebacks. Otters, water voles and water shrews are mammals which can dive and swim well. But they, too, must come to the surface to breathe.

Amphibians, such as frogs, toads and newts, can live quite happily away from water. But they return to the pond to lay their eggs. In spring, frogs' spawn can be seen floating like a mass of jelly in the water. The eggs hatch into tadpoles which swim around in the pond until they have grown legs and developed into frogs.

A small pond can support a number of animals. The tall reedmace shelters insects such as the damselfly. Frogs and newts visit the pond in spring to breed. Their spawn hatches into tadpoles. Birds such as the great crested grebe and coot nest in the reeds. On the surface are small creatures such as pond skaters and backswimmers, while below are water scorpions and caddis worms. The water spider carries air bubbles down to its nest. The fierce diving beetle will even attack small fish like the stickleback.

See also DRAGONFLY; FROG AND TOAD; LEECH; MOSQUITO; NEWT; OTTER.

POPE The Pope is the head of the Roman Catholic Church and bishop of Rome. The word *pope* means 'father'. St Peter was the first bishop of Rome, and most popes have lived in Rome. But at times there have been two popes, each supported by different rulers. And for a long time the popes themselves were powerful rulers, with their own lands.

Today the Pope lives in the Vatican, which is a tiny independent state in Rome. His chief advisers are the cardinals. It is they who elect a new pope.

PORCUPINE Porcupines are rodents. They live in forests and eat twigs, leaves and fruit. The porcupines of Africa and Asia live on the ground, but the American porcupines are good climbers. The porcupine's quills are good protection against enemies.

POST OFFICE In early times messages were carried by runners or by riders on horseback. Fresh messengers and horses waited at 'posts', usually inns, along the road. Later, post coaches were used.

In the United States, the first postal service was begun in 1639 when Richard Fairbanks of Boston was authorized to receive and then distribute mail which arrived from abroad. He charged 1 penny per piece. In 1775 Ben Franklin was appointed head of the American postal system. He was largely responsible for the establishment of our postal system.

This was how the post office began. Today we can send letters, parcels and telegrams almost anywhere in the world. Telephone calls can be sent through undersea cables and bounced off space satellites.

Every day millions of letters are mailed. They have to be collected, sorted and delivered. Sorting is done either by hand or by machines.

See also STAMPS.

POTATO Potatoes are important food plants. The part you eat is a *tuber*. This is not a root, but a swollen underground stem, in which the plant stores food. New plants grow from the 'eyes' in the tubers.

The potato plant grows wild in the Andes Mountains of South America. Explorers brought potatoes to Europe for the first time in the 1500s. Soon they became an important crop.

PREHISTORIC ANIMALS Life on Earth has existed for millions of years. The animals we know today are descended from animals which died out long ago. Life is always changing, and we describe these changes as 'evolution'. Many of the animals which lived millions of years ago looked very different from those of today. But they were well-suited for the conditions they lived in. Those animals which were able to change, as conditions changed, survived. Animals which could not change died out.

By 'prehistory' we mean the time before written records were kept by human beings. People have been on Earth for only a short time, compared with the prehistoric animals that lived before them. We know about these early animals from their fossils. Fossils are remains, such as shells and bones, that have been preserved in the rocks, and become like rocks themselves.

The first animals appeared in the sea more than 700 million years ago. They may have been shaped as tiny blobs of jelly. Later some kinds developed protective shells. One common group, called trilobites, looked like woodlice. They had legs and feelers, and crawled over the sea bed looking for food. There were also animals like shellfish and squids. All were invertebrates – that is, they had no backbones.

The first vertebrate animals (animals with backbones) were fishes. Fishes first appeared about 450 million years ago. The first fishes were strange, ugly creatures with armored bodies and heads. The armor protected them from the great sea scorpions that preyed on them.

The seas were now full of life, but the land was almost empty. There were plants on the land, and insect-like creatures but no vertebrates. Then, about 400 million years ago, some fishes crawled out of the water on to the land. They slowly developed legs instead of fins, and

Mailboxes from (above) USA and Victorian Britain; (below) France and Denmark.

A potato plant, showing the underground tubers.

Old World porcupines live in Africa, Asia and parts of Europe. The long quills are a good defence.

lungs through which they could breathe. They were the first amphibians. Some of the early amphibians were much bigger than the amphibians of today, such as frogs and toads. But like them, these amphibians had to return to the water to breed. They were not true land animals.

The next step came with the appearance of reptiles. Unlike the amphibians, the reptiles did not have to lay their eggs in water. Instead, they laid eggs with hard shells, inside which the baby reptiles developed until they were ready to hatch and look after themselves.

About 200 million years ago some reptiles gave rise to dinosaurs. For millions of years dinosaurs were the most important animals on the land surface of the Earth. Some, such as *Tyrannosaurus rex*, were large and fierce, hunting other dinosaurs which browsed on plant food. The large plant-eating dinosaurs, such as *Brachiosaurus* and *Diplodocus*, were the largest land animals which have ever lived.

The first mammals were small, insect-eating animals. For a long time they remained unimportant, while the dinosaurs ruled supreme. But when the dinosaurs died out, the little mammals took over.

No one is sure why the dinosaurs became extinct. Most people think it was because they were cold-blooded and could not adapt when the climate grew cooler. But other people think that they were warm-blooded and must have died out for another reason.

The mammals had larger brains than the reptiles. They were warm-blooded and had fur to keep out the cold. They gave birth to live young and fed them on milk. Many different kinds of mammals developed. There were giant deer, giant sloths and giant armadillos. These animals are now extinct. So, too, are the woolly mammoth, the woolly rhinoceros and the fierce saber-toothed cat. Many mammals became extinct during the Ice Ages, when they were killed by a new enemy — man the hunter.

People evolved from prehistoric apes. Some apes began walking on two legs. This left their hands free to use tools and weapons. From these primitive man-like apes, the first human beings developed.

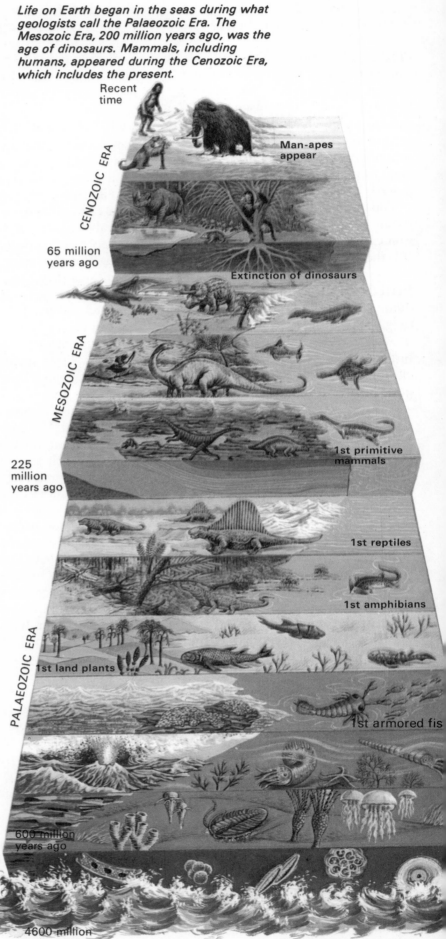

Life on Earth began in the seas during what geologists call the Palaeozoic Era. The Mesozoic Era, 200 million years ago, was the age of dinosaurs. Mammals, including humans, appeared during the Cenozoic Era, which includes the present.

Recent time

CENOZOIC ERA

Man-apes appear

65 million years ago

Extinction of dinosaurs

MESOZOIC ERA

1st primitive mammals

225 million years ago

1st reptiles

1st amphibians

PALAEOZOIC ERA

1st land plants

1st armored fis

600 million years ago

4600 million years ago

PRE-CAMBRIAN TIME

See also CAVE MEN; DINOSAUR; EVOLUTION; FOSSIL; ICE AGE; MAMMOTH.

PRESIDENCY OF THE UNITED STATES

When the Founding Fathers wrote the Constitution, they planned the presidency to be an office of great honor and dignity but little real power. In the two centuries since America had its first president, the powers and responsibilites of the president have grown considerably. Still, the Constitution provides Congress with checks against any president who may try to assume too much authority.

An example of the increased load of responsibilities may be seen if one considers how many people are needed to assist the president in his duties: George Washington, the first president, had as staff one secretary, one or two clerks, and household servants who acted as messengers.

The Presidents of the United States
George Washington 1789-97
John Adams 1797-1801
Thomas Jefferson 1801-09
James Madison 1809-17
James Monroe 1817-25
John Quincy Adams 1825-29
Andrew Jackson 1829-37
Martin Van Buren 1837-41
William Henry Harrison 1841 (died in office)
John Tyler 1841-45
James K. Polk 1845-49
Zachary Taylor 1849-50 (died in office)
Millard Fillmore 1850-53
Franklin Pierce 1853-57
James Buchanan 1857-61
Abraham Lincoln 1861-65 (assassinated)
Andrew Johnson 1865-69
Ulysses S. Grant 1869-77
Rutherford B. Hayes 1877-91
James A. Garfield 1881 (assassinated)
Chester Alan Arthur 1881-85
Grover Cleveland 1885-89, 1893-97
Benjamin Harrison 1889-93
William McKinley 1897-1901 (assassinated)
Theodore Roosevelt 1901-09
William Howard Taft 1909-13
Woodrow Wilson 1913-21
Warren G. Harding 1921-23 (died in office)
Calvin Coolidge 1923-29
Herbert Hoover 1929-33
Franklin D. Roosevelt 1933-45 (died in office)
Harry S. Truman 1945-53
Dwight D. Eisenhower 1953-61
John F. Kennedy 1961-63 (assassinated)
Lyndon Baines Johnson 1963-69
Richard M. Nixon 1969-74 (resigned)
Gerald R. Ford 1974-77
James Earl Carter, Jr. 1977-

Today the president requires the assistance of about 500 people, called the White House Office Staff.

As the head of the executive branch of the government, the president is responsible for carrying out the laws of Congress. He has the power to appoint important officials, such as ambassadors, federal judges, heads of government agencies, and U.S. attornies. The president may recommend legislation and has the power to veto any bill passed by Congress. He is also the country's chief diplomat, receiving ambassadors and representatives of foreign countries. The president is the commander-in-chief of the armed forces, and in some emergencies can act without Congressional consent.

PRINTING

Every day millions of words and pictures are printed to make books, magazines and newspapers. Before the 1400s, the usual way of producing books was to copy them by hand, so they were rare and expensive. About 1450, Johannes Gutenberg made copies of the Bible on a printing press. The printing press was one of Man's most important inventions, for it enabled many books to be produced in a short time.

Gutenberg's method of printing was to build up his words from separate pieces of *type*, ink the type then press paper against it. Printing by inking metal type (called *letterpress*) is still widely used for newspapers, books and magazines. But many books are now printed by a photographic process (called *lithography*). The words are made up on a piece of film, and flat printing plates are made from the film. The plates are treated so that they pick up the ink only where the words are.

Ink roller

Letterpress

Lithography

The two basic printing processes are letterpress and lithography.

PYRAMID

The ancient Egyptians buried their pharaohs (kings) in pyramids. These were stone hills, each with four triangular sides meeting at the pointed top. It took many years to build a pyramid. Thousands of people dragged the huge stones slowly into place. Inside was a tomb where the mummy (preserved body) of the pharaoh was laid, surrounded by treasure. Some pyramids are made of more than two million blocks of stone.

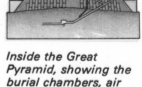

Inside the Great Pyramid, showing the burial chambers, air shafts and gallery.

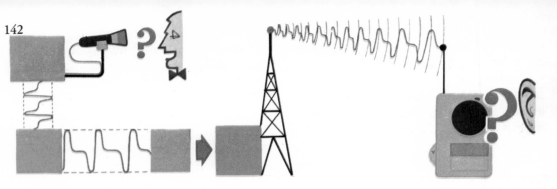

How radios work. Sounds are changed into electric currents, and carried by radio waves broadcast from a transmitter. The receiver separates the sound signals from the 'carrier' waves, and makes them stronger.

The rabbit (below) and hare (above) have many enemies. They are always alert and ready to run from danger.

The raccoon often dabbles its food in water before eating, as if washing it.

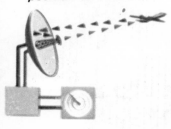

A radar station sends out radio signals. These are reflected back from an aircraft and show its position on a screen.

RABBITS AND HARES
Rabbits make good pets. They are also kept in captivity for their fur and meat. But wild rabbits damage crops and pastures, nibbling plants down to the roots with their large front teeth. To the farmer the rabbit is a pest.

Rabbits are burrowing animals, and live in colonies called warrens. Rabbits breed rapidly. There were none in Australia until the 1850s. Then a few English rabbits were set free. Soon there were rabbits everywhere.

Hares look like rabbits. But they are bigger, with longer ears and legs. Hares are swift runners. Unlike rabbits, they live alone, and do not dig burrows. Instead, they live in hollows in the ground called forms. In spring, male hares dash wildly about, leap in the air and fight one another with their front legs. From this comes the expression 'as mad as a hare'.

RACCOON
The inquisitive raccoon looks as if it is wearing a black face mask. It is an intelligent animal, which swims and climbs trees. Raccoons can use their front paws like hands. They eat plant food, fish and small mammals.

The North American raccoon lives mainly in the forest. But it often wanders into towns and raids trash cans. The crab-eating raccoon of South America prefers the seashore and river banks.

RADAR
means 'radio direction and ranging'. It is a device that can 'see' far away objects by bouncing radio waves off them. The waves travel like echoes back to the radar. They are picked up by the radar antennae and show up as small dots of light on a screen, rather like a television screen. From the position of the dot, the direction and range (distance away) of the object can be worked out. The radio waves are sent out from a rotating aerial or scanner. These scanners can be seen on ships' masts and at airports. Radar is important to ships and planes because it can pick up objects at far greater distances than the eye can see.

RADIO
is a means of sending signals over long distances. By means of radio we can listen to people talking on the other side of the world, and even astronauts on the moon. The Italian Guglielmo Marconi did most to make radio possible in the 1890s. But large-scale broadcasting did not begin until the 1920s.

The radio is sometimes called a 'wireless' because wires are not needed to carry the messages. Radio depends on radio waves. These invisible waves travel as fast as light waves. And they can travel in space as well as in the air. Radio works because radio waves can be made to carry signals which represent sound. In a radio broadcasting studio sounds go into a microphone, where they are changed to electrical signals. These signals are combined with a radio 'carrier' wave, which is transmitted by a tall aerial. The aerial of a radio receiver picks up the carrier wave. Circuits in the receiver remove the carrier wave and leave only the sound electrical signals. These are fed to a loudspeaker. This then gives out the same sounds as went into the studio microphone.

See also MARCONI, G.

RADIOACTIVITY
The atoms of most chemical elements do not change. An atom of gold always remains an atom of gold. But the atoms of some elements do change. They are unstable and emit (give out) atomic particles or radiation. We call this process radioactivity, and we call these elements radioactive. Uranium and radium are well-known radioactive elements.

See also ATOM.

RAILWAYS Two hundred years ago travel by road was uncomfortable and very slow. In summer, carriage axles broke on the rutted, dusty road. In winter, the wheels sank in deep pools of mud. And there was always the danger of being attacked by Indians.

When the steam engine was invented several people tried to build a steam-driven automobile. But none was successful on the bad roads. A British engineer, Richard Trevithick, thought of mounting a steam powered car on rails to give a smoother ride.

The idea of making a track for the wheels of vehicles was not new. The Ancient Greeks cut smooth grooves in their roads for the wheels of chariots. Much later, iron tracks were used in coal mines to make the heavy wagons move more easily. But with the invention of the steam engine railways completely changed travel on land.

The first public railway to use steam locomotives was the Stockton and Darlington line in Northern England. It was opened in 1825. George Stephenson, a self-taught engineer, built the ten-mile track and its first engine, called *Locomotion*. A few years later Stephenson built his most famous locomotive, *The Rocket*.

The railway age had begun. Within 25 years there were railways in most European countries, and enough track had been laid to stretch around the world.

It was not long before people and goods could travel right across North America, Europe and Asia by rail.

Bigger and more powerful steam locomotives were built over the years. But they all worked in much the same way as the early engines. Coal burning in a firebox heated water and turned it to steam. The pressure of the steam forced large pistons back and forth in cylinders. Pistons, connected to driving wheels, turned them around.

Steam locomotives belching smoke hauled passenger trains and freight cars for over one hundred years. But there are few left today. They have been replaced by diesel and electric locomotives which are cleaner, quieter and cheaper to run.

Diesel locomotives are powered by oil-burning diesel engines similar to those used in large trucks. Electric locomotives are driven by powerful electric motors. They are connected to an electricity supply by overhead wires or by a 'live' third rail.

Until the beginning of this century the railways had no rivals. Then the automobile and the airplane were invented. Railways were used less and less and some lines closed. Now, new trains are being built which travel twice as fast as a car. And hover-trains which glide on a cushion of air have been invented. In the future, trains will be faster and more comfortable than ever before.

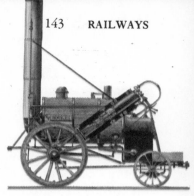

George Stephenson's 'Rocket' of 1829.

An electric locomotive of the present day.

A huge diesel locomotive.

This monorail runs on an overhead track.

A cutaway diagram of a steam locomotive. Steam was raised by burning coal, wood or oil, and the pistons were linked by rods to the driving wheels.

Boiler

Firebox

Driving rod   Piston

RAIN The rain which falls from the clouds starts off as water in seas, lakes, rivers and soil. The Sun's heat 'evaporates' some of this water, turning it into water vapor which disappears into the air. The water vapor remains invisible until the air rises and cools. Air rises when it is warm, or when it meets a heavier mass of cold air, or when it is forced upward by high ground. As the rising air cools, some of the water vapor 'condenses' or turns back to water droplets and becomes visible as clouds. As the air rises higher, more and more vapor turns back to water and the clouds grow bigger and darker. Finally, water droplets from the clouds fall to the ground as rain.

Places close to the sea usually get most rain, especially high areas. In the middle of large land masses it is often dry because the winds blowing from the sea have lost most of their moisture

Rain provides water for plants and animals. It soaks into the ground, and some water runs out again in the form of springs. Springs feed streams and rivers, which flow into lakes and seas. In this way, the 'water cycle' continues.

RAT Few people like rats. These rodents eat and spoil our food, and also spread disease. The black rat and the brown rat often live in or near buildings.

Rats are bigger than mice. They eat almost anything; and they can swim, burrow and climb. The black rat often lives on ships. In the Middle Ages it helped spread the disease, the plague.

See also MOUSE.

RECORDING Most of us have listened to our favorite music or stories on phonograph records. Records are one way of recording sound. Thomas Edison invented the first phonograph in 1877. Modern records are disks of plastic which 'store' sound in their grooves. Another way of recording sound is on tape. Here, the sound is recorded in the form of a magnetic pattern. Both disks and tape can be made to carry left-hand, and right-hand sounds. This gives a more realistic 'stereo' effect. Television programs can now be recorded on disk and tape. The sound

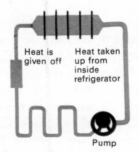

In a refrigerator the cooling fluid is pumped around a long coil. When it is compressed (squeezed) by the pump, it gives up most of its heat. The cool fluid takes heat away from inside the refrigerator (because heat always moves from a warm place to a cool one). Then it returns to the pump, ready to be compressed and cooled once more.

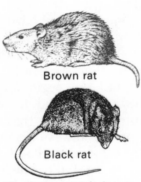

The brown rat is larger and more common than the black rat, which spread the plague in the Middle Ages.

The powerful reindeer can travel long distances over snow or marshy ground without tiring.

track on films is often recorded as an image on the film. It is changed into sound by light-sensitive photocells.

RED CROSS The Red Cross organization helps the victims of wars and disasters. In 1859 the armies of France and Austria fought a terrible battle in Italy. A Swiss traveler named Jean Henri Dunant visited the battlefield and saw thousands of wounded soldiers, with no one to help them. Dunant tried to help, and wrote a book describing what he had seen.

As a result, the Red Cross was formed at Geneva in Switzerland (a country which never takes part in war). Its flag is a red cross on a white background. In Moslem countries the organization called the Red Crescent or Red Lion.

REFRIGERATION Foods last longer when they are kept cool in a refrigerator. Cooling slows down the processes which make food go bad. Deep-freezers keep foods fresh by freezing them.

The first refrigerators were boxes surrounded by ice. Some people still call refrigerators 'ice-boxes'. But modern refrigerators usually run on electricity. They have a pump that turns a vapor into liquid. The liquid is turned into vapor again inside the freezing compartment. As it does so it takes up heat from the food. In another part of the refrigerator the vapor is changed back into a liquid and recirculated.

At ice rinks, the water is frozen and kept frozen by pipes carrying very cold brine (salt solution). Portable ice chests can be packed with dry ice (solid carbon dioxide gas). It is very cold and changes into gas without melting.

REINDEER Most deer are wild, shy animals. The reindeer is the only deer which has been tamed. The Lapp people of Scandinavia keep herds of reindeer. The reindeer provide them with skins, meat and milk, and also pull sleds.

Both male and female reindeer have antlers. In winter reindeer feed on lichens growing beneath the snow.

In North America reindeer are called caribou. Caribou migrate southward to escape the harsh Arctic winter.

WORLD RELIGIONS

Menorah
(Judaism)

Cross
(Christianity)

Eastern orthodox bishop
(Christianity)

Crescent of moon
(Islam)

Statue of Buddha
(Buddhism)

Hindu carving
(Hinduism)

RELIGION A religion is a belief, a way of living, or both. It may mean belief in a god or gods with powers greater than our own, and in another life after this one. It may involve prayer and worship. There are many religions, but most try to explain how the world and life began.

More advanced religions developed after people began living in towns. The ancient Egyptians believed in life after death, and preserved their dead as mummies inside tombs hidden beneath a pyramid of stone, with food and jewels ready for the next world. The ancient Greeks, in their myths and legends, told of gods who lived on top of Mount Olympus. The Romans borrowed some of the Greek gods, as well as religions from other countries which they conquered.

All the world's great religions began in Asia. The oldest religion to teach that there is only one god is *Judaism*, the religion of the Jews. Its history is told in the Hebrew Bible, which Christians call the Old Testament. *Islam* is followed in Africa and Asia. Its founder was the prophet Mohammed, and its followers are called Moslems. They believe in Allah, the one god. Moslems pray in a mosque and obey the teachings of the Koran, their holy book.

Hinduism is the chief religion of India. Hindus believe people's souls are reborn many times until good enough to join Brahman, a supreme power. Their gods include Vishnu and Shiva. The River Ganges is sacred to Hindus. So are some animals, especially the cow, monkey and cobra. *Buddhism* is another important Eastern religion. Its founder, Buddha ('The Enlightened One'), taught people how to escape from suffering and find peace. Buddhists do not worship a god. They believe that people have many lives, and move gradually towards perfection.

People who follow the teachings of Jesus Christ are *Christians*. All Christians do not belong to one Church, but most share certain basic beliefs: they believe that God made the world, that Jesus was His Son, and that through faith in Him people can gain eternal life.

Other important world religions are Confucianism, Taoism, Zoroastrianism, Shintoism and Sikhism. The Chinese philosopher Confucius taught how people should behave, rather than what they should believe about God. In the Persian religion of Zoroastrianism both good and evil are thought to be powerful forces.

People who believe in no god and have no religion are called atheists. An agnostic is someone who does not know whether or not there is a god.

See also BIBLE; BUDDHA; JESUS CHRIST; MAGIC; MOHAMMED; MYTHS AND LEGENDS.

RENAISSANCE The word 're-naissance' means 'rebirth'. In the 1300s there began a rebirth of learning in Europe. Scholars rediscovered and studied the ancient writings of Greece and Rome, which had been forgotten during the Middle Ages. Artists such as Michelangelo and Leonardo da Vinci recaptured the beauty of 'classical' Greek sculpture and architecture. Scientists such as Copernicus and Galileo questioned the old ideas about the Universe. Explorers such as Columbus brought back new knowledge from their voyages. Erasmus and other 'humanist' thinkers taught that human beings were important, and not just weak, miserable creatures ruled by God.

These new ideas were spread by a new invention, printing. But powerful kings built strong nations that kept the peoples of Europe divided. And the widespread power of the Church weakened as Christians began to argue over its teachings. The Renaissance lasted into the 1600s. It was an exciting age. People no longer wanted to be told what to think. They wanted to find out for themselves.

REPRODUCTION All animals and plants can reproduce. They can make other living things like themselves. If this were not so, life on Earth would come to an end.

All living things are made up of cells. Simple animals and plants can reproduce on their own. They either divide in two (like the amoeba) or make special cells which grow into new plants (like the fungi).

More advanced forms of life reproduce sexually. All but the simplest animals do this. So do flowering plants (which can also often reproduce by splitting as well).

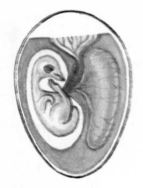

Inside a fertile bird's egg, the developing embryo is protected by the shell. It feeds on the yolk and takes its first breath from an air pocket at the large end of the egg.

Both produce special sex cells. When a male cell joins with and fertilizes a female cell, this grows into a new individual.

In flowering plants a male sex cell stored in a pollen grain joins a female sex cell in the part of the flower called the carpel.

In animals, the male cells are called sperms, and the female cells, eggs. Most female fishes lay their eggs in water. Male fishes fertilize them by dropping sperms over the eggs. In reptiles and birds, fertilization takes place inside the female. Then she lays her eggs, which are protected by shells. Inside the egg, the young have food and shelter until they are ready to hatch.

Most mammals, including human beings, give birth to live young. The male's sperms fertilize the female's eggs inside her body. But the female does not lay eggs. Each tiny embryo develops inside its mother, until it is ready to be born. It gets its food from the mother's bloodstream, and is much safer than the young of egg-laying animals.

See also CELL; ANIMAL; FLOWER; GENETICS; HUMAN BODY.

REPTILE Crocodiles, tortoises, lizards, snakes and the lizard-like tuatara from New Zealand are all reptiles. They all have tough, scaly skins and most lay leathery-shelled eggs. Baby reptiles hatch fully developed and are not cared for by their parents. A few reptiles give birth to live young—the eggs hatch inside the female's body.

Reptiles are cold-blooded animals—their body temperature is the same as the temperature of their surroundings. For this reason reptiles cannot live in very cold lands. And in places where there are cold winters, reptiles hibernate. They are most at home in warm lands where they can often be seen basking in the sun and then moving into the shade when they become too hot.

There are about 5500 kinds of reptile. Most are small. Once there were some much larger reptiles. But these are now extinct. Most reptiles eat insects and small animals, but some eat plants.

See also CROCODILE; DINOSAUR; LIZARD; SNAKE; TORTOISE AND TURTLE.

REVOLUTION The word *revolution* means 'turn around' or 'complete change'. If a country has a revolution, its government and laws are overthrown, often by war and bloodshed.

The most famous revolutions in history happened in America, France and Russia. In 1776 the American colonies broke away from Britain and became an independent republic. The French Revolution (1789) brought about the overthrow of the king and the nobles who ruled France. In 1917 the rule of the Russian Tsar (emperor) was ended, and the world's first Communist government was set up.

Another kind of revolution is economic, and changes the way people live. The Industrial Revolution, which began in the 1700s, is still changing our lives today.

RHINOCEROS The rhinoceros is like an armored tank. It is the second largest land animal, after the elephant.

On the African plains live the black rhinoceros and the white rhinoceros. Actually, both are gray. The rhinoceroses of India, Java and Sumatra live in dense forests.

Rhinoceroses are shortsighted and rather bad-tempered. But they eat only grass, shoots and twigs. Their only enemies are hunters. Many rhinoceroses have been killed because people believed their horns had magic powers.

White rhinoceroses grazing on the African plains. The white rhino is the largest of the rhinoceros family, and is much rarer than the smaller black rhino also found in Africa.

Green rice seedlings are planted in flooded fields.

Major Rivers	
Africa	4186 miles
Nile	6737 km
	2716 miles
Zaire	4370 km
Asia	3433 miles
Yangtze	5525 km
Australia	1702 miles
Darling	2739 km
Europe	1774 miles
Danube	2855 km
North America	
Mississippi-	3860 miles
Missouri	6211 km
South America	
Amazon	3999 miles
	6436 km

RICE More than half the people in the world eat rice as their main food. Rice is a cereal, like wheat, but it grows in warmer and wetter parts of the world. Because young rice plants need plenty of water, they are grown in flooded 'paddy' fields. The water is drained off before the rice is harvested.

Rice does not make good flour. It is usually boiled and eaten with sauces. Many people eat brown rice – which still has some of its husk, or skin. The white rice eaten in Europe and North America has been polished to remove the husk. This takes away some of the goodness.

RIVER Rivers begin their lives as small streams in hills or mountains. Some begin as trickles of water from melting glaciers. Others bubble up through the ground as springs.

Gravity makes water flow downhill. At first the river rushes along, fed by rain and melting snow. It is narrow but fast-flowing, forming rapids and waterfalls, and carrying along with it stones and pebbles which help to deepen and widen its course.

When it reaches flatter country, the river flows more slowly. Other streams, called tributaries, may join it. The river valley gradually becomes wider and flatter. Mud and sand borne by the river are dropped on its bed and banks, and it meanders or loops from side to side. Finally, the river flows into the sea, sometimes through a fan-shaped network of channels known as a delta. The fresh water of many a river meets the salt water of the sea in a river mouth, or estuary.

From earliest times, people have lived close to rivers, where there was water for their crops and animals. It was often easier to travel by boat than overland, so river transport became important. People met beside rivers to trade, and so settlements began. Later these grew into great cities.

Rivers provide us with water to drink, and for farms and factories. By building dams across rivers, we can create huge lakes to store water and to provide power to make electricity. Many rivers are rich in fish. And some rivers are so large that sea-going ships can sail up them.

See also AMAZON; NILE.

ROADS form a vast network linking town to town and even country to country. Almost everywhere new roads are being built to cope with the increasing number of vehicles using them. Most old roads follow the pattern of the land, twisting and turning and going up and down. New roads are built especially for fast moving traffic. They are very straight and have few ups and downs. Traffic moving in different directions travels in separate lanes. They are called such names as motorway (Britain), expressway (United States), autobahn (Germany) and autostrada (Italy).

Italians built the first modern motorway in the 1920s. Two thousand years before, their ancestors, the Romans, were building fine roads throughout Europe, North Africa and the Middle East. Their roads were built in layers and paved with flat stones. They had a curve, or camber, to let the rain run off. Modern roads are also built with a camber and are made up of layers. Tarmac roads

The animal life of the river and its banks include birds such as the kingfisher and dipper, and mammals such as the water vole and the otter.

Sedimentary rocks are formed when sediment (mud and small stones) hardens. Limestone is formed from lime-mud; pebbles are pressed into conglomerate. Igneous rocks, such as granite and obsidian, were once hot and molten and were brought to the surface of the Earth by volcanoes.
Metamorphic rocks are formed when other rocks are changed by heat or pressure.

have layers of tar and stones on top of well-rammed soil. Concrete roads are made up of layers of concrete, laid by a long 'train' of vehicles.

ROCK The inside of the Earth is a hot, molten mass. But the outer skin, or crust, is made up of solid rock. Where there is soil covering the rock, plants can grow. But in places, including some deserts and mountains, wind and water have carried away the soil, leaving bare rock at the surface.

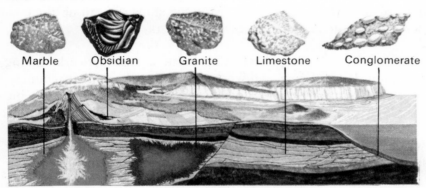

Marble   Obsidian   Granite   Limestone   Conglomerate

Saturn V space rocket

Lunar module

3rd stage

2nd stage

1st stage

USA

ROCKET A rocket is a kind of engine. It works by shooting out a stream of gases backward. As the gases go backward the rocket goes forward, like a balloon when you suddenly let the air escape from it.

The rocket works rather like a jet engine. Both burn fuel to make hot gases, which shoot out in a stream. But the rocket carries its own oxygen to burn the fuel. The jet engine gets its oxygen from the air. This is why the rocket can work in space, where there is no air.

The simplest rocket is a firework rocket. It is a long tube packed with a solid fuel, and fixed on a stick to help it fly straight. Some space rockets also have solid fuel. Others have liquid fuels. The most powerful rockets are liquid-fueled. Very cold liquid hydrogen and liquid oxygen are important fuels. They are pumped from storage tanks into a chamber when they are burned.

Space rockets are made up of two or more separate rockets on top of one another. They are called step rockets. Each rocket fires in turn and pulls away when its fuel runs out. Only in this way can the small top rocket be made to travel fast enough to get into space.

ROCKY MOUNTAINS The Rocky Mountains of North America are very rugged. There are snow-capped peaks, rushing rivers, deep gorges and narrow passes. The highest peak in the Rockies is Mt Elbert at 14,433 feet, (4399 meters). The Rockies stretch down the western side of North America from Alaska in the north to Mexico in the south.

The Rockies have a rich animal life, including bears, pumas, wild sheep and deer. National parks have been set up so that visitors can enjoy the scenery. The hot springs and geysers in the Yellowstone Park are a sign that there is still volcanic activity beneath the mountains.

Some of North America's big rivers begin in the Rockies. They include the Missouri, the Colorado, the Rio Grande and the Columbia.

RODENT There are more rodents than any other kind of mammal. Rodents have chisel-like front teeth, which they use to gnaw their food.

Most rodents are small. The largest is the water-loving capybara. Beavers, coypus and water voles also live near water. Squirrels and some porcupines live in trees, while jerboas and gophers live on the ground. Some kinds of mice and rats live in human dwellings.

Rodents have many enemies. They are preyed on by hawks, owls, snakes, foxes and other animals. But rodents are always alert for danger. And most kinds breed rapidly.

The chinchilla is valued for its fur, while guinea pigs, hamsters and gerbils are popular rodent pets.

See also BEAVER; MOUSE; PORCUPINE; RAT; SQUIRREL.

ROME, ANCIENT About 2700 years ago small villages lay on hills above the River Tiber in Italy. The people were farmers, who lived in thatched huts. From these humble beginnings grew the great city of Rome. Its people won a mighty empire, whose armies ruled lands from England to the Middle East.

According to legend, Rome was founded by twin brothers called Romulus and Remus, who were raised by a she-wolf. At first the Romans were ruled by

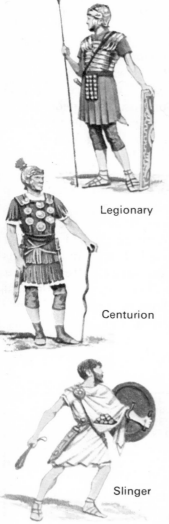

Legionary

Centurion

Slinger

Above: Three Roman soldiers. Below: The Colosieum, a huge amphitheatre in Rome.

foreign kings. But in 509 BC the people set up a republic, in which they elected their own rulers. They fought against their neighbors and built a powerful army.

Without this army, the Romans would never have conquered and ruled their Empire. Roman soldiers were tough and well trained. The army was divided into legions. A hundred soldiers made up a century, six centuries a cohort, and ten cohorts a legion.

The Roman Empire was divided into provinces, ruled by governors. The capital of the Empire was the city of Rome, built on seven hills. To the Romans, Rome was the center of the world. Its fine buildings included the Forum (meeting place), the Senate (parliament), triumphal arches, temples, shops and villas (houses).

As Rome grew stronger, its citizens grew richer. They began quarreling among themselves. In 45 BC Julius Caesar became dictator (sole ruler). And in 27 BC his nephew Augustus became Rome's first Emperor. At the height of its power, Rome was a city of great splendor. Rich people, such as the aristocrats or 'patricians', lived in fine houses, with central heating, baths and fine furniture. They gave great banquets where the guests lay on couches, watching dances or listening to music and poetry. The ordinary working people,

or 'plebeians', had few luxuries. But they too were citizens of Rome.

However, Rome was also a cruel place. The Romans kept thousands of slaves. Huge crowds watched fights to the death between gladiators in the arena, or jeered as Christians were killed by lions. They cheered the 'triumph' of a victorious general as he led his army into Rome, dragging his captives in chains.

In AD 395 the Empire was divided into two. One half was ruled from Rome, the other from Byzantium (Constantinople). Rome was no longer strong. Its government was dishonest, and the army could no longer fight off the barbarian raids. Around AD 476 the western empire fell, and Rome was destroyed. In the east, the Byzantine Empire lasted until 1453 when Constantinople was captured by the Turks.

But Roman ways and ideas survived, and many Roman customs were continued by the invaders. Many modern languages, such as French, Italian and Spanish, are related to Latin, which for hundreds of years was Europe's language of learning. The remains of fine Roman buildings can be seen in many places in Europe, South-West Asia and North Africa. The Romans copied much of their art, literature and religion from ancient Greece. They are remembered for being skilled builders and engineers, fine soldiers, and wise rulers.

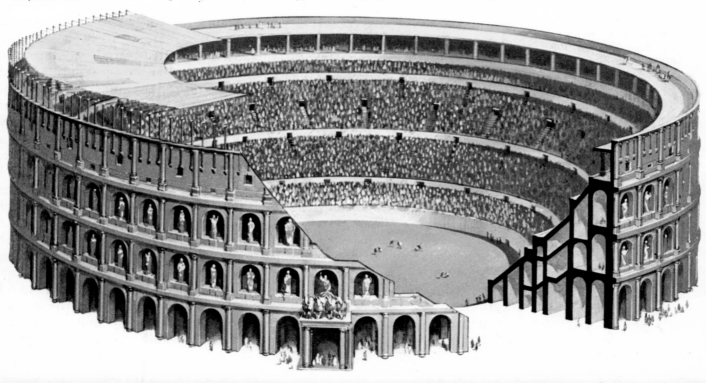

Rubber trees are 'tapped' to drain off the milky sap.

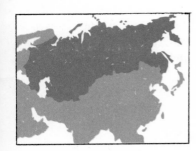

Russia stretches from Europe to Asia. It is the largest country in the world.

St Basil's Cathedral, with its onion-shaped domes, stands in Red Square in Moscow, the capital of Russia.

RUBBER is an elastic material that can be made from the sap of the rubber tree. Rubber trees grow in tropical countries such as Malaysia and Indonesia. Cuts are made in the bark of the tree and a milky sap (latex) oozes out. The sap is treated with acid to produce crude rubber. Other things are mixed with it, and then it is molded to make soles of shoes, tires, tubes and numerous other things. Much of the rubber used now, however, is made by the plastics industry.

RUGS AND CARPETS are heavy fabrics used to cover floors. Man probably made the first rugs from animal hair for use in caves. For many centuries only rich people could afford rugs since they were woven by hand. Nowadays most are made on machines.

Rugs and carpets serve to keep rooms warm. Some are considered works of art because of their beautiful colors and patterns.

RUSSIA When people talk about 'Russia' they usually mean the 'Union of Soviet Socialist Republics', for this is the country's full name. Fifteen republics make up Russia, the largest country in the world, stretching from Europe right across Asia to the Pacific Ocean.

There are many different regions in such a huge land, and many different climates. In the east, the country is flat and marshy in places. The Caucasus Mountains stretch between the Black Sea and the Caspian Sea. And the rugged Ural Mountains separate Europe from Asia. Beyond are wide treeless plains called steppes. The highest mountains are in the Pamir and Tien Shan ranges, and the longest rivers are in the vast wilderness of Siberia.

In each region there are different plants and animals. The north has a cold Arctic climate. But in the warm south fruit, tea and even palm trees grow. In the cool *taiga* zone the forests provide huge amounts of timber, while on the fertile steppes wheat and other crops are grown.

Farming is important and so are fishing, the fur trade and mining. There are rich deposits of minerals, including coal, oil, iron ore, manganese and gold. All farms, factories, mines and shops are run by the government.

Until 1917 Russia was an empire. The emperor was called the Tsar and had great power. But most of the people were poor peasants. There were few factories or schools. During World War I conditions became so bad that there was a revolution. The Tsar, Nicholas II, was overthrown, and Vladimir Lenin set up a communist government.

Later Russia was ruled by the dictator, Josef Stalin. During World War II Germany invaded Russia and millions of Russians were killed. After the war Russia controlled the communist countries of Eastern Europe. Science and industry were developed rapidly, until Russia rivaled the United States as the richest and strongest country in the world.

Facts and Figures
Area: 8,610,030 square miles
     (22,300,000 square kilometers)
Population: 253,000,000
Capital: Moscow
Government: Communist federation
Money Unit: Ruble
Longest River: Ob-Irtysh, 3,461 miles
     (5569 kilometers)
Highest Mountain: Communism Peak,
     24,591 feet (7495 meters)

RUST If you leave a shiny new nail out of doors all year long it will soon become covered with a brownish film. This is rust. Rust is produced when iron or steel is attacked by damp air. The oxygen in the air joins with some of the iron to form brown iron oxide. To stop iron and steel from rusting they must be coated with paint, plastic, or a metal which does not rust, such as zinc.

SAFETY Every day people are injured or killed in accidents, many of which could have been avoided if rules of safety had been followed. For example, falls are the most common accidents at home. One way to avoid falls is to pick up toys and tools so no one will trip over them. It is also important to wipe up spilled liquid as soon as possible so no one will slip.

SAILBOAT A sailboat is different from other boats because it uses the wind to move it through the water instead of a motor or oars. Sails are large pieces of cloth which catch the wind.

The ancient Egyptians and Greeks used sails on their boats. Through the centuries sailboats were used for exploring, making war, and moving people and things from place to place. Nowadays sailboats are mostly used for pleasure and sport.

SALMON are fish with an unusual life history. They are born in fresh water, but swim down to the sea to spend their adult lives. When they are ready to breed, they swim back up the river to the place where they were born. To reach it, they leap up rapids and waterfalls. The salmon lay their eggs in quiet streams; then, worn out, most of them die.

SALT Salts make up a class of chemicals. There are many different salts, but the one we know best is the salt we eat – common salt. Chemists call it sodium chloride, because it is made up of the two elements, sodium and chlorine. Our bodies need salt. There is salt in our blood, in our sweat and in our tears.

Salt is obtained in three ways. It is mined from deep underground, it is pumped up as a liquid from salt wells and dried out, and it is dried out from sea water.

SAND Rocks are very hard. But the pounding of ocean waves, the grinding of glacier ice and the scouring of winds can break up rocks; first into small pebbles, and then into tiny grains of sand.

Sand washed down by rivers forms sand banks. The wind often blows sand from a beach into heaps called dunes. Desert dunes look like giant waves of sand. They can be whipped up by the wind into fierce sandstorms.

Sand is used in making concrete and glass. Because it is hard and gritty, it is good for cleaning and smoothing rough surfaces.

SATELLITE A satellite is a small body which circles around a larger one. The

Eggs

Fish hatches from egg

Mature salmon

Young salmon (parr)

Moon is the Earth's satellite. It circles around the Earth once a month. Most of the planets have satellites circling round them. We often just call them moons.

To stay up in space a satellite must have a very high speed — more than 17,000 miles (28,000 km) an hour. Then gravity will not be able to pull it back to Earth. Satellites can be very useful. Some help in weather forecasting. Some relay telephone and television signals between the continents.

Salmon lay their eggs in fresh water. Each baby fish feeds on the yolk in its egg sac. When they are older, the young salmon are called parr. When they are about two years old, the salmon swim to the sea where they grow into adult fish.

The Orbiting Astronomical Observatory (OAO) satellite gives scientists on Earth a clearer view of the stars. Its solar panel 'wings' change the Sun's rays into electricity.

SAUDI ARABIA This desert kingdom is an important Arab nation. It supplies much of the oil for the world (including the United States). Located on a tilted platform of ancient rocks, higher on its western boundary, the Red Sea, and sloping gently to its eastern boundary, the Persian Gulf, over one-third of Saudi Arabia's 830,000 square miles is desert. The biggest desert area, Rut-al-Khali (the Empty Quarter, as it is called) covers 250,000 square miles in the southern part of the country.

This map shows the countries which make up Scandinavia.

SCANDINAVIA is the name of a region in northern Europe. It includes the countries of Norway, Sweden, Denmark and Finland. History and trade have brought them close together.

The Scandinavian peninsula is a long strip of land, surrounded by cold seas. There are high mountains, and on the west coast are long, narrow inlets called fiords. The northern part of Scandinavia is inside the Arctic Circle. The people who live there are the wandering Lapps, who have herds of reindeer. There are also iron ore mines. The forests of Scandinavia produce timber. And farming, fishing and lumbering are important occupations.

Vultures and ravens scavenge on the body of a dead animal. The birds' keen eyesight enables them to spot a carcass from a long way off.

The scorpion carries its tail arched over its back. The sharp sting at the end is connected to a poison gland and can be very painful. The largest scorpions are over 3.9 inches (10 centimeters) long.

SCAVENGER When an animal or plant dies, its body soon disappears. This is thanks to the work of scavengers. These animals are nature's sanitation men.

The most important scavengers are too tiny to be seen without a microscope. These are bacteria, which break down all living things when they die. In this way essential chemicals are returned to the soil.

Many insects, especially flies and beetles, are useful scavengers. They lay their eggs on dead animals or on animal waste, such as dung. When the eggs hatch, the larvae have a food supply.

The largest scavengers include crows, vultures, kites, jackals and hyenas. When an animal dies, or is killed for food by another animal, the scavengers gather to finish off the remains.

SCHOOL In most countries there are schools, where children are educated. In rich countries the law usually says that all children must attend school. But in poor countries there are not enough schools or teachers, and not all children can go to school.

Some of the first schools were started in ancient Egypt. Greek and Roman children learned reading, writing and arithmetic. However, few girls went to school, and for a long time only wealthy parents could afford to educate their children. During the Middle Ages most teachers were monks.

Nowadays, government-run schools are usually free. There are also private schools, which charge fees. All children go to primary and secondary schools and some go on to study at a university or college.

SCIENCE The word 'science' just means knowledge. In science, people try to find out about the world around them by observing things and carrying out experiments. When some information is found out, scientists try to classify it, or fit it in with other knowledge they already have. Observation, experiment and classification are common to all the sciences.

Chemistry, physics and biology are the main branches of science. Chemistry studies the way matter is made up. Physics studies the properties of matter and energy. And biology studies living things. Each of these branches has many divisions. Biology, for example, has two main divisions – botany, the study of plants, and zoology, the study of animals.

SCORPION This creature lives in the warmer parts of the world. People living in these places watch out for scorpions because they have a dangerous poisonous sting.

Scorpions are relatives of spiders. During the day they usually hide in the shade. At night they come out to catch insects and small mammals. The scorpion uses its pincers to grab its prey. It keeps the sting in its tail for defense.

If two scorpions meet they often fight to death. But the female scorpion is a good mother. She carries her young around on her back.

SCULPTURE Since people began using tools, they have made models and figures, or statues. This form of art is called sculpture. Early sculptors modeled animal shapes in wood and bone, and also made religious statues or 'idols' to please their gods or frighten away evil spirits.

The ancient Egyptians cut huge figures of solid rock, and there is wonderful ancient sculpture too in the Far East, India and in Central America. But the masters of sculpture were the ancient Greeks. They decorated their temples with marble statues of athletes, heroes

The seahorse has a stiff, bony body and a tube-like mouth. It can hold on to seaweed with its tail.

and gods. Roman sculptors copied the Greeks. Their work is not so beautiful, but the faces on the statues are more like those of ordinary people. Sculptors often made stone portraits, showing a person's head and shoulders. These are known as 'busts'.

In the Middle Ages wood carvers and stone masons decorated churches with figures of saints. But they also showed people going about their everyday work. During the Renaissance, or 'rebirth of learning', sculptors such as Michelangelo imitated the 'classical' lifelike style of the Greeks. Modern sculptors do not copy the human body or natural shapes so closely. Instead they make beautiful patterns or shapes which express feelings and ideas. This kind of sculpture is called 'abstract'.

Sculpture is done in two ways: by *carving* and *molding*. In carving, the sculptor cuts into a block of wood or stone with sharp tools. In molding, he

Top: A sculptor at work on a clay model in his studio.
Above: In the 1600s sculptors loved to show off their skill. This style is called Baroque, and is full of movement and amazing detail. These marble figures of Apollo and Daphne were carved by the great Italian sculptor Giovanni Bernini (1598–1680).

makes a model in soft clay, then bakes the clay to harden it. From the hard model he makes a mold, and pours into it wet concrete or hot, liquid metal (such as bronze). When this hardens, a perfect 'casting' of the model is left. Today sculptors also make shapes out of pieces of metal, glass and plastic. Some modern sculpture has moving parts, and is known as a 'mobile'. A 'relief' is a kind of raised picture made by cutting into a flat piece of wood or stone.

SEAHORSE The seahorse is actually a small sea fish. It gets its name from its horse-like head.

The seahorse swims in a curious upright position, fanning its dorsal (back) fin. It can cling on to seaweed, using its coiled tail.

Seahorses take unusual care of their young. The female lays her eggs in a pouch on the male's body. He looks after them until they hatch.

SEALS AND SEA LIONS are mammals which spend most of their time in the sea. Their legs have become flippers, and they are expert swimmers. But they have to come to the surface to breathe.

Seals and sea lions catch fish underwater. Seals swim by moving their bodies from side to side. Sea lions use their front flippers like oars.

These animals come ashore to breed. They gather in large colonies on rocky coasts. Seals are slow and clumsy on land. But sea lions can turn their back flippers forward and gallop along quite quickly.

See also WALRUS.

Above: Weddell seal and pup from the Antarctic.
Right: The huge elephant seal. Below: Arctic ringed seal.

Life on the seashore: A puffin, its beak full of sand-eels, watches as black-headed gulls squabble and an oyster catcher probes the sand for shellfish. Along the water's edge are razor shells, cockles, whelks and shore crabs, and also sea urchins, starfish and jellyfish left stranded by the tide. In small pools live fish, such as gobies, hermit crabs, sea anemones and shrimps, while edible crabs hide in rock crevices. Clinging to the rocks are limpets, mussels, barnacles and periwinkles. Shore plants include marram grass, sea holly, pink thrift, yellow Hottentot fig and samphire.

SEASHORE

Between the land and the sea is the seashore. Every day it is washed by tides. The animals and plants of the seashore lead interesting lives.

There are several kinds of seashore. Shingle beaches are not good places for animals and plants, because of the pounding waves and churning pebbles. But river estuaries and mud flats are ideal for shellfish, such as cockles, snails muscles and oysters. Here too gulls, waders and other birds can find plenty of food, particularly at low tide.

A sandy beach is the best place to look for empty shells. However, most of the shore animals hide beneath the sand. Shrimps like sandy shores. So do worms such as ragworms and lugworms. Cockles and razor shells dig themselves into the sand and suck for food through a siphon tube. When the tide goes out, it often leaves jellyfish and starfish stranded on the beach.

A rocky shore is the best place for plants and animals. Seaweed clings to the rocks. Green seaweed grows on the higher shore. Lower down, where they are covered with water for most of the time, grow brown and red seaweed. Barnacles and limpets also fasten themselves to rocks. When the tide goes out, they close their shells tightly.

In rock pools, exposed at low tide, you may find crabs, sponges, sea cucumbers, sea squirts and sea urchins. The sea anemone looks like an underwater flower. But it is actually an animal with stinging tentacles. Some sea worms bore into the rocks and breakwaters (manmade barriers).

Fish which live close to the shore include blennies, gobies, wrasse, rockling, pipe-fishes, sand eels and flatfish, such as dabs and flounders. The lumpsucker, or sea hen, is sometimes left stranded on the beach. The male guards the eggs, clinging onto a rock with a sucker disk on his underside. He can live out of water until high tide. A fish to watch out for is the weaver. It hides in the sand, with just the tips of its poisonous spines showing.

Many birds are seen on the seashore. Some like sandpipers, avocets, plovers, curlews and oystercatchers, gather to feed on the mud flats or sandy shores at low tide. Other birds, such as gulls, terns and gannets choose cliffs or sand dunes as nesting places.

See also CRAB; JELLYFISH; SEAWEED; SHELLS; SHRIMPS AND PRAWNS; STAR — FISH.

SEASONS The different times of the year are called seasons. Many lands have four seasons. In spring plants begin to grow and animals have their young. Summer is the hottest time of the year, when the days are longest. In autumn crops are harvested, and the leaves fall from the trees. (Another name for autumn is the *fall*.) Winter is the coldest time of the year. The days are short and plants stop growing.

In the northern half of the Earth spring comes in March, April and May. But in the southern half these are the autumn months. Summer and winter also occur at opposite times of the year in northern and southern lands.

The seasons are caused by the way the Earth orbits, or travels around, the Sun. When the North Pole leans towards the Sun, northern lands have their summer and southern lands their winter. At the opposite point of the orbit, when the North Pole leans away from the Sun,

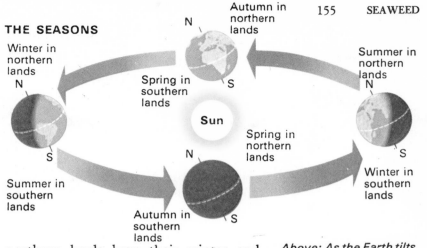

THE SEASONS

Winter in northern lands

Autumn in northern lands

Summer in northern lands

Spring in southern lands

Summer in southern lands

Sun

Spring in northern lands

Autumn in southern lands

Winter in southern lands

northern lands have their winter and southern lands their summer. Spring and autumn are the points in the orbit when the Equator, at the middle of the Earth faces the Sun, so northern and southern lands have roughly the same amount of warmth.

At the Equator there is little difference between the seasons. The Sun is always high in the sky. But at the poles there is a great difference. During the summer the Sun never sets, and during the winter it never rises above the horizon.

SEAWEED Seaweed are simple plants of the algae group. They have no flowers or proper roots.

Green seaweed grows high up the beach. Lower down grows brown sea-

Above: As the Earth tilts on its axis, the Sun warms different parts of the surface. When the Earth shows its northern face to the Sun, the northern hemisphere has its summer and the southern its winter. Six months later the Earth is on the other side of the Sun, and the seasons are reversed. Spring and autumn occur when the Earth's tilt is sideways to the Sun.

Seaweeds provide food and shelter for many sea animals. There are green, brown and red seaweed.

weed, while red seaweed lives in deeper water. Seaweed need light. None grow deeper than 250 feet (75 meters).

Most seaweed are tough and slippery. They can survive being pounded by waves and dried by sun and wind. The brown channeled wrack stores water in its fronds so that it can live out of water. The bladderwrack has air bladders to keep it floating near the surface. They pop when you squeeze them.

Some seaweeds can be eaten. Other kinds make good fertilizers.

SENSES tell us what is happening around us and inside us. We have external senses of hearing, taste, touch, sight and smell. Each sense comes from nerve endings or sense organs which send signals to our brain along the nervous system. For example, we have nerve endings on our tongue, called taste buds. When we eat, these tell us whether the food is salty, sour, sweet or bitter. Internal senses tell us when we are hungry, tired or thirsty. And our muscle sense tells us the position of different parts of our body. For example, we do not have to look at our arm to know where it is.

See also NERVOUS SYSTEM.

SEVEN WONDERS OF THE WORLD Travelers in ancient times marveled at the Seven Wonders of the World. People came from far and wide to see them, just as today tourists visit the Eiffel Tower and the Taj Mahal.

1 *The Pyramids of Egypt*. The largest of these tombs of the pharaohs took 30 years to build.

2 *The Pharos of Alexandria*. This was a lighthouse, almost 400 feet, (120 meters) high. Its light came from a fire reflected in curved mirrors.

3 *The Colossus of Rhodes*, was a bronze statue of the Sun-God, Helios. It stood at the mouth of Rhodes harbor.

4 *The Statue of Zeus at Olympia*. Made by the sculptor Phidias, it was seven times life-size.

5 *The Hanging Gardens of Babylon*. These gardens terraced the slopes of a stepped pyramid, 'or ziggurat', crowned by a temple.

6 *The Temple of Artemis* stood near Ephesus in Greece. Some of its 127 stone columns are now in the British Museum.

7 *The Mausoleum at Halicarnassus*. This was the tomb of Mausolus, an ancient King of Asia Minor.

Of these wonders, only the Pyramids can still be seen.

SHAKESPEARE, William (1564–1616) is often called the world's greatest writer. He was born in Stratford on Avon and later went to London to be an actor. Here he began writing plays. Some were about history. Others, like a *Midsummer Night's Dream*, were comedies. *Hamlet*, *Macbeth* and *King Lear* are great tragedies. The plays are written in poetry which is among the most beautiful in the English language.

Herding sheep on horseback in Australia.

Mako shark (left); thresher (right); and hammerhead (below).

SHARK Sharks are the most feared hunters of the sea. Drawn by the smell of blood, sharks will kill fish, seals, porpoises and even whales. Some sharks, such as the great white shark, the blue shark and the tiger shark, are maneaters.

Although people are frightened of sharks, most kinds are harmless. Some sharks, such as the dogfish, are small. The huge whale shark is the largest of all fish; but it eats only tiny sea animals and plants.

Sharks are strong, fast-swimming fish. Their gaping jaws are full of sharp teeth. Instead of bones, sharks have gristly skeletons. Their skins are rough like sandpaper.

Skates and rays are related to sharks. They live on the sea bottom. They have flat bodies and whip-like tails.

SHEEP Wild sheep live in the mountains in parts of America, Europe and Asia. They have curling horns and look rather like goats. Sheep are also important farm animals. People began keeping flocks of sheep thousands of years ago, making their wool into cloth, eating their meat, drinking their milk and wearing their skins. Sheep are easy to keep. They can feed on rough pasture, and their thick coats keep out bad weather.

A male sheep is called a ram and a female a ewe. The Merino is a breed which has very fine wool. Men who look after sheep are called shepherds. Often they use trained sheepdogs to help them with their flocks. In Australia and New Zealand a flock may contain 10,000 sheep.

See also WOOL.

SHELL The shells you find on the beach were once the homes of animals called mollusks. Mollusks have soft bodies. Instead of bones, they have hard shells. Inside its shell, a mollusk is protected from enemies.

There are many kinds of shell. Snails, winkles and whelks have one-piece shells, coiled round in a spiral. The cone-shaped shell of the limpet is very strong. Other mollusks have two shells, held together by hinges of muscle. These mollusks are called bivalves. They can open their shells to feed or move about. Oysters, cockles and clams are bivalves. The nautilus shell has several 'rooms'; the animal lives inside the largest room.

Collecting unusual and colorful shells is an interesting hobby. Shells are made from carbonate of lime which is produced by the mollusk. As the mollusk grows, so does its shell.

See also MOLLUSK; SEASHORE; SNAIL.

1. Textile cone shell 2. Tiger cowrie 3. Scorpion shell 4. Nautilus 5. Royal comb Venus 6. Chiton 7. Spindle shell 8. Thorny oyster 9. Left-handed whelk 10. Bishop's miter 11. Harp shell 12. Elephant's tusk 13. Northern scallop.

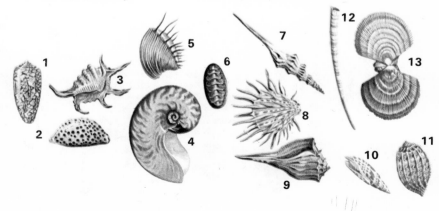

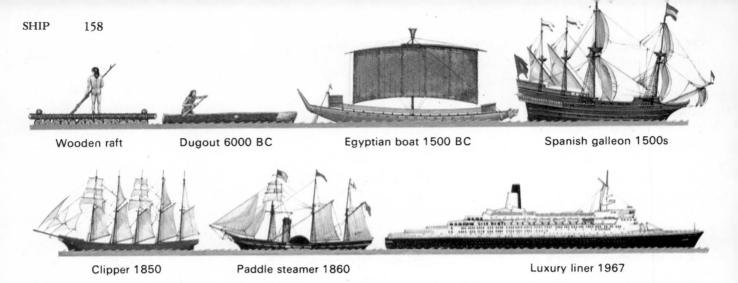

Wooden raft   Dugout 6000 BC   Egyptian boat 1500 BC   Spanish galleon 1500s

Clipper 1850   Paddle steamer 1860   Luxury liner 1967

SHIP For at least 4000 years ships have been sailing across seas. They still transport most of the world's cargo between the continents. But few carry passengers. Most long-distance travelers now go by air. Compared with planes, ships are extremely slow. Many travel only slightly faster than you can pedal on a bicycle! But what they lose in speed, they more than make up for in carrying capacity. Ships can carry thousands of tons of cargo, far more than any plane.

In warfare, ships are not as important as they once were. Being so slow, they are an easy target for bombs and missiles. The most dangerous ship of the present day is the submarine, which travels under water. The warships of the last war were fully armored and heavily gunned. The large navies had aircraft carriers. Today, few aircraft carriers remain. Instead navies have smaller, lighter and faster craft armed with rockets and guided missiles. Some of these crafts carry vertical take-off and landing planes.

Ships that carry passengers and cargo are called merchant ships. Biggest of them all are the giant oil tankers designed to carry oil from the Middle Eastern oil fields to Europe and the United States. Among the largest is the French tanker *Batilus,* 1312 feet (400 meters) long and carrying over half a million tons. Tankers are long and low and have little or no superstructure.

Along with tankers, there are other kinds of cargo ships, called freighters. These ships carry their cargo in open or closed holds. They have small cranes, or derricks, on deck to help load and unload. Freighters which sail at regular intervals to regular ports are called cargo liners. Those which sail when and where there is work to be done are called tramps.

Liners are passenger ships. They tend to have a large superstructure (containing cabins for passengers). Before air travel became common many larger liners sailed the seas. Today, there are few on regular routes. Most liners now are cruise ships taking people on vacation to sunny places. The *Queen Elizabeth II* is the largest liner afloat. It is a floating luxury hotel with restaurants, pools, shops, lounges and bars.

There are many other kinds of ships: trawlers are common fishing boats; tugs

The first log rafts were floated on rivers. Later hollowed-out tree trunks were shaped into dugout canoes. The first seagoing ships, with sails and oars, were built in Egypt. In time, extra sails and masts were added, and in the 1500s great galleons sailed the seas. The fastest of all the sailing ships were the tea clippers. But in the 1800s sails were replaced by steam engines, driving first paddle wheels, and then screws.

Life below decks on a galleon was cramped. The ship carried stone ballast, and stores including spare sails. Cannons fired broadside through ports in the side. The captain's cabin was in the stern.

tow larger ships into and out of port and go to the aid of ships in distress; ferries carry passengers and cargo on short crossings at regular times; lightships warn other ships of danger; and ice-breakers have very strong bows (fronts) to smash through ice in winter.

Until about a hundred years ago most ships were propelled by sails. For many years ships had only one square sail on a single mast. They could only sail well with the wind and relied on oars to propel them at other times. The Viking longships were an example of this. By the 1400s ships were built with several masts, one of which carried a triangular sail which made sailing easier in all winds. Soon came the three-masted caravels and galleons. Last of the sailing ships were the graceful and speedy clippers, which carried wool or tea from Australia or the Far East to Europe and America.

When the steam engine was invented, ships no longer had to rely on the wind. In time steam turbines propelled huge ships built of steel. Most ships nowadays are propelled this way. They get up steam by heating water in oil-fired boilers. The steam spins the turbines, which turn the ship's propellers. Some ships are motor ships. They have a diesel engine to spin their propellers. A few speedy naval craft have gas-turbine engines, which work much like a jet engine.

Ships are built in shipyards close to water. The body, or *hull*, is built by welding sheets of steel together. For strength and safety the hull has a double wall, or double bottom. The *keel*, or backbone of the ship is usually laid first. And the hull, together with horizontal decks and crosswise compartments, are built up from it. After the hull is finished the ship has a naming ceremony and is launched down a slipway. Once it has been tested the ship can go into service.

See also SAILBOAT; SUBMARINE; YACHT.

SHOES probably began as pieces of animal hide that cavemen wrapped around their feet to keep them from being frozen or bruised. While shoes are meant to protect, for a long time they were used as signs of a person's rank. During the Middle Ages the pointed toes of some handmade shoes were so long they had to be held off the ground by ribbons around the knees. Shoes today are much more practical and are made by mass production.

SHRIMPS AND PRAWNS are crustaceans, with hard shells to protect their soft bodies. Many live in shallow sea water, and eat seaweed, worms and small sea animals.

Shrimps bury themselves in the sand by day, and come out at night to feed. Prawns are larger than shrimps. When frightened, they swim backwards.

Shrimps and prawns are good to eat. Most kinds are brown or grey. They turn pink when they are cooked.

The prawn (top) and the shrimp (bottom) are shellfish related to lobsters and crabs.

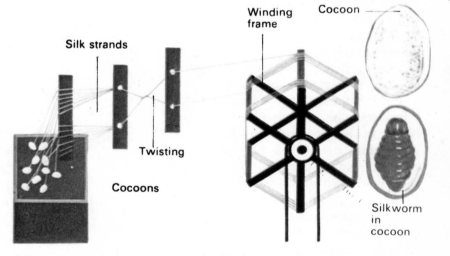

Silk strands

Cocoons

Twisting

Winding frame

Cocoon

Silkworm in cocoon

Silkworm cocoons are placed in hot water to melt the gum that holds the silk threads together. Then the threads from several cocoons are pulled out together and twisted. The silk is wound on a frame, then onto reels.

SILK The beautiful smooth cloth called silk is made from threads spun by the silkworm. This is actually the caterpillar of a moth. It eats only mulberry leaves.

When the caterpillar is fully grown, it wraps itself in a cocoon of fine silk, stuck together with gum. The ancient Chinese discovered how to wash away the gum and unwind the silk on to reels. It was then dyed and woven into cloth.

The Chinese may have kept their secret for more than two thousand years. But they sold silk to merchants who traveled the 'silk road' from Europe. Then in the year AD 552 two monks smuggled some silkworms out of China. People in Europe began keeping silkworms. Today, silk is also made in Japan.

SILVER is a beautiful shiny metal which is widely used to make jewelry and expensive tableware. It is a scarce, precious metal that does not readily lose its shine. It can be shaped easily by bending and hammering. To the scientist, silver is interesting because it conducts (passes on) heat and electricity better than any other substance. It also forms compounds that are sensitive to light. They are used in photography.

SKELETON The skeleton is the framework of bones which gives the body its shape. Our skeletons support and protect the soft parts inside. We can move easily because the skeleton is made of many different bones.

Bones are held together by *ligaments*, which are rather like elastic bands. Some bones are fastened so tightly they cannot move. Others are connected by *joints*, which can open and shut like hinges. Muscles attached to the bones by *tendons* make the body move.

The skull is a very light but strong case. It protects the brain. The bones in our arms and legs are long and thin. The backbone consists of a lot of little bones called *vertebrae*. Inside it is the important part of the nervous system called the spinal cord.

Animals with backbones are called *vertebrates*. Animals which do not have backbones are called *invertebrates*. Some of them, such as insects and crustaceans, have a shell-like covering called an external skeleton.

SKIING For thousands of years, skiing existed in Scandinavia as a means of cross-country travel. It became popular as a sport in the 19th century when people became inspired by the feat of Norwegian explorer Fridtjof Nansen who crossed the Greenland icecap on skis in 1888. Suddenly mountaineers realized they could be up on the mountains in the winter and they began to develop Alpine skiing techniques. Today there are two types of skiing, Nordic and Alpine.

Nordic skiing includes cross-country and ski jumping. Cross-country

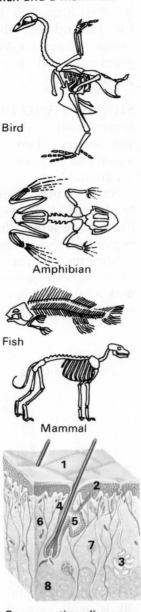

Below: The skeletons of a bird, an amphibian, a fish and a mammal.

Bird

Amphibian

Fish

Mammal

Cross-section diagram of the skin showing: (1) Surface cells (2) Epidermis (3) Sweat gland (4) Hair (5) Sebaceous gland (6) Blood (7) Nerve (8) Fat.

Above: The skunk's raised tail is a warning.

skis are narrow and the shoes are flexible. They attach to the skis at the toe which allows the heel to lift with each step. Ski jumping involves skiing down a steep slope, jumping, then landing further down the hill.

When a skier goes Alpine skiing, he usually takes a lift to the top of the mountain, then skis down. Alpine boots are stiff and fasten with buckles. They attach to the skis by means of safety bindings which are designed to release the boot if the skier falls. There are three types of competitive Alpine racing—downhill, slalom, and giant slalom.

SKIN is more than just the covering of the body. It keeps us from getting too hot or too cold. It helps keep out harmful germs. And it helps the body get rid of waste.

The skin is in two layers. The outside layer is called the *epidermis*. It grows all the time, to replace dead skin cells which are rubbed off. Our fingernails and toenails are made from these hard cells.

Underneath the epidermis is a thicker layer called the *dermis*. It contains nerves and blood vessels. Hair grows out of it. Here too are the sweat glands. When we sweat, tiny holes in the skin (called pores) open to let out water and waste.

SKUNK Skunks live in North America. They are relatives of badgers and weasels, and are animals of the woodlands. They eat insects, birds' eggs and small mammals.

Other animals keep well away from the skunk, because it has an unusual and effective defensive weapon. If attacked, the skunk turns its back, raises its bushy tail, and squirts out a foul-smelling spray of liquid from a special gland. With this protection, the skunk wanders about quite fearlessly. The only enemy which will attack it is an owl.

SLAVERY In the past rich people often kept slaves. Slaves were servants who could be bought and sold. They were often forced to do hard, cruel work and many died because their owners treated them badly. In ancient Egypt, Greece and Rome there were a great many slaves.

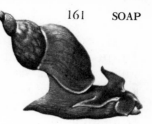

Few were lucky enough to gain their freedom.

When Europeans began settling in America, they took black slaves from Africa to work on the plantations. This slave trade was not stopped until the 1800s. All the black slaves in the southern United States were freed in 1865 after the American Civil War. However, in parts of Europe poor peasants or 'serfs' were treated like slaves right up until the 1900s.

SLEEP We spend about a third of our lives asleep. Our minds and bodies do not stop working while we sleep, but they do slow down. Without sleep, we feel tired and angry, and we cannot concentrate on what we are doing.

Part of the brain is active during sleep. Though our eyelids are closed, our eyes move rapidly. When this happens, scientists know we are dreaming.

Children need more sleep than adults because their bodies are growing. Babies sleep in the day as well as at night. But as we get older we get used to sleeping at a certain time. Our 'body clock' tells us when it's time to go to bed.

SMUGGLING means carrying goods secretly and illegally from country to country. Usually this is done to avoid paying government taxes called custom duties on goods which come from abroad. In the 1700s, when there were high duties on such goods as brandy and tobacco, smuggling was common. Landing in lonely coves by night, gangs of smugglers would bring in smuggled goods or 'contraband' by ship.

Any traveler who avoids paying duty on an article he has bought abroad is smuggling. But nowadays the real smuggler is a criminal, smuggling gold, diamonds or dangerous drugs. Narcotic drugs, such as heroin, are smuggled from the Far East to Europe and the United States.

SNAIL A snail cannot run away from an enemy. Instead it hides inside its shell. Snails are mollusks. There are land snails, fresh water snails and sea snails. Most snails eat plant food. But some water snails eat other mollusks.

A snail's eyes are on stalks. It also has feelers to help it find food. Snails like dark, cool places, and die if they get too dry and hot.

See also MOLLUSK.

SNAKE Snakes are legless reptiles. Unlike lizards, snakes have no eyelids. Most snakes lay eggs, but some give birth to live young.

All snakes prey on other animals, such as insects, birds, frogs and small mammals. Poisonous snakes kill their prey by biting it with their fangs and injecting poison, or 'venom', into its body. Many snakes have no poison but grab their prey with their sharp teeth. Some large snakes coil their long bodies around their prey and crush it until it suffocates.

Snakes swallow their food whole. After a meal, a snake rests until the food has been digested. Some snakes can go many months without eating. Snakes move by zig-zagging their bodies or by using scales on their stomachs to pull themselves forward.

Many people are frightened of snakes. But of some 2500 different kinds, only about 150 are dangerous to people. The most poisonous snakes include the cobra, mamba, puff adder and rattlesnake. The largest snakes are the python, boa and anaconda. These snakes constrict, or crush their prey.

SNOW Inside a cloud are millions of tiny water droplets. At the top, where the air is coldest, the water freezes to ice. Sometimes the drops of ice melt as they pass into warmer air and they fall as rain. But if the air is cold enough, they fall as snowflakes.

Snowflakes are tiny crystals. Each one has a beautiful pattern and always has six sides. A large snowflake is made of thousands of crystals stuck together.

Hailstones are little balls of ice. They are formed inside thunderclouds.

SOAP is a substance which helps wash away dirt and grease. The tiny soap particles are able to stick to and surround specks of dirt, and float them away in the water. Soap is made by boiling animal fat with a chemical called an alkali.

A water snail. Most snails eat plants, but some pond snails feed on other water animals.

The anaconda lives in the rivers and swamps of South America. This snake kills its prey by crushing it.

In a single large snowflake there may be thousands of tiny ice crystals.

SOIL is made from crumbled rocks. The process of wearing down rocks into small pieces is called weathering. It takes millions of years. Slowly a layer of soil is built up. Plants begin to grow, using minerals in the soil to make their food. Animals burrow through the soil, loosening it and letting in water and oxygen. Their waste products enrich the soil. When plants and animals die, their remains are broken down by bacteria into 'humus'. Humus holds moisture in the soil and binds the soil together.

SOLAR ENERGY refers to energy which comes from the sun (solar comes from the Latin word for sun). The energy is created by nuclear reactions taking place in the sun.

Scientists have long been working on ways to make electric current from solar energy. Already there are houses heated by solar energy which is collected by special devices, such as large mirrors.

SOUND A violin and a road drill are very different objects. But they do have one thing in common – they make sound. The violin makes a pleasant sound, which we call music. The road drill makes an unpleasant sound, which we call noise. Sound is produced by objects that are vibrating back and forth.

If you touch the strings of a violin, you can feel them vibrating. A vibrating string gently nudges the molecules of the air as it goes back and forth. These air molecules nudge other air molecules

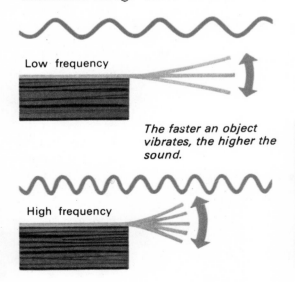

Low frequency

The faster an object vibrates, the higher the sound.

High frequency

and a wave spreads from the string though the air, just as ripples spread on a pond. When the sound wave strikes our ears, it causes our eardrums to vibrate and nerves send signals to the brain. This is how we hear. If there were no air, there would be nothing to carry the sound. That is why there is no sound in space.

Sounds are described in various ways. They can be loud or soft; high or low. High sounds, or, rather, high-pitched sounds, are made by things that vibrate rapidly. Low-pitched sounds are made by slow vibrations.

Some things produce sound waves pitched too high for us to hear. We call these waves *ultrasonic*. Bats find their way in the dark by bouncing ultrasonic waves off objects. In a similar way, ships carry ultrasonic equipment called *sonar* to find objects under water.

SOUTH AFRICA The republic of South Africa lies at the southern end of Africa. It is a warm, sunny land and many wild animals roam in its huge national parks. But there are also large cities, such as Johannesburg, Cape Town and Durban. South Africa is a rich country. Farming and mining (for gold, diamonds and uranium) are the chief activities.

South Africa was settled by Dutch people in the 1600s. Today their descendants are called 'Afrikaners'. Later, British settlers came. The Dutch or 'Boers' fought them, but in the end the British won. In 1910 South Africa became an independent country.

Although most South Africans are black, Colored (of mixed race) or Asian, the whites control the government. The whites also live separately, as part of a policy called *apartheid* or 'separate development'.

South American Indians from the Andes Mountains. Life for these villagers is often hard.

South Africa lies at the tip of the continent.

Facts and Figures
Area: 471,814 square miles
      (1,222,000 square kilometers)
Population: 25,000,000
Capital: Pretoria
Government: Republic
Money unit: Rand
Longest River: Orange, 1300 miles
      (2092 kilometers)
Highest Mountain: Thabana-Ntelyana,
      11,425 feet (3482 meters)

SOUTH AMERICA

Panama Canal

VENEZUELA

Atlantic Ocean

Amazon

PERU

ANDES

Pacific Ocean

BRAZIL

Gran Chaco

Pampas

River Plate system

ARGENTINA

Cape Horn

The narrow Isthmus of Panama joins South America to North America. Here the Panama Canal links the Atlantic and Pacific Oceans. South America has high mountains, such as the Andes, enormous rain forests in the Amazon basin, and rolling pampas plains. Its products include coffee, oil, cattle and minerals. Its people include primitive Indians, whose way of life is being changed as the jungle is cleared to make way for new cities such as Brasilia. Among other important cities of South America is Rio de Janeiro, where a colorful carnival is held every year.

SOUTH AMERICA The continent of South America is the fourth largest in the world. It has dense rain forests, barren deserts, wide grasslands and high mountains. In large areas there are hardly any people at all.

South America is joined to Central America by a thin strip of land called the Isthmus of Panama. The widest part of the continent is toward the north, where the climate is mostly hot and wet. Further south the land narrows, finally tapering to a point at Cape Horn. Here the climate is generally cold.

The Andes Mountains, the highest in South America, stretch for over 4350 miles, (7,000 kilometers) down the western side, overlooking the Pacific Ocean. In the Andes is Lake Titicaca, the highest large lake in the world. From the mountains several great rivers flow east across the continent to the Atlantic Ocean. The most important river is the mighty Amazon, which flows through thick forest. Other rivers are the Orinoco, the Sâo Francisco and the River Plate system.

In the center of the continent are vast plains. They include the forests of the Amazon basin which cover an area the size of Western Europe, the endless swamps and lakes of the Gran Chaco, and the grassy pampas of Argentina where gauchos (South American cowboys) herd cattle and horses.

South America has many wild animals, most of which live in the Amazon rain forest. There are tapirs, jaguars, monkeys, armadillos, anteaters, sloths, porcupines and many different birds and insects. The anaconda is one of the largest of all snakes. In the Andes mountains live llamas, which are relatives of camels. But South America has no large herds of animals, like those of Africa.

Because it has a variety of climates and soils, South America can produce many kinds of crops. In the hot regions coffee, cocoa, sugar and bananas are grown, and fruit, wheat, tobacco and cotton are also important. Rubber trees brought from Brazil were used to start the rubber industry in Asia. The trees of the forest give valuable woods such as mahogany, logwood and balsa. The potato came from South America, and so does the tree from which the drug quinine (used to treat malaria) is made.

South America is rich in minerals, such as copper, tin, iron, platinum, manganese, nitrates, bauxite, diamonds and emeralds. Mining is an important industry, and there are also large oilfields, particularly off the coast of Venezuela.

Despite this, most of the people of South America are poor. In the more remote regions the people live in small villages, without schools or hospitals. Many people work on plantations. Others are fishermen. New factories are being built, but one obstacle is the difficulty of transportation across mountains and

through the forests. People are crowding into the towns to find work, and South America has some of the largest and fastest-growing cities in the world.

The first people to reach South America were the Indians, who came from North America. The most advanced Indians were the Incas, who built a mighty empire. Christopher Columbus reached South America in 1498, and by the 1600s the Spanish and Portuguese had conquered most of the continent. Many Indians were killed by the Spanish or died from diseases brought from Europe. In the 1800s the countries of South America, inspired by the great Venezuelan general Simón Bolívar, fought for their independence and set up republics. Today, South America is a continent which is changing rapidly. Its governments are sometimes democratic, but more often are controlled by military leaders.

See also AMAZON; ANDES; COUNTRIES OF THE WORLD; INCA.

SPACE FLIGHT Today we live in an exciting Space Age. At last we can leave the Earth and travel in space. We can circle around the Earth in roomy space stations. We can travel to the Moon and return safely. We can also send spacecraft deep into space to explore the other planets.

The Space Age began in October 1957. That month the Russians launched the first spacecraft, *Sputnik 1*. A month later they launched *Sputnik 2*. This spacecraft contained the first space traveler, a dog called Laika. Man first went into space in April 1961, when Russian cosmonaut Yuri Gagarin flew once around the Earth. John Glenn became the first American to circle the Earth in 1962.

Sputnik was a tiny manmade moon, which circled around the Earth in space. We call such spacecraft artificial satellites, or simply satellites. They carry such equipment as measuring instruments, tape recorders, radios and cameras. They have special solar batteries, which produce electricity from sunlight. Satellites and other spacecraft are launched by huge rockets. The rocket which carried America's astronauts to the Moon was over 330 feet (100 meters) long.

Apollo command and service module

Above: The Skylab orbital space station was launched by the United States in 1973. Three astronauts could stay for 80 days inside Skylab, observing the stars and studying the Earth's surface.

The Russians launched Sputnik 2 in 1957. Inside was a dog called Laika, the first animal to fly in space. In 1961 the Russian cosmonaut Yuri Gagarin became the first man in space, making one orbit of the Earth in Vostok 1.

Apollo telescope mount

Orbital workshop

Multiple docking adaptor

The spacecraft which travel to the Moon and other planets are usually called probes. Some of them are designed to land. They have a rocket motor to help slow them down for a soft landing. Probes have already photographed all the planets out to Jupiter, and have landed on Venus and Mars.

A spacecraft designed to carry men is much more complicated than an unmanned probe. It must protect the astronauts when they take-off and keep them alive while they are in space. It must also bring them safely back to Earth. Until now most manned spacecraft have been made up of several sections. Only the crew section comes back to Earth.

Soon American astronauts will fly into space in a space shuttle. This is a craft that can be used again and again. It has wings like an airplane and can land on an ordinary runway.

See also ASTRONAUT.

SPAIN is a country in southwest Europe. It is separated from France by the Pyrenees Mountains. With Portugal, Spain makes the Iberian Peninsula.

Much of the center of the country is a high plateau, where few trees grow. Northern Spain is wet and cool, but the south is hot and dry. The best farmland is near the coast.

Most Spanish people work on farms. Spain is famous for olives, oranges and onions. The most famous Spanish wine is sherry. Cork is obtained from cork-oak trees. A great many sheep and goats are kept. Important industries are mining, steel-making, shipbuilding and engineering. Many tourists visit Spain every year.

During the 8th century the Moors from North Africa conquered Spain. But by the 13th century Christian kings had recaptured most of the country. Spain became rich and strong, especially after the 1500s when Spanish soldiers conquered much of South America. Later, however, Spain grew weak and lost its overseas lands.

In 1931 Spain became a republic. From 1936 to 1939 there was a terrible civil war, after which General Francisco Franco ruled as a dictator. When he died in 1975 Spain became a kingdom again.

Facts and Figures
Area: 194,980 square miles (505,000 square kilometers)
Population: 35,500,000
Capital: Madrid
Government: Monarchy
Money unit: Peseta
Longest River: Ebro, 565 miles (909 kilometers)
Highest Mountain: Teide (on the island of Tenerife), 12,199 feet, (3718 meters)

A magnificent hilltop castle overlooking a village in the Spanish province of Almería.

Spain occupies most of the Iberian Peninsula.

SPICES come from plants. They are used in cooking to flavor food. In the Middle Ages, when meat had to be salted or dried to keep it from going bad, spices made it taste better. Europeans first sailed to India and the Far East in search of spices.

Today, we use many spices, including nutmeg, vanilla, saffron and the pepper pods called chilies. Caraway, sage, parsley, dill, thyme and mustard are also used as herbs. Some spices are sweet and scented. Others, such as those used in curries, give food a hot taste.

See also HERBS.

The water spider carries
air bubbles down to its
nest underwater.

The bite of the tarantula
is poisonous but it is not
fatal to man.

*Above: Some spiders
spin webs. But the
trapdoor spider hides in
a hole, and waits for its
prey.*

SPIDER

Spiders are not insects. Their bodies are made up of two parts (not three) and they have eight legs (not six). Spiders are related to scorpions.

All spiders make silk inside their bodies. Some spiders use the silk to make webs to trap insects for food. When an insect is caught in the web, the spider wraps it in silk before killing it with its poisonous fangs.

Not all spiders build webs. Wolf spiders chase their prey on the ground. Crab spiders lurk inside flowers, while trapdoor spiders lie in wait in holes. The largest spider is the South American bird-eating spider. The black widow and some other spiders have a bite that is dangerous to people.

Female spiders are usually bigger than males. After mating, the male escapes quickly before the female can eat him.

SPIES

A spy is a person who is sent secretly into enemy territory to gather information (called *intelligence*), usually for political or military purposes. The practice of spying is called *espionage*.

Spies have been around for centuries. Historians say that the ancient Egyptians, for example, hid spies in flour sacks on ships they wished to capture.

Modern spies are highly trained in the use of microphones, X-rays, and microdots—tiny film messages printed on what look like periods.

SPINNING AND WEAVING

Cotton is our most useful textile material. It grows as short fibers around the seeds of the cotton plant. The harvested fibers are much too short to be made into fabric. First they have to be twisted into longer threads, or yarns. This is called spinning. The yarns are then joined to form a fabric. This is usually done by weaving.

For thousands of years women spun cotton and wool by hand. First they collected the fibers together in a loose rope. Then they twisted and drew out the rope into a tighter and finer thread. About 700 years ago they began using spinning wheels to twist and draw out the thread.

In a modern spinning mill the fibers go through carding and combing machines before they are spun. There they are cleaned and untangled, and formed into loose ropes. The ropes are drawn out and twisted into yarn by machines and then wound on to reels.

Yarn is woven into cloth on a loom. In weaving, one set of yarns (weft) is threaded at right angles under and over another set (warp). The warp yarns run lengthways on the loom. Each of the warp yarns is raised and lowered by a device called a harness. A shuttle carries the weft yarn sideways through the gap between the raised and lowered threads. On some modern high-speed looms a jet of air or water carries the weft through.

See also COTTON; DYES; SILK; TEXTILES; WOOL.

Below: How cloth is woven on a loom, showing how the shuttle carries the weft threads backward and forward across the warp. All weaving was done by hand until the 1700s when power looms were invented.

Plain weave cloth

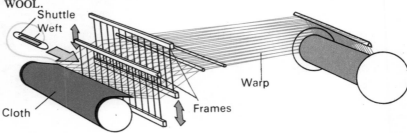

Shuttle / Weft / Warp / Cloth / Frames

SQUIRREL

Squirrels are small furry animals with bushy tails. They belong to the rodent family. Most squirrels live in trees. The red squirrel lives in Europe and Asia. The North American gray squirrel has spread to other countries. Flying squirrels can glide from the tree tops, using folds of skin between their legs as 'wings'.

Some squirrels live in holes in the ground. Gophers, prairie dogs and chipmunks are ground squirrels which live in America.

Below: Red squirrel.

STAMPS Postage stamps were first used in Britain in 1840. They were the idea of a man called Rowland Hill. Soon people began collecting stamps as a hobby. Another name for stamp collecting is philately.

The first stamps issued in the United States, called Postmaster's Provisinals, were issued by postmasters of individual towns. It was not until 1847, though, that the federal government issued the first two stamps. A 10 cent stamp bore a portrait of George Washington; a 5 cent issue carried a likeness of Ben Franklin.

Perforations (little holes) round the edges make it easier to tear stamps from the sheet on which they are printed. To stop stamps being used twice, the post office 'cancels' them with an ink postmark. This shows where and when the letter was posted. To start a stamp collection, you can buy packets of stamps. The stamps should be mounted in a stamp album, using special gummed mounts or paper hinges.

See also POST OFFICE.

STAR The stars we see in the night sky are balls of glowing gases. They are so far away that they seem very tiny. But if we could get closer, they would look like the Sun. For the Sun is a star, and a very ordinary one. Some stars are very much bigger and brighter than the Sun. Others are much smaller and dimmer.

Most stars shine steadily year in, year out. But some change their brightness. They are called variable stars. Some stars suddenly explode and blast themselves apart. Others wink on and off so quickly you don't even notice. The **brightest star in the sky is called Sirius** or the Dog Star. Stars shine by nuclear power; heat and light are produced in the heart of a star when atoms of hydrogen gas fuse, or join together.

Every night the stars appear to circle overhead. And different stars come into view every month. This is because the Earth spins like a top in space, and moves around the Sun during the year.

See also NUCLEAR POWER; SUN.

STARFISH A starfish is not a fish, but a spiny-skinned sea animal. Some have up

The spiny-skinned starfishes use their sucker feet to cling to rocks and to open shells.

Taurus

Cancer

Sagittarius

Groups of stars are called constellations. Each group is named after the pattern its stars form. Shown here are Taurus (the bull); Cancer (the crab); and Sagittarius (the archer).

In 1788 James Watt built this steam engine. The steam drove pistons connected to a beam. As the beam rocked, gears turned a drive wheel.

to 44 arms. But most starfish have five. A starfish uses its strong arms to pull open the shell of a mollusk. Then it pushes its stomach inside the shell to digest the mollusk's soft body.

STEAM ENGINE A hundred years ago the most important kind of engine was the steam engine. It powered machines in industry, locomotives on the railways and ships at sea. In the modern world it has been replaced by better engines, such **as gas and diesel engines, and by** electrical machines.

James Watt built the first really efficient engines in the late 1700s and made them suitable for driving industrial machinery. Earlier engines had only been used for pumping water from mines.

In Watt's type of engine, steam pushes a piston back and forth in a cylinder. The piston is connected to whatever is to be driven – for example, the wheels of a locomotive. Steam is produced by burning coal or wood in a furnace beneath a boiler. In a steam locomotive most of the engine is taken up by the boiler. Hot gases from the furnace pass through tubes in the boiler and heat the water. The steam produced goes to the cylinders and drives the pistons. When it has done its job, it goes up the chimney. This is what causes the puffing noise a steam locomotive makes.

A rather different kind of steam engine is the steam turbine. Huge steam turbines **power most electrical generators and** many ships. Each has a shaft on which there are many blades. When steam is forced through the blades, it causes the shaft to spin, just as the wind turns the sails of a windmill.

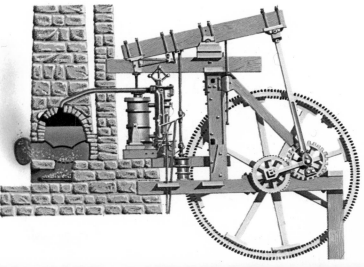

STORK

Storks live in many parts of the world. The natural home for these long-legged birds is marsh or grassland. The stork uses its long beak to catch frogs, insects and small mammals.

White storks migrate every spring. They fly from Africa to Europe. Often they nest on the roofs of houses. People encourage this because they think the storks bring them good luck.

In parts of Europe white storks nest on chimneys. These birds spend the winter in Africa but return every spring.

SUBMARINE

Ships that can sail under water are called submarines. A submarine dives by letting water into tanks around the hull (body). This makes it heavier than water. To surface it blows the water out, making it lighter again. It is steered under water by fins at the sides and a rudder at the rear. A periscope enables the captain to see above the surface while the submarine is still submerged.

Ordinary submarines are propelled under water by a propeller driven by electric batteries. They have to surface when their batteries run down. On the water they are propelled by diesel engines, which also charge the batteries.

Nuclear submarines are powered by a nuclear reactor. They can remain under water for months at a time. These submarines are deadly weapons, for they can launch nuclear missiles from under the water at a target thousands of miles away.

SUBWAYS

are railroads which run underground. Sometimes, in big cities, they are the quickest way to travel. Nearly six million passengers a day ride on New York City's subway. In Paris and Moscow, the subway is called the Metro. In London, it is simply called the Underground. The London Underground is the world's biggest and oldest subway. It dates back to 1863.

Subways are powered by electricity.

They have cars which can hold many people standing up and sitting down. They have sliding doors to save space. Some, like the Bay Area Rapid Transit (BART) System in San Francisco, California, are controlled by signals from a computer. They operate automatically.

SUGAR

Plants make sugar for their own food. The sugar we use to sweeten food is called *sucrose*. It comes from sugar beet and sugar cane. Other sugars are *fructose* (from fruits), *glucose* (from fruits, vegetables and grain), and *lactose* (from milk).

Sugar cane looks like bamboo. It grows in hot, wet lands. The cane is cut and crushed to squeeze out the juice. Sugar beet is a root vegetable. It grows in cooler climates. The beets are sliced and boiled to make sugar. Maple trees also provide sugar. Raw sugar is brown. It is refined (purified) to make it white.

SUN

The Sun is our nearest star. It is a great ball of very hot gases swirling in space. All the time it pours out heat and light as atoms of hydrogen gas join together inside it to form atoms of another gas – helium. Life on Earth depends on this heat and light. Without it, the Earth would be a dark, cold and dead lump of rock. All living things need warmth, and plants need sunlight to make food.

The Sun is very much like many other stars in the sky. It appears bigger and hotter only because it is much nearer than the other stars. But compared with the Earth, the Sun is very big indeed. You could get more than a million Earths inside the Sun.

The Earth is part of the Sun's family, or solar system. It is one of nine planets. *Comets* are other members of the Sun's

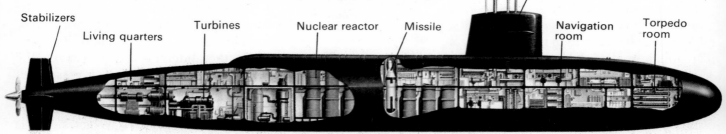

Stabilizers — Living quarters — Turbines — Nuclear reactor — Missile — Conning tower — Navigation room — Torpedo room

This cutaway diagram of a nuclear submarine shows the navigation room below the conning tower, and the nuclear reactor and steam turbine engines in the stern. Guided missiles can be fired from underwater. The submarine can stay submerged for long periods.

family. All these bodies constantly circle around the Sun. The Sun is moving, too. It travels through space with all the other stars in the sky.

SUPERMARKETS Before supermarkets became popular in the 1930s, shoppers used to make separate stops to buy meat, canned goods, vegetables, etc. Supermarkets are large, self-service stores where all sorts of merchandise—from food to housewares to cosmetics—is gathered under one roof, making it easier to shop.

SUPERSONIC means faster than the speed of sound (which is about 760 miles, 1,223 km, per hour, at sea level). The first airplane which flew at supersonic speed was the U.S. Air Force's X-1 in 1947. In recent years engineers have developed supersonic transports (SST's) which can carry passengers at speeds of 1,550 miles (2,494 km) per hour.

Sometimes a loud, explosive noise is heard when airplanes go at supersonic speed. This is called *sonic boom*.

SWIMMING Most animals can swim naturally. But human beings have to learn to swim. They learn to float in the water, and to use their hands and feet in the different swimming strokes.

There are four main strokes. They are the crawl (the fastest), the butterfly, the back stroke, and the breast stroke. Most people swim for fun in indoor pools or at the seaside. But swimming is also an important sport. There are competitions in swimming and diving. And there are long distance swims, such as across the English Channel.

TAX The government needs money in order to run the country. It gets this money mainly from the taxes we pay. Taxes pay for roads, schools, hospitals and many other services the country needs.

There are several kinds of taxes. Most people pay tax on their income – the money they earn. Income tax is a direct tax. So is the tax paid by companies on their profits. Indirect taxes are taxes on goods and services. Some taxes have to be paid

when goods enter the country. These are called customs duties. A value added tax (VAT) is a tax paid on goods we buy, such as candy or clothes. The government also puts special taxes, called excise duties, on goods such as tobacco and alcohol.

A government department called the Treasury looks after the country's money. Each year the government works out how much money it plans to spend and how much will have to come from taxes. This is called the budget, and Congress has to approve the government's plans.

There are also local taxes on land paid by homeowners to the local governments.

TCHAIKOVKSY, Peter Ilych (1840-1893) was a Russian composer whose music is among the most popular ever written. He was a rather unhappy man and much of his music sounds sad. Tchaikovsky composed for orchestras, the violin and the piano. He also wrote operas. But he is perhaps best remembered for ballets like *Swan Lake*, *The Sleeping Beauty* and the *Nutcracker Suite*.

Tea pickers at work in Sri Lanka. Only the top bud and the leaves just below are picked. The best tea comes from bushes grown on high ground, where it is cooler.

TEA is a popular drink. It is made by pouring boiling water onto tea leaves. The leaves come from tea bushes, which are grown mainly in India, Sri Lanka and China. The young leaves are picked, dried and crushed. Then the tea is packed in boxes and sent abroad.

Tea came to Europe from China in the 1600s. At first it was brewed and stored in barrels, like beer. Today most people make tea in a teapot.

TEETH cut and chew food into pieces small enough to be swallowed. They also help to make sounds when we talk.

The kinds of teeth an animal has **depend on the kind of food it eats.** Beasts of prey, such as wolves and lions, have long sharp teeth. They use them to kill their prey and to tear the meat. Rodents, such as squirrels, have gnawing teeth. Grazing animals, such as cattle, have flat grinding teeth. Some snakes have special teeth called fangs which inject poison into their prey.

Human beings have sharp cutting teeth *and* flat grinding teeth. This is because we eat both meat and plant food. Babies are born without teeth. Our first 'baby' teeth drop out. Permanent teeth grow in their place, 16 in each jaw.

TELEPHONE The telephone was invented in 1876 by Alexander Graham Bell. The first telephone calls could only be sent through wires. Now a telephone call may travel by way of wire, or by radio, sometimes bounced off man-made moons in space. Many telephone calls may one day travel as beams of light through glass fibers.

By picking up a telephone and dialing a number, we can get in touch with someone anywhere in the world. When you dial a number, the telephone sends out electrical pulses. They go to an exchange, which automatically connects your line to that of the person you are calling. The exchange then rings the bell of that person's telephone. In some country districts, calls may have to be routed through an operator.

The telephone receiver contains a small microphone in the mouthpiece and a small loudspeaker in the earpiece. When you talk, the microphone changes your voice into electrical signals. These travel down the wires to the earpiece of the person you are talking to. There they are changed back into the sound of your voice.

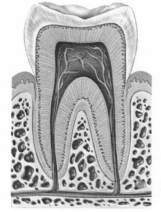

A molar (grinding) tooth. Above the gum is the crown, below it the roots. The tooth is protected by hard enamel.

The simple telescope consists of a single tube containing lenses.

As you speak, a diaphragm in the telephone mouthpiece vibrates. Carbon granules 'translate' the vibrations into electric current which can travel through wires. At the earpiece, an electromagnet and another diaphragm reproduce the original sounds.

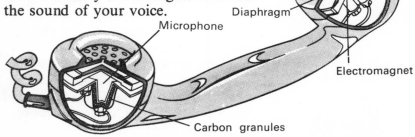

Earpiece

Diaphragm

Microphone

Electromagnet

Carbon granules

TELESCOPE A telescope is an instrument that makes distant objects appear nearer and larger. Astronomers use telescopes to observe the heavenly bodies.

The simplest type of telescope consists of a tube containing two lenses – pieces of curved glass. The lenses bend the light rays from the distant object and make it appear as if the object were nearer. This kind of telescope is called a refracting telescope because the lenses bend, or *refract*, the light.

Most astronomers, however, use reflecting telescopes, which have a mirror to collect and bend the light. Reflecting telescopes can be made much bigger than refracting telescopes and can 'see' more clearly. Astronomers do not often look through big telescopes. Rather they take photographs through them. Photographic film stores pictures of stars. And it can record stars too faint for the eye to see.

As well as light telescopes, astronomers use radio telescopes. They are large metal dishes which gather radio waves sent out by heavenly bodies.

TELEVISION brings us 'pictures from a distance'. That is what the word 'television' means. Our television set can show us live pictures of sports programs and festivals taking place on the other side of the world. Television brings news, educational programs and entertainment of all kinds right into the home. The British Broadcasting Corporation (BBC) transmitted the first regular television programs in 1936.

The two main pieces of television equipment are the camera and the receiver. The camera records an image of the scene it views on an electrically charged plate. A beam of electrons then sweeps back and forth in a series of lines across this plate. The result is electric signals which represent the brightness in different parts of the scene. These signals are combined with a radio wave and sent out by a transmitter.

The aerial of the television set picks up the wave. Circuits in the set separate the signal from the wave. These signals then go to the picture tube. In the tube a 'gun' fires a beam of electrons at the screen causing a spot of light. The television signals alter the strength of the beam

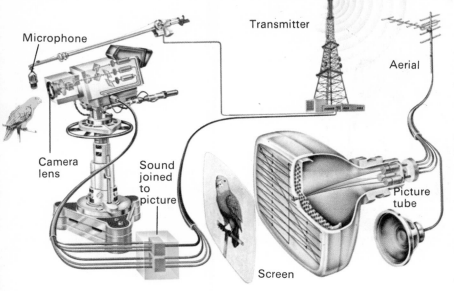

The television camera changes light waves into electrical 'vision' signals. With 'sound' signals from the microphone, these are transmitted on radio 'carrier' waves. The receiver's cathode ray tube and loudspeaker change the signals back into pictures and sounds.

and thereby the brightness of the spot. They also cause the beam to sweep back and forth in a series of lines just as the beam of the television camera did. The result is lines of spots of varying brightness. The lines are very close together, and our eyes see them as a complete picture.

TENNIS is one of the oldest sports. It was played in various forms by the ancient Egyptians, Greeks, and Persians. For many hundreds of years, the upper classes played an indoor game called court tennis. It wasn't until the 19th century that lawn tennis, a game played outdoors with a racket and ball, became popular.

In recent years there has been a tennis explosion, with estimates of more than 34,000,000 tennis players in the U.S. alone.

There are five basic tennis strokes: forehand (hitting the ball from the right); backhand (hitting the ball from the left); service (beginning of a point); volley (hitting the ball before it bounces); and smash (hitting the ball overhead, except when serving).

TEXTILES are materials made by weaving, looping or twisting threads of fibers together. The most common type textile is woven cloth. In cloth the threads go under and over one another at right angles in a regular way. Knitted textiles are different. They are formed by rows of loops. Each row hangs on the one above it. Lace is a textile made by twisting threads together.

Many different kinds of fibers are used to make textiles. Cotton is the most important natural fiber. It comes from the cotton plant. Another important plant fiber is flax which is made into linen. Wool from sheep and silk from silkworms are the most widely used animal fibers. A great many textiles used nowadays are manmade.

See also COTTON; SILK; SPINNING AND WEAVING; WOOL.

THANKSGIVING DAY was first celebrated in October 1621 by the Pilgrims in Plymouth, Massachusetts. They had had a bitter winter since the *Mayflower* had brought them to the new country, and they wanted to give thanks that at last they had good crops, friendly relationships with the Indians and better health. The first Thanksgiving lasted three days.
(See also AMERICAN COLONIES)

THEATER The first theaters were in ancient Greece. People watched plays as part of a religious festival. They sat in the open air on a hillside, while below actors and dancers performed on a space called the orchestra. Behind the actors was a changing room called the skene. This later became a stage, and it gives us the modern word 'scenery' and 'scene'.

England's first real theaters were built in the 1500s. Each had a jutting stage almost surrounded by the audience. Rich people sat under cover. Poor spectators stood in the 'pit', and got wet if it rained. But soon all theaters had roofs. Complicated scenery and stage machinery began to be used. And to hide the workings from the audience, a 'picture frame' was put round the stage.

THERMOMETER A thermometer is an instrument that measures temperature, or in other words how hot it is. Some simple thermometers consist of a thin tube with a bulb at the bottom containing liquid. When liquids are heated, they expand, or grow bigger. So when the liquid in the thermometer becomes hotter, it expands and rises up the tube. The hotter it is, the higher it rises. The liquid in these thermometers is often mercury or colored alcohol.

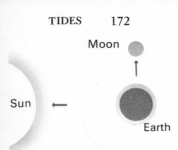

NEAP TIDES

SPRING TIDES

Spring tides are caused by the Sun and Moon pulling together. Neap tides occur when the Sun and Moon are at right angles to one another.

The Bengal tiger lives in India. In its jungle home, its striped coat becomes part of the pattern of sunlight, shadows and long grass. This makes it hard to see. Tigers prefer thick cover, and seek out cool places, such as caves or swamps, during the heat of the day.

TIDES Twice a day the tide comes in and goes out again. At high tide the sea floods up the beach. Then it ebbs, or falls, until at low tide a wide stretch of beach may be left dry.

Tides are caused by the Moon and the Sun pulling the world's oceans towards them. This is the result of gravity. Because the Moon is closer to Earth than the Sun is, its pull is stronger. The land is pulled as well, but because water moves more easily, the effect on the oceans is much more obvious.

There are roughly two high tides and two low tides every 24 hours. When the Moon and Sun are on the same side of the Earth, their combined pull produces the biggest tides, called spring tides. When the Moon and Sun are pulling at right angles to each other the smallest tides, called neap tides, occur.

TIGER The tiger is the largest of the big cats. Its home is Asia. Most tigers live in hot forests. But the largest come from cold Siberia.

Tigers hunt alone and at night. They prey on deer, wild cattle and pigs. Only an old or sick tiger will attack people. The tiger's stripes camouflage it in long grass. Unlike other cats, tigers often bathe to keep cool.

Many tigers have been killed for their handsome skins. Now they are protected in India.

TIME Most of us live our lives by the clock. We go to school, have our meals and go to bed at regular times. Life would be very difficult to arrange if we did not have a reliable way of time-keeping. We measure time, or rather the passage of time, with clocks and watches. They help us split each day into 24 hours; each hour into 60 minutes; and each minute into 60 seconds. Day, hour, minute and second are units of time.

We can say what time it is in two ways – by a 12-hour clock or a 24-hour clock. On a 12-hour clock school starts at 9 o'clock in the morning. We also call this 9 a.m. (a.m. stands for *ante meridian*, meaning before noon). School finishes at 3 o'clock in the afternoon, or 3 p.m. (p.m. means *post meridian*, or after noon). On the 24-hour clock school starts at 0900 hours and finishes at 1600 hours.

The day is a natural unit of time. It is the time the Earth takes to spin around once in space. Our other main natural unit of time is the year. This is the time it takes the Earth to travel once around the Sun. There are $365\frac{1}{4}$ days in the year.

The Moon circles the Earth about every 27 days. This gives us another unit of time – the month. Our calendar has 12 months each year.

Our calendar is a way of arranging the units of time in a regular way so that we can plan the time ahead. For three years out of four, we have a year 365 days long. It is split up into 11 months of 30 and 31 days and one month (February) of 28 days. Every fourth year, however, February has 29 days. It is called a leap year. The extra day makes up for the $\frac{1}{4}$ missed out of the calendar year.

See also CALENDAR; CLOCKS AND WATCHES.

TOBACCO is made from the dried leaves of the tobacco plant. Its home is America. The Spaniards carried tobacco back to Spain in the 1500's and today to

bacco is grown in Asia, Africa and Europe as well as America.

Tobacco leaf can be made into pipe, cigar or cigarette tobacco, or snuff. Smoking tobacco is a bad habit, because it contains substances which harm the body. It is especially bad for the lungs.

TORNADO Another name for a tornado is whirlwind. It is a violent storm, which usually begins in open country during thundery weather. The winds whirl at great speed, creating a black funnel of cloud which spins its way down towards the ground. When it touches the ground, the air is sucked up into the funnel and buildings in the tornado's path are blown apart.

Tornadoes follow a narrow, zigzag path, doing great damage. Over the sea they cause water-spouts, and in the deserts similar storms produce whirling sandstorms called dust-devils.

TORTOISE AND TURTLE Unlike other reptiles, tortoises and turtles have hard shells to protect their bodies.

Tortoises are land animals. They live in warm countries and eat plant food. A tortoise cannot run away from an enemy. Instead, it tucks its head and legs into its shell. Some tortoises can live to be much more than 100 years old – older than any other animals.

Turtles live in the sea. They have flatter shells than tortoises, and use their legs as paddles for swimming. On land they are clumsy. Some turtles eat fish and mollusks, others prefer plants. Small freshwater turtles are called terrapins.

Because people have hunted them for food, sea turtles are rare. Female turtles crawl ashore to lay their eggs in the sand. The eggs hatch in the heat of the sun, and the baby turtles scuttle down the beach to the safety of the sea.

Small tortoises and terrapins can be kept as pets. But they need proper care.

TOYS are objects that provide fun and amusement, such as dolls, rattles, pull toys, metal soldiers, music boxes, and blocks. Miniature versions of everyday objects used by grown-ups are also toys—there are tiny dishes, pots and pans, and typewriters.

Above: A tornado over town in Texas. These violent wind storms can travel across country at speeds of up to 50 miles (80 kilometers) an hour.

The African leopard tortoise (above) is a land reptile. It feeds mainly on plants. The snapping turtle (below), also from Africa, is a flesh-eater with strong jaws.

Toys also can be educational, and help a child learn about the world even before he or she enters school. Rattles and bell toys help a baby become familiar with different shapes and sounds. Mobiles hanging over his crib teach him to distinguish colors. Toy clocks teach children to tell time, while alphabet blocks help them learn to spell.

TRADE UNION Trade unions are organizations or associations of workers. By joining together in a union, workers are better able to negotiate, or bargain, with their employers for higher wages or improved working conditions.

TREASURE is a hoard of gold, silver, precious stones or other valuables, often hidden in a secret place. In fairy tales treasure is often guarded by a fierce monster. In real life rich people sometimes buried their valuables in time of war. Such treasures occasionally remain hidden for hundreds, even thousands of years. Sometimes they are discovered by some lucky person. "Treasure Trove," as these riches are called, belongs to the government. But the finder usually gets its value in money.

The ancient Egyptians buried their dead pharaohs (kings) in tombs beneath great stone pyramids. They filled the tombs with treasure. Most of the tombs were later broken into and robbed. But in 1923 two British archaeologists opened the tomb of the pharaoh Tutankhamun and found a wonderful treasure. In the past, gold coins, ornaments, jewels and weapons were often buried with dead kings or chieftains. In 1939 a wooden ship, laden with treasure, was found buried at Sutton Hoo, in England. It had been buried by the Saxons in honor of a great chieftain.

When the Spaniards conquered the Incas of Peru in the 1500s they found temples decorated with gold. They captured the Inca king Atahualpa, who filled a room with gold as a ransom for his release. But the greedy Spaniards killed Atahualpa and melted down the beautiful ornaments and statues so that they could more easily carry the gold back to Spain.

Many exciting stories are told of pirate treasure buried on lonely islands. Mysterious maps are said to mark the spot where the treasure lies. There is certainly treasure hidden beneath the sea, in the wrecks of sunken ships. Sometimes divers are able to swim down to a wreck and recover its treasure.

TREE Trees are the largest of all plants. The world's biggest tree is the California redwood which reaches a height of over 330 feet (100 meters). Trees also live longer than any other actively living thing. There are bristlecone pine trees more than 4000 years old.

Trees grow a little each year. The tips of their branches grow longer, and a ring of tissue in the main trunk and the older branches produces more cells to make them thicker.

Evergreen trees keep their leaves all year round. Conifers, such as spruce, pine and fir, are evergreens. They grow in colder climates, and most are cone-shaped (so that snow slides off their branches). Their leaves are thin and hard, and look like needles. Conifers do not have flowers; instead, they have winged seeds hidden inside 'cones'.

Many tropical trees are also evergreens. But they have broad leaves, and flowers. Broad leaved trees grow in cool countries too. Those that shed their leaves in autumn are called 'deciduous' trees. All trees take in water through their roots and give out water through their leaves. Deciduous trees stop doing this when they are leafless and start again when they grow new leaves in the spring.

Once most of Europe and North America was covered by thick forests. There are still great forests in Canada, Siberia, South America, Africa and Asia. But many trees have been cut down to make room for farms and towns, and to supply timber for factories and homes.

Trees are useful in many ways. Besides wood, they also provide us with many fruits and nuts, and with products such as rubber, turpentine, maple syrup and palm oil. Tree roots bind the soil and stop erosion by wind and water. Trees provide shelter for birds and they make our surroundings more attractive. Trees

Beech   Common oak   Aspen   Yew
Black poplar   Sycamore   Ash   Walnut
Horse chestnut   London plane   White willow   Lime
Elm   Bird cherry   Larch   Sweet chestnut
Silver birch   Lombardy poplar   Whitebeam   Holly
Scotch pine   Wynch elm   Alder   Field maple
Hornbeam   Rowan   Norway spruce   Sessile oak

take a long time to grow. So it is important to look after them, and to replace those that die or are cut down.

See also FOREST; WOOD.

UNITED KINGDOM

England, Scotland, Wales and Northern Ireland together make up the United Kingdom of Great Britain and Northern Ireland. The head of state is the queen, but parliament makes the laws, and the government is led by the prime minister.

The United Kingdom is an island nation, and has always lived by trade. The narrow English Channel separates it from the rest of Europe. Although it is a small country, it has many different kinds of scenery. The climate is mild, with plenty of rainfall.

In this rather crowded country, most people live in towns. But farming is important.

There is coal underground, and natural gas and oil offshore beneath the sea. Together these fuels help to provide power for the nation's many industries. Heavy industries are mainly in northern England, South Wales and Scotland. Many people live in and around London, the capital and business center.

By exploration, trade and wars from the 1500s onwards, the United Kingdom gained colonies in America, Africa, Asia and Australia. The Industrial Revolution turned it into the world's leading industrial country, with railways and factories. By the middle of the 1800s it was the center of a huge empire.

Almost all the countries once governed by the United Kingdom are now independent. Many are members of the Commonwealth. After World War II, the United Kingdom was much less powerful.

Map of the United Kingdom.

Facts and Figures
Area: 94,594 square miles
(245,000 square kilometers)
Population: 56,000,000
Capital: London
Government: Monarchy
Money unit: Pound
Longest River: Severn
180 miles
(290 kilometers)
Highest Mountain: Ben Nevis
4406 feet
(1343 meters)

UNITED NATIONS

In the present century there have been two terrible world wars. The United Nations Organization was set up in 1945 to try and prevent wars.

The U.N. tries to settle quarrels between countries peacefully. It helps refugees and children, and sends experts to fight hunger, disease and ignorance in poor countries. The headquarters of the U.N. are in New York. Here the General Assembly and the Security Council meet to discuss world problems.

UNITED STATES OF AMERICA

Fifty states make up the United States of America. This huge country is often called simply America or the USA. It consists of the middle part of North America, and also Alaska in the north and Hawaii in the Pacific Ocean.

There are many kinds of land. The highest mountains include the Sierra Nevada in the west and the Alaska Range. There are thick forests and great rivers, including the long Mississippi, Missouri, Ohio and Rio Grande. The Colorado River winds through the awe-inspiring Grand Canyon. In the north are the five Great Lakes, on the border with Canada. The Great Salt Lake, seven times as salty as the sea, is in the west. In the center of the country are wide plains called prairies; in the south there are deserts and swamps.

The climate varies from region to region. Some areas are hot in summer and cold in winter, but the south and west coasts have mild winters. Most regions get good rainfall.

There are many kinds of animals; the largest are the moose, bison (called buffalo) and bears. There are also deer, pumas, wolves, coyotes, beavers, alligators and rattlesnakes.

The United States has very great natural resources. Its farmland is fertile. Huge crops of wheat are grown on the prairies, and maize (corn), tobacco, cotton, fruit and vegetables are also grown. From the forests comes timber, while underground are valuable minerals, including coal, oil, natural gas, iron, copper, zinc, gold and uranium. Many rivers and lakes have been dammed to produce electricity.

The stately white dome of the Capitol building in Washington DC. The Capitol was designed by William Thornton, who won a contest for its design in 1792.

The United States grew from 13 colonies on the east coast to a republic stretching from the Atlantic to the Pacific oceans.

landed astronauts on the Moon. It has become the strongest and richest country in the world.

See also NORTH AMERICA.

More than half the people live in towns and cities, for the United States is the greatest industrial country in the world. Its factories make aircraft, computers, cars, machines, foodstuffs and many other kinds of goods. The biggest city is New York; and other large and important cities are Los Angeles, San Francisco, Chicago, Philadelphia, Pittsburgh, Detroit and New Orleans. The central or federal government is in Washington, the capital. The President lives in the White House.

The republic grew into a union of 50 states. Many poor people from European countries came to the United States. Industry developed so quickly that the Americans soon enjoyed a higher standard of living than any other people in the world.

In the 20th century the United States has played an important part in world affairs, especially since World War II. Its rivalry with Russia led to a period of bad relations, known as the 'cold war'. During the 1960s the United States fought the Vietnam War and

UNITED STATES OF AMERICA, HISTORY OF

When Columbus discovered America there were about 500,000 Indians who lived by farming and hunting. Today, there are still about the same number of Indians in the U.S. but their numbers are dwarfed by the more than 200,000,000 other Americans.

The first settlers had begun arriving in 1585. About 90 percent of the early settlers were farmers, although fishing, whaling and fur trapping were also businesses. The British government felt that if they could keep the colonists from becoming too industrial, they would continue to buy manufactured goods from the mother country. Britain therefore made many laws which restricted commerce.

Not all the first Americans came inspired by the desire to settle a new land. It was common that prisoners were offered a choice between a jail sentence or being sent to America. Orphans, beggars, and the unemployed in England were often taken by force from their villages and sent to the new country since they were considered a burden on the rest of the village. And several hundred Africans came to America in chains to serve as slaves.

Some men and women who couldn't afford to buy the ship passage to the new land came as servants to the wealthy.

By 1776, the 13 colonies, feeling a desire to be independent of Great Britain, sent representatives to the First Continental Congress in order to decide on how they could get greater freedom from England. Later in 1776, this same Congress would declare independence starting the Revolutionary War.

During the war years, the Congress governed the colonies, appointed George Washington commander-in-chief, printed money, and sent ambassadors abroad. In 1781, the colonies

Facts and Figures
Area: 3,615,000 square miles
(9,363,000 square kilometers)
Population: 211,900,000
Capital: Washington, D.C.
Government: Federal Republic
Money unit: Dollar
Longest River: Mississippi-Missouri
3860 miles
6211 kilometers
Highest Mountain: Mt. McKinley
20,300 feet
6194 meters

FACTS ABOUT THE 50 STATES

State	Capital	Admitted to Union	Rank By Sq. Area	Nickname
Alabama	Montgomery	1891	29	Heart of Dixie
Alaska	Juneau	1959	1	The Great Land
Arizona	Phoenix	1912	6	Grand Canyon State
Arkansas	Little Rock	1836	27	Land of Opportunity
California	Sacramento	1850	3	Golden State
Colorado	Denver	1876	8	Centennial State
Connecticut	Hartford	1788	47	Constitution State
Delaware	Dover	1787	49	The First State
Florida	Tallahassee	1845	22	Sunshine State
Georgia	Atlanta	1788	21	Peach State
Hawaii	Honolulu	1959	46	Aloha State
Idaho	Boise	1890	13	Gem of the Mountains
Illinois	Springfield	1818	24	Land of Lincoln
Indiana	Indianapolis	1816	37	Hoosier State
Iowa	Des Moines	1846	25	Hawkeye State
Kansas	Topeka	1861	14	Sunflower State
Kentucky	Frankfort	1792	36	Bluegrass State
Louisiana	Baton Rouge	1812	31	Pelican State
Maine	Augusta	1820	38	Pine Tree State
Maryland	Annapolis	1788	41	Old Line State
Massachusetts	Boston	1788	44	Bay State
Michigan	Lansing	1837	23	Water-Winter Wonderland
Minnesota	Saint Paul	1858	12	Gopher State
Mississippi	Jackson	1871	48	Magnolia State
Missouri	Jefferson City	1821	19	"Show Me" State
Montana	Helena	1889	4	Treasure State
Nebraska	Lincoln	1867	15	Cornhusker State
Nevada	Carson City	1864	7	Silver State
New Hampshire	Concord	1788	43	Granite State
New Jersey	Trenton	1787	45	Garden State
New Mexico	Santa Fe	1912	5	Land of Enchantment
New York	Albany	1788	30	Empire State
North Carolina	Raleigh	1789	28	Tarheel State
North Dakota	Bismarck	1889	17	Flickertail State
Ohio	Columbus	1803	34	Buckeye State
Oklahoma	Oklahoma City	1907	18	Sooner State
Oregon	Salem	1859	10	Beaver State
Pennsylvania	Harrisburg	1787	32	Keystone State
Rhode Island	Providence	1790	50	Little Rhody
South Carolina	Columbia	1788	39	Palmetto State
South Dakota	Pierre	1889	16	Sunshine State
Tennessee	Nashville	1796	33	Volunteer State
Texas	Austin	1845	2	Lone Star State
Utah	Salt Lake City	1896	11	Beehive State
Vermont	Montpelier	1791	42	Green Mountain State
Virginia	Richmond	1788	35	Old Dominion
Washington	Olympia	1889	20	Evergreen State
West Virginia	Charleston	1863	40	Mountain State
Wisconsin	Madison	1848	26	Badger State
Wyoming	Cheyenne	1890	9	Equality State

now states, signed the Articles of Confederation, which declared a new government of the "United States of America". This was an unusual government for the time since there was no king, and almost all other countries had a king.

The United States did not begin to become an industrial nation until the 19th century, although small factories did exist. The new country continued to buy manufactured goods from abroad, and stayed a nation of farmers. When the U.S. fought the War of 1812 against Britain, the country was cut off from a supply of manufactured goods, so Americans had to build their own factories. Between the War of 1812 and the Civil

War was a period of great development. Pioneers traveled west, looking for gold and new lands to farm. In the Northeast cities and factories grew.

The Civil War lasted from 1861 to 1865 and was the result of many differences between the southern states, which were mainly farming states, and the industrial North. The South believed, among other things, that slavery was needed to support its agricultural system while the North wanted to abolish slavery. The South declared its independence from the United States, trying to *secede* or leave the union. The northern states, under the Presidency of President Abraham Lincoln, won the war.

In 1865, slavery was outlawed by a Constitutional amendment. While he watched a play in Washington, D.C., Lincoln was shot by John Wilkes Booth, a supporter of the South.

As the U.S. grew in power and economic influence, many people from around the world came in search of freedom and a better life. These people, called *immigrants*, came to the U.S. mainly through New York Harbor.

The last part of the 19th century and the beginning of the 20th century saw many important inventions. In 1876 Alexander Graham Bell invented the telephone. In 1879 Thomas Edison perfected the incandesant light bulb. The Wright Brothers made the first successful airplane flight in 1903 and, just about the same time Henry Ford's automobiles were becoming more visible on America's streets, thanks to his invention of the mass production line.

In 1898, the U.S. and Spain fought the Spanish American War over Spain's interference in American affairs. After a series of sea battles, during which much of Spain's navy was destroyed, the U.S. gained control over Puerto Rico, the Philippines and Guam.

The U.S. finally entered World War I in 1917, although many other countries had been fighting Germany since 1914. The war ended on November 11, 1918, a day still celebrated as Veteran's Day. The U.S. was important in the settlement of the war, and President Woodrow Wilson went to Paris to sign the peace treaty.

Following the war came a period of prosperity known as the Roaring Twenties. Many changes took place in American life. Perhaps the most important was the passage of the Nineteenth Amendment to the Constitution in 1920, which gave women the right to vote for the first time in history.

This period came to an end on October 29, 1929, a day known as "Black Thursday," when the stock market "crashed". Many people's life savings were wiped out, and the country plunged into the Depression.

Under President Franklin D. Roosevelt, the government began helping citizens in 1933, with such programs as the Works Progress Administration (WPA), the National Recovery Act (NRA), Social Security and others. It was a long process, but soon business had improved, more Americans were back to work and the country seemed on the road to better times.

A surprise attack by Japanese planes at Pearl Harbor in Hawaii on December 7, 1941 plunged the U.S. into World War II. Many Americans lost their lives in the war, which ended August 9, 1945, after atomic bombs were dropped on Japan.

In the 1950s, a "cold war" broke out between the U.S. and Russia, and the 1960s saw the war in Vietnam, the assassinations of President John F. Kennedy, his brother, Robert, and Martin Luther King. The first men to walk on the moon in 1969 were Americans, thus ending the space race against the Russians which had begun in the early 1960s.

In 1974, after the Watergate scandal, President Richard Nixon resigned. He was the first American president to do so.

UNIVERSE When we talk of the universe, we mean everything that exists. This includes the air, the sea, the Earth, the other planets, the Moon, the stars

Vegetables add variety to our food and provide valuable salts and vitamins. Common garden vegetables include lettuces (1), peas (2), cauliflowers (3), beans (4), onions (5), carrots (6) and red beets

and space. Years ago people thought that the Earth was the center of the universe. They thought that all the other heavenly bodies circled around it. About 500 years ago people began to realize that the Earth was not the center.

Now we know that the Earth is only a tiny speck in the universe. It belongs to the Sun's family of planets. The Sun itself belongs to a family of stars called the Galaxy. The Galaxy belongs to a family of galaxies. And there are millions of such families in the universe. But most of the universe is just empty space.

Astronomers think that the universe is thousands of millions of years old. It probably was once a solid lump of matter. Then it exploded, and gas and dust were scattered in all directions. From the gas and dust the stars and planets were born.

See also EARTH; MOON; PLANETS; STARS; SUN.

VEGETABLE Many of the plants we eat are called 'vegetables'. Vegetables are good food, supplying energy or body-building substances. Although vegetables have a lot of water in them, some are rich in carbohydrates, fat, protein, minerals or vitamins. Vegetables also provide solid matter, or 'roughage', which helps the body's digestive system to work properly.

Some plants, like turnips, parsnips, carrots and red beets, store food in their roots. They are "root vegetables." One of the most common is the potato. It has tubers or swollen underground stems which we eat.

'Green vegetables' are eaten for their leaves and flowers. For example, we eat the leaves of spinach, kale, cabbage, and lettuce. Brussels sprouts are leaf buds. Cauliflower and broccoli have swollen flower heads which are good to eat.

Some fruits and seeds are eaten as "vegetables." Tomatoes, squash and cucumbers are fruits. Peas and beans are seeds, which grow inside pods. Both beans and pods of French and runner beans are eaten. Onions are edible bulbs.

We eat some vegetables raw as salads. Others are cooked, often by boiling them. Cooking makes vegetables easier to digest, but takes away some of the goodness. Root vegetables can be stored in a dark, dry place. Other vegetables are preserved by freezing, drying or canning them.

VIKING In the 8th century fierce Vikings from Scandinavia began raiding the coasts of western Europe. They burned villages, robbed churches, stole cattle and carried off slaves. People were terrified of them, especially as Vikings often fought like madmen, as if eager to die in battle.

But the Vikings were not just pirates

When the Viking longships appeared, people fled in panic, for the fierce warriors came to kill, burn and plunder. But as well as being cruel raiders, the Vikings were also great traders and explorers.

and robbers. They were also farmers and traders, and they sailed to find new lands, braving great dangers. In their longships (wooden boats with oars and square sails) they crossed the Atlantic Ocean to settle in Iceland and Greenland. They probably reached America around AD 1000. Vikings from Denmark settled much of eastern England.

VIRUSES are very small organisms or living things which cause diseases in humans and in animals. Viruses cause such diseases as polio, influenza, and rabies.

VITAMIN Vitamins are chemicals our bodies need for healthy growth. We get vitamins from food.

Vitamin A comes from lettuce, carrots, butter and eggs. It helps us grow. There are several kinds of *Vitamin B*. We eat them in cereals, milk, meat, fruit and vegetables. They keep us healthy. So does *Vitamin C*, found in tomatoes, oranges and other fruits. Years ago sailors got a disease called scurvy because there was no vitamin C in their food. *Vitamin D* is important to babies. It prevents a bone disease called rickets. Codliver oil, egg yolks and liver are rich in vitamin D. Sunlight has the same effect too.

Other vitamins are known as E and K. The body only uses vitamins in tiny amounts. A good varied diet gives it all the vitamins it needs.

VOLCANO Volcanoes are openings in the Earth's surface, which may hurl out gases, ash and red-hot molten rock called lava. Volcanoes occur where the Earth's crust is being squeezed or stretched as new mountains are formed. The enormous pressures melt the solid rock to liquid lava. When the pressures become too great, gases and hot liquid rock may burst through the center of a volcano and out of a crater at the top.

It is a terrifying sight, as smoke and cinders are flung into the air. Molten lava flows down the sides of the volcano, covering everything in its path. As the lava cools, it hardens.

Active volcanoes erupt fairly often. Those which have been quiet for hundreds of years are called extinct volcanoes. In 1883 the volcanic island of Krakatoa in Indonesia exploded. The explosion was heard thousands of miles away and caused huge waves which killed 36,000 people. Other famous volcanoes are Vesuvius (Italy), which buried the Roman town of Pompeii in AD 79, Etna (Sicily) and Fujiyama (Japan).

WALRUS With its drooping moustache and long tusks, the walrus is rather a comical-looking animal. Walruses are related to seals. They live in the Arctic and eat shellfish, which they dig up from the sea bed with their tusks.

A large bull (male) walrus can weigh over a ton. Although killer whales and polar bears sometimes attack walruses, the walrus's worst enemy is man. So many walruses have been killed for their meat, blubber (fat) and tusks that there are not many left. The walrus herds are now protected, but they keep away from people, often gathering on ice floes.

See also ARCTIC.

WAR People have always found it difficult to live in peace together. Even in prehistoric times envy and greed made one tribe attack another, in order to steal its land or animals. Great empires were founded by conquering armies.

In ancient Greece and Rome soldiers were armed with swords, spears, slings and bows and arrows. Foot soldiers, or infantry, made up the largest part of an army. The Roman armies were so well trained that for hundreds of years they were almost unbeatable. Civilizations built walls and forts to keep out invading barbarians. For example, the Great Wall of China was built to stop the raids of fierce nomadic horsemen.

Horsemen, or cavalry, played an important part in wars throughout the Middle Ages. Knights in armor, armed with lances, swords and clubs, battered their way through the enemy ranks. But if a skilled archer with a longbow killed his horse, the clumsy knight was helpless on foot.

In wartime, people sought safety inside castles. The attacking army would besiege the castle and try to break down its walls with battering rams and giant

Three kinds of volcanos: quiet Hawaiian volcano (top); explosive volcano (middle); and intermediate Vesuvian volcano (bottom).

Above: A large male or bull walrus.

catapults hurling rocks. With the invention of gunpowder in the 1300s, castles were not safe, for cannons could smash down the thickest walls.

From now on wars were fought increasingly with guns. But it took many years before soldiers had guns light enough to carry easily. In the 1600s

In the 1700s armies moved slowly and fought according to certain 'rules'. During the American War of Independence, the British soldiers in their bright red uniforms advanced in a line. The Americans, who were good shots with their muzzle-loaders, often won battles by breaking the 'rules'.

weapon. Even more deadly was the airplane. For the first time civilians were attacked in their homes by bombs dropped from the air.

World War II was fought in Europe, Africa and Asia. Most of the world's leading nations took part. It was a war of rapid movement. At sea, the aircraft carrier was more important than the battleship. Submarines sank many ships with their torpedoes. On land tanks were used in great numbers. The importance of air power was shown by the Battle of Britain (1940). British fighters shot down many German bombers, and so prevented a German invasion of Britain. Both sides dropped bombs on towns and factories. Radar was developed, and towards the end of the war Germany

musketeers took so long to load their muskets that they had to be protected by pikemen, armed with long spears or 'pikes'. By the 1800s the musket was replaced by the repeating rifle, and in the 1800s the machine gun, which could fire several hundred bullets a minute was invented.

The invention of gunpowder also brought great changes to war at sea. Ramming and boarding an enemy ship gave way to battles between tall galleons firing broadside from one hundred or more guns. Then wooden sailing ships were replaced by 'ironclad' steam warships, with guns mounted in revolving turrets. War was becoming mechanical.

By 1914 guns were so powerful that soldiers had to dig trenches for protection. During World War I whole armies remained bogged down in trenches, unable to move more than a few miles. Millions of soldiers were killed. Cavalry was now out of date. The tank, first used in 1916, was a powerful new

Above: The German Me 109 fighter of World War II.

World War I was the first mechanized war, in which vehicles such as the Italian Cerrano 75 mm motorized gun and the Renault field ambulance played a part.

Famous Wars

This list shows some of the most important wars fought since the Fall of the Roman Empire.

476	Fall of the Roman Empire
1066	Normans conquer England
1337–1453	Hundred Years' War
1455–1487	Wars of the Roses
1588	English defeat Spanish Armada
1618–1648	Thirty Years' War
1642–1651	English Civil War
1701–1713	War of Spanish Succession
1740–1748	War of Austrian Succession
1756–1763	Seven Years' War
1775–1783	War of American Independence
1803–1815	Napoleonic Wars
1854–1856	Crimean War
1861–1865	U.S. Civil War
1870–1871	Franco-Prussian War
1899–1902	Boer War (South Africa)
1904–1905	Russio-Japanese War
1914–1918	World War I (Germany, Austria and Turkey against Russia, France, Britain, Italy and U.S.)
1936–1939	Spanish Civil War
1939–1945	World War II (Germany, Italy and Japan against Allies, including Britain, U.S. and Russia)
1950–1953	Korean War
1965–1975	Vietnam War

introduced the V1 flying bomb and the V2 rocket. In 1944 the Allies crossed the English Channel to invade France. This was the largest sea invasion of all time. The war against Japan ended with the dropping of the first atomic bombs on the cities of Hiroshima and Nagasaki.

Nuclear weapons are the most terrible ever known. To use modern hydrogen bombs in war would almost certainly mean the destruction of much of the world. So no nation is prepared to risk using them. In this way they are a 'deterrent' – they stop quarrels between nations from turning into large wars.

WASHINGTON, D.C. Soon after George Washington was inaugurated as the first president of the United States, Congress decided to establish a permanent headquarters for the new country. Since several cities and areas of the country wanted the honor of being the capital, a compromise was reached: a new city was built on a swampy tract of land betwen Virginia and Maryland (both states donated the land).

Washington, D.C., designed by a French officer in the Revolutionary War, Pierre Charles L'Enfant, is one of the most beautiful cities in the world—with white government buildings and memorials, wide avenues, and large parks. The city is not part of any state; it covers an area of 69 square miles (179 square kilometers) called the District of Columbia.

One of the central points in Washington is the Capitol, where Congress meets and where presidents are inaugurated. Wide avenues raidate from the Capitol like spokes of a wheel, dividing the city into four sections.

The White House, home of U.S. presidents, was the first public building to be built in the city. The original building was burned during the War of 1812. Since then the White House has been renovated several times.

WASHINGTON, George (1732–1799) The first President of the United States of America was a farmer from Virginia. His name was George Washington. When the American colonists fought against Britain in the War of Independence (1775–1783), Washington became general of their army. Often he turned defeats into victories. In 1789 he became President, although he did not think he was fit for such an important task. Washington, the capital city of the United States, is named after him.

WASP Wasps are related to ants and bees. They are hunting insects, and many wasps will sting if annoyed.

Social wasps live in colonies. Inside the nest, the queen lays eggs, while workers care for the eggs and larvae. Adult wasps eat nectar. But the larvae are fed on insects and caterpillars. In the autumn all the wasps die, except for the young queens. They hibernate, and start new nests in the spring.

Solitary wasps live alone and build small nests. To make sure her young have enough food, a female wasp may catch a caterpillar, sting it, and lay her eggs on its body.

The common wasp has black and yellow stripes. Its stinger is at the end of its body.

WATER is the most precious liquid on Earth. For without it, nothing can live. Fortunately there are large amounts of water on the Earth. Seas cover two-thirds of the world's surface. More than two-thirds of our own bodies are water.

Water is the only mineral that is liquid. It is made up of the chemical elements hydrogen and oxygen. Its molecules contain two atoms of hydrogen (H) to one atom of oxygen (O). We write it as the chemical formula H_2O.

Water plays an important part in our weather. The Sun warms up the water on the surface of the Earth. Some of it changes into vapor, rather the way water turns into steam when it is boiled.

Roman centurion

Crusader knight

French sailor (WW1)

Australian infantryman (WW2)

US marine (present day)

SOLDIERS THROUGH THE AGES

The vapor is carried along and up by the wind It cools and condenses, or turns back into water droplets. These form clouds, and when the droplets get too heavy, they fall back to the ground as rain. If it is cold, they may fall as snow. This continuous process is called the water cycle.

Water also shapes the Earth. In the form of rain or ocean waves, it beats against the rocks and gradually breaks them down. Flowing rivers cut deep canyons in rock. Frozen water, or ice, forms into huge masses, called glaciers, in mountain regions. Glaciers move slowly over the land, gouging a path through the rocks and soil.

The power of water can be tremendous. Flood waters can smash houses to pieces. So can huge tidal waves set off by earthquakes. But water power also helps Man. Great dams can harness the power of water to make electricity. We call this hydro-electric power.

We use large amounts of water every day for washing, cooling and drinking. Drinking water is made safe by passing it through fine sand and adding some chlorine to purify it. Waste water and sewage from our houses is purified in special treatment plants before it is allowed back into the rivers.

Industries use large quantities of water for cooling and processing. Recently many rivers and lakes have become polluted by chemical wastes from factories. And oil spilled from tankers at sea has caused pollution of the ocean waters.

See also ENERGY; GLACIER; ICE; LAKE; RAIN; RIVER; OCEANS.

WATERFALL

WATERFALL A waterfall is a beautiful sight. A river pours over a cliff with a noise like thunder, sending spray high into the air.

A waterfall is caused by water wearing away rock at different speeds. If a river flows over a join between hard rock and soft rock, it wears away the soft rock more quickly and makes a deep 'step'. Some waterfalls are quite small, but in some places wide rivers fall over huge cliffs. The most famous waterfalls are Niagara, between Canada and the United States and the Victoria Falls in Africa.

Above: The weasel hunts by scent and will attack prey much larger than itself, such as a rabbit.

Below: The world's highest waterfall is the Angel Falls in Venezuela.

Weather forecasters use instruments to measure windspeed, air pressure and temperature.

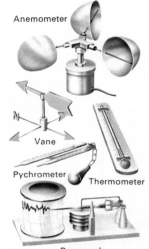

Anemometer

Vane

Pychrometer   Thermometer

Barograph

WEASEL The fierce little weasel is only about ten inches (25 centimeters) long. But it will hunt and kill animals up to twice as big as itself.

Weasels hunt by scent. They can climb and swim, and will chase mice and voles into their burrows. Weasels help to keep down the numbers of these rodents.

The stoat is a larger relative of the weasel. In cold countries weasels and stoats change their reddish-brown summer coat for a white winter one.

Other members of the weasel family include otters, pine martens and minks.

WEATHER When we ask, 'what is the weather like?', we want to know several things. We want to know about temperature, air pressure, wind and cloud; we want to know if it is going to be fair and dry or warm and rainy.

The weather of a particular part of the Earth over a long period is called its climate. The weather at any place depends on conditions in the Earth's atmosphere. The most important cause of weather is wind. Hot air rises and cool air moves in underneath it. Huge masses of air, some hot and some cool, are always moving over the Earth's surface as wind.

At the Equator and at the North and South Poles the weather changes very little. It is hot most of the time at the Equator and cold most of the time at the Poles. Between Equator and Poles there are areas known as the temperate zones. Here the weather is generally mild but changes a good deal. Hot air and cold air are constantly meeting to form regions of low pressure called depressions, which bring unsettled weather.

Weather forecasters show what is happening on charts, showing winds, temperatures and pressures. Weather ships at sea, balloons, and satellites in space collect information about the changing weather. In this way storms can be spotted as they start to grow, and warnings sent out to ships and people in their path.

See also CLOUD; FOG; HURRICANE; RAIN; SNOW; TORNADO; WIND.

WEST INDIES The islands known as the West Indies lie between the Caribbean Sea and the Atlantic Ocean. In the north are the Bahamas. Next come the Greater Antilles, which include the four largest islands: Cuba, Jamaica, Hispaniola (which is divided into two countries: Haiti and the Dominican Republic) and Puerto Rico. In the south are the Lesser Antilles, which are smaller. They include a group called the Leeward Islands and another known as the Windward Islands.

Except for the Bahamas, the West Indies have a tropical climate. Many islands are hilly. Sugar, tobacco, cocoa, coffee, coconuts, bananas and other fruits are grown. Iron ore, bauxite (aluminium ore) and asphalt (for road-making) are important products.

Christopher Columbus discovered the West Indies in 1492. But he thought he had reached the Indies of Asia. The native Indians, called Caribs, were killed when Spain conquered the islands. Later the British, French and Dutch set up West Indian colonies. African slaves were brought to work on the plantations. Most of the islands now run their own affairs.

WHALE Although whales spend all their lives in the sea, they are mammals, not fish. Whales are warm-blooded. They have skin, not scales. The females give birth to live young and feed them on milk. Although a whale can dive to great depths, loading its blood with enough oxygen to last for up to 45 minutes, it must surface to breathe. As it breathes out, the whale spouts used, hot, moist

The islands of the West Indies lie in a curving line between Florida (United States) and Venezuela (South America). Most are hilly and almost all lie in the tropics.

The blue whale is probably the largest animal which has ever lived. It lives in the Antarctic seas and feeds on tiny sea animals called krill.

air as a fountain of fog. Whales use their flippers for steering; they swim by beating their broad tails up and down.

There are two families of whales: toothed whales, and whalebone or baleen whales. Toothed whales have normal teeth. They catch fish and squid. Killer whales, sperm whales, dolphins and porpoises are all toothed whales. Whalebone whales have no teeth. Instead they have ridges covered with bristles inside their huge mouths, and they use these to strain tiny sea animals and plants called plankton from the water. Whalebone whales include the blue, right, gray, fin, humpback and sei whales. The blue whale is probably the largest animal that has ever lived. It may be 100 feet long (30 meters) and weigh 150 tons.

See also DOLPHIN.

WHEAT Like other cereal plants, wheat belongs to the grass family. It is an important food. The ripe seeds, or grain, can be ground into flour and used to make bread, pasta (macaroni and spaghetti), and breakfast foods.

People have grown wheat for thousands of years. During that time they have produced a great many hybrid (crossbred) kinds. Wheat is grown in many lands, even in parts of the tropics and Arctic. Much of the world's wheat is grown on the plains of Canada, the USA, Australia and Russia.

WHEEL Without the wheel our transport systems would be primitive. There would be no cars, buses, trucks or trains. There would be little industry either, because most engines and machines contain wheels of one kind or another.

Our world would be much like it was before the discovery of the wheel, more than 5000 years ago. Men traveled on foot and pulled loads for short distances on sleds. Then someone had the idea of putting logs under the sleds. The sleds moved more easily because the logs rolled over the ground. There is less resistance to rolling than there is to sliding. Later, pieces of wood shaped like slices of log were placed on wooden axles, and the wheel was born.

WIND is the movement of air over the Earth's surface. The chief cause of wind is the unequal heating of the Earth's surface. At the Equator, which gets most heat from the Sun, the air becomes warm and rises. At the Poles, which are the coldest places, cold air sinks. As the warm air rises, cool air moves in to take its place.

Changing temperatures over the sea and land also affect the pattern of the winds. Certain winds blow steadily in the same direction. The most reliable winds are the *trade winds* which blow towards the Equator.

Winds are named after the direction from which they come; so a north wind blows from the north, and so on.

WOLF The howling of wolves is a frightening sound. But wolves rarely attack people. Wolves belong to the dog family, and the gray timber wolf of North America, Europe and Asia is the largest kind.

Wolves are strong, intelligent animals and often hunt together in packs. They will chase a deer for many hours until the prey is exhausted. Wolves also eat smaller animals, and will attack cattle and sheep. For this reason men have hunted and killed them. Wolves are now quite rare.

There are stories of children being raised by wolves. The most famous story is about Romulus, who is said to have founded Rome, and his brother Remus.

WOOD is one of our most useful raw materials. It is used in building, in making furniture and is even burned as fuel. Cut wood is called timber. The timber we get from coniferous trees, such as pine, is called soft-wood. The timber we get from deciduous trees, such as oak, is called hardwood. Softwoods are used mainly in building construction, hardwoods for furniture.

Wood is also made into paper, textile fibers, plastics, explosives and other useful chemicals. The main chemical substance in wood is called cellulose.

WOOL is the fine hair obtained from the fleece of sheep. It is one of the oldest fibers used for making clothes and other textiles. Wool fibers are naturally crinkled which help woolen garments keep their shape. Each fiber is covered with tiny overlapping scales so that the fibers lock together when they are spun into yarn. The Merino breed of sheep produces the heaviest fleeces.

WORM Worms are animals with soft bodies. Some live underground or in water. Other worms live as parasites inside plants or other animals.

The flatworms include such harmful parasites as the liver fluke and the tapeworm. The tapeworm enters an animal's body as an egg, usually in food. It hatches and lives inside its host's stomach. Roundworms, hookworms and threadworms are also parasites.

Segmented worms are not harmful. Their bodies are made up of segments or rings. This group includes the ragworms and lugworms of the seashore, and the earthworm. Earthworms feed by swallowing soil and passing it through their bodies. In this way they help break down plant matter in the soil. They also help air to circulate through the soil. Another segmented worm is the leech.

Some bristle worms are sea worms that live inside tubes made of mud and sand. The fan worms use their brightly colored tentacles to gather food.

See also LEECH; PARASITE.

Above: Arctic musk oxen form a circle as a defense against a pack of hungry timber wolves.

Each year a tree adds a new growth ring of cells round the solid core or heartwood.

Earthworms leave 'casts' of soil on the surface.

Flatworms often live as parasites inside the bodies of other animals.

YEAST is a tiny plant which brewers use to make beer and bakers use to make bread. In brewing the yeast feeds on the sugar in the brewing liquor. It changes it into alcohol and bubbles of carbon dioxide gas. This process is called fermentation. A similar process changes grape juice into wine. When yeast is added to dough in bread making, it produces bubbles of carbon dioxide which make the dough rise.

X-RAY Invisible rays that can pass through materials are called X-rays. They pass through flesh, for example. In hospitals doctors take X-ray photographs to look inside the body. A patient stands in front of a photographic film and X-rays are passed through him. When the film is developed, the patient's bones show up. This is because the bones block some of the rays and cast a shadow on the film. The doctors can see if any of the bones are broken. Some new X-ray machines can photograph body organs as well.

Zebras at a waterhole. They move about the grassy African plains in herds, and are often killed by lions.

ZEBRA The zebra is a wild African relative of the horse. There are three kinds, but they all have similar striped markings. The zebra's stripes help to camouflage it on the grasslands where it lives.

Zebras live in herds. Their worst enemy is the lion. But zebras run swiftly, and also kick and bite savagely. Zebras cannot be tamed easily. In the past many were hunted for food. The quagga was a kind of zebra which became extinct about 100 years ago.

YACHT A yacht is a boat or ship used for pleasure, for example, racing or cruising. Some yachts are small sailing boats, suitable only for sheltered waters. Others are large motor yachts and steam yachts rugged enough for ocean crossings. Small yachts sometimes have only a cockpit or simple cabin to shelter the crew, while large ones may have spacious accomodations with every modern luxury and convenience.

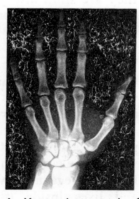

An X-ray photograph of a human hand, showing the bone structure.

ZOO A zoo is a place where wild animals are kept in captivity. People enjoy going to zoos to see animals from other countries. But more important, zoos help to save rare animals from becoming extinct. Zoos around the world exchange animals and try to breed them.

In the past kings collected wild animals in zoos. The first public zoos began in the 19th century. Often the cages were too small for the animals and the bars made it hard for people to see them properly.

YAK In the cold, high mountains of central Asia lives the yak. Yaks are among the largest wild cattle, yet they climb as nimbly as goats. Although there are wild yaks, most yaks are domesticated.

To the people of the Himalayas the yak is a very useful animal. It can live on poor pasture. It gives milk, butter and meat, its skin is made into leather, and its long hair is woven into cloth.

Today zoos have enclosures in which the animals feel more at home. Ditches, moats and glass keep the animals and visitors apart. Birds fly about inside large aviaries. Mountain goats climb man-made hills, while penguins, polar bears, seals and even elephants have pools to splash in. In special darkened buildings, people can see animals which are normally active only at night.

Each animal needs special care. Its food must be carefully prepared. Some animals need warm houses, but others live happily in large open enclosures. Some zoos have a special children's zoo, with goats, rabbits, guinea pigs and other small animals.

The yak is sure-footed and strong. It can carry heavy loads, even at high altitudes. The yak's shaggy hair protects it from the cold.

Index

Note: Subjects and page numbers in **bold type** are main entries in the encyclopedia.

ACKNOWLEDGEMENTS

Photographs: Page 6 Zefa *top left,* British Museum *center left,* Musee de l'air *center right;* 8 British Airways *top,* Scalá *bottom;* 14 R. I. Lewis-Smith; 19 Sonia Halliday *top,* J. Allan Cash *center;* 21 Dave Collins; 25 ANIB; 26 ANIB; 28 BBC; 31 NSP; 34 NHPA; 33 Mansell Collection; 36 Dave Collins; 39 NHPA; 40 Zefa; 42 Sonia Halliday; 44 Michael Chinery *top,* Danish Agricultural Products *bottom;* 45 Zefa; 47 Zefa *top,* Martin Borland *bottom;* 48 Sonia Halliday; 53 NHPA *center* 54 Novosti *top left,* National Tourist Office of Italy *center left,* Martin Borland *center;* 55 Royal Netherlands Tourist Office *top,* Dave Collins *bottom left,* ANIB *bottom left;* 58 NHPA *center,* Dancing Times *bottom;* 59 Mander and Mitchenson; 66 NHPA; 62 Vickers *top,* Seaphot *center;* 63 P. Morris; 66 Martin Borland; 74 Sonia Halliday; 79 Asbestos Information Committee *bottom;* 82 Michael Chinery; 84 British Museum; 85 Zefa *bottom;* Mansell Collection; 87 French Toursit office *top,* National Geological Museum *bottom;* 88 Aldus Books; 89 P.J.E. Clapham; 91 Michael Chinery; 94 Westland Helicopters; 95 Dave Collins; 97 NSP; 100 NHPA *left,* Danish Tourist Office *right;* 101 Michael Holford *top,* Dave Collins *bottom;* 105 Japan Information Center; 109 New Zealand House *top,* ANIB *bottom;* 108 International Research and Development Co.; 109 Heather Angel; 110 Robert Harding Assoc. *center* NHPA *right;* 111 P. Morris; 113 NSP; 114 Red Cross *top,* Brompton Hospital *bottom;* 115 Paul Brierley *top,* AM & S, Europe Ltd. *bottom;* 118 Giraudon; 117 National Coal Board; 120 California Institute of Technology; 124 Mansell Collection *top,* Syndication International *center;* 124 Sonia Halliday; 125 New Zealand High Commission; 129 Seaphot; 130 P. Morris *top,* National Gallery *center* Pitti Gallery, Florence *bottom;* 131 National Gallery *top left,* Museé du jeu de Paume *center,* V & A *bottom;* 132 Zoological Society of London; 133 Dave Collins *center right,* Zefa *bottom right;* 135 NHPA; 137 National Portrait Gallery *center,* Mansell Collection *top, bottom* 137 National Portrait Gallery; *center* 139 P. Morris; 141 Barnaby's Picture Library; 146 NHPA; 150 Zefa; 152 P. Morris; 153 Heather Angel *top,* British Tourist Authority *center,* Italian Cultural Institute *center bottom;* 157 ANIB; 164 Novosti; 165 Zefa; 173 Blake Allison; 182 Michael Chinery; 183 P. Morris *top,* Adrian Warren *center;* 186 Sonia Halliday.

Artwork: Artist Partners Ltd.; Faulkner/Marks Partnership; Linden Artists; John Martin & Artists Ltd.; Sackett Publishing Services Ltd.; Temple Art; George Thompson; The Tudor Art Agency.